What Every

Middle School Teacher

Should Know

WHAT EVERY

Middle School Teacher

SHOULD KNOW

THIRD EDITION

Dave F. Brown and Trudy Knowles

AMLE

HEINEMANN
Portsmouth, NH

Heinemann
361 Hanover Street
Portsmouth, NH 03801–3912
www.heinemann.com

Association for Middle Level Education
4151 Executive Parkway, Suite 300
Westerville, OH 43081
www.amle.org

Offices and agents throughout the world

The authors and publisher wish to thank those who have generously given permission to reprint borrowed material:

Excerpts from the Free Press edition of *Why Do They Act That Way? A Survival Guide to the Adolescent Brain for You and Your Teen* by David Walsh, Ph.D. Copyright © 2004 by David Walsh, Ph.D. Reprinted with the permission of Atria Publishing Group, a Division of Simon & Schuster, Inc.

Credits continue on page x.

Library of Congress Cataloging-in-Publication Data
Brown, Dave F.
    What every middle school teacher should know / Dave F. Brown and
Trudy Knowles. — Third edition.
        pages cm
    Includes bibliographical references.
    ISBN 978-0-325-05755-2
    1. Middle school education—United States.   2. Adolescence—United States.
I. Knowles, Trudy.   II. Title.
    LB1623.5.K56 2014
    373.236—dc23   2014014757

Editor: Tobey Antao
Production: Hilary Goff
Cover and interior designs: Suzanne Heiser
Typesetter: Valerie Levy, Drawing Board Studios
Manufacturing: Steve Bernier

Printed in the United States of America on acid-free paper
7 8 9 10 RWP 24 23 22 21
January 2021 Printing

◆▌ Dedication

In memory of our esteemed colleague and friend, Dr. Vince Anfara, Jr., who
elevated the international knowledge base in the development of genuine
middle level schools through his exceptional research, visionary leadership,
and tireless efforts.

—D.F.B.

To Rachel, who continues to inspire me with her love of middle school.
I love being your mom.

—T.K.

◆◖ **Contents**

Chapter 11 *This* Is Learning: Making Instruction Meaningful   181

Chapter 12 Assessment That Promotes Active Learning   208

Acknowledgments

The endeavor of writing is seldom a solitary venture. It takes the support of family, friends, and colleagues to encourage us when other distractions arise. I want to first acknowledge the support, encouragement, and guidance I receive from my coauthor, Trudy. Co-writing can be a challenge on so many fronts, from disagreements on the basic premise of the text to the minute details of every sentence.

I never experience any stress or frustration when working with Trudy, and often it seems we are of one mind on so many details. It's our philosophies, though, that make this a symbiotic relationship as coauthors. Trudy and I didn't know this when we wrote the first edition in 2000, but through that initial process we soon realized how compatible our views were and continue to be as we completed this third edition. Thank you, Trudy, for suggesting we write a book to begin with, sound advice in all matters, and knowing exactly what was needed this time to make it better. As usual, it's been more fun than work.

Trudy, of course, has influenced her daughter Rachel's educational philosophies. I have known Rachel since she was ten, and now she's a middle level educator—naturally! Rachel's thoughts on how to make connections with students and on the direction advisories have gone are essential aspects of this edition. Thank you, Rachel, for guiding your mom and me through this new edition.

Danielle Bajus and Dave Mercurio have welcomed me into their curriculum integration classroom whenever I want to "intrude"—which is often. They contributed on many fronts to this edition, particularly by permitting me to gather their students' thoughts on several topics—from how teachers should act to the challenges of being a young adolescent. Danielle and Dave are model middle level teachers, and I thank them immensely for their essential contributions to this edition.

Several teachers and an assistant principal at a local middle school near Philadelphia were kind enough to offer their time and enlightening comments about the challenges of teaching middle school. Thank you Kevin, Kristi, Leah, Heather, Tim, Amy, and Kristina for your contributions. I would also like to thank the Radnor Township School District and Cedarbrook Middle School for their assistance in completing this book.

Kevin Burke has been instrumental in paving the path for me to gain access to teachers in his school, and is a true friend and colleague in improving the lives of middle level teachers and students. His energy as a middle level administrator is exemplary. Heather Barsky is an amazing teacher. She has a heart of gold that shines brightly for her students, and it excites me to know that she is with young adolescents every day! Thank you, Heather, for contributing to this edition, inspiring me, and being a genuine friend.

John Gulick provided expert knowledge on using technology with young adolescents—thank you for jumping onboard to help us "sight unseen." I'd like to thank one of my undergraduate students, Tynika, who was kind enough to share her insights on her journey as an adolescent. Thank you, Dr. Frances Spielhagen—fellow researcher, exceptional author on adolescent issues, and colleague—for providing wise advice for this revision. My colleagues on the Pennsylvania Association for Middle Level Education executive council are quality educators and consummate professionals; they help me understand the plight of young adolescents through their frequent stories. I would be honored to have any one of them teach or be an administrator for my own children.

Our editor, Tobey Antao, guided us with great professionalism and has made this the best of the three editions. Every conversation we have confirms her commitment to students with a philosophy that Trudy and I share about what matters in classrooms every day. Thank you, Tobey, for taking us on for this journey and joining in the madness of helping us choose all the "right" words.

My closest friends and my family have been especially patient with me throughout this writing process. My colleague, Dan, provides me with the sanity and humor to get through the toughest times—thanks again, Dan, for listening and helping me plan my future. My siblings, Carol Ann, Bob, Brian, and Ken, always support me. Our frequent conversations help steer me in the right direction when I don't have the "right" answers to life's vexing questions. Thank you all.

Nothing beats the joy—and challenge—of parenting, and my daughters make being a dad a pretty simple process because they are caring souls. My adult daughter, Lindsay, has become a necessary sounding board for me as I handle the challenges of parenting and teaching. I so appreciate our frequent conversations about everything that affects us both. Thank you, Lindsay, for being there for me. To my younger daughter, Taylor, please know how much I enjoy our conversations and our travels, too. I enjoy listening to you as you mature socially, emotionally, and intellectually. Enjoy the journey of young adulthood—and leave the stress behind. Life will be much more fun for you that way.

—Dave F. Brown

The voices of middle school students and teachers continue to inform the work we have done in the third edition of this book. My ongoing thanks and gratitude go out to all those who have spoken to us through all three editions of this book and who have allowed us to use their words. It is their voices that guide us. I am also continually grateful to those professors, teachers, and college students who have embraced this book as a framework and resource for their work with middle school students. For all who work in the middle, thanks. You are the difference makers.

There are a few special people I want to thank for their contributions to this edition. Thanks to Wilma Ortiz for her contribution about language and identity. She is an amazing educator and I am lucky to have an office next to hers. Thanks to Sue Luppino who shared her thoughts on how she connects with her middle school students. She teaches me something new about education every day. Thanks to Ellen Jordan, a middle school math teacher, and to her eighth graders who shared their insights on what it means to be in middle school. It's encouraging to see middle school teachers like Ellen at work. Thanks to Gregory Wironen who shared his thoughts on what it was like to be in middle school on 9/11. He will make an excellent teacher.

I have to give a special thanks to my daughter, Rachel Knowles, who shared many insights for this edition. I love the conversations we have about education. Rachel teaches middle school social studies with passion and love. Her students are lucky to have her.

My thanks go to Nancy Doda and Mark Springer for writing the Foreword to this edition. Nancy is an amazing educator and she keeps me grounded. Her friendship is one of the joys of my life. Mark's amazing career has inspired hundreds of students and professionals. I feel fortunate to know Mark and to call him my friend.

I have met some amazing middle level educators throughout my career. Their heart, passion, vision, and belief in democratic classrooms continue to inspire me in ways they will never know. These are the educators who speak out against the abuses that we dump on kids every day in the name of education reform and accountability. They encourage me to never give up speaking the truth about education, to use my voice to always advocate for what's best for kids. Thanks forever particularly to Jim, Barb, and Ann. It is educators like them who keep me going when I want to give up. My hope is that through this book other educators will gain a vision of what school can be like for young adolescents when our classrooms are focused on them and not on data.

Our editor, Tobey Antao, is amazing. She has guided us with incredible skill, an educational philosophy that enriches ours, and a keen eye for what should stay in and what should come out. Every author should be so lucky.

And then there's Dave. Dave and I met more than a quarter century ago in a Sociology of Education class at the University of Tennessee. Through the years we have remained colleagues and friends. After the second edition of the book I said, "That's it." And yet, here is the third edition. I think I had more fun with this edition than the other two. Dave keeps reminding me that what we know to be true in our hearts about the right thing to do with kids is backed up by the research. He is an amazing researcher himself, and I thank him for letting me go off the handle while he finds the research to back it up. He is fun to write with and fun to talk with. I feel grateful to have had such a friend for so many years.

And always, always, always, I thank my family, born and created, who have been the most important thing throughout my life. My mom and dad were my first supporters. I feel them around me and miss them daily. Thanks to my kids and kids-in-law—Mellissa, Rachel, Robert, Ariel, Austin, Juliano, Jereme, Jeanna—and my husband, Dan. They support me, are proud of me, and love me unconditionally. And a shout out to my grandkids, Isaac, Orion, and Denali. They are the future. My hope is that when they reach middle school, we will again have classrooms that are student-driven, not data-driven. They deserve it. All kids deserve it.

—Trudy Knowles

◆❙ Foreword

A Better Map for Teaching Young Adolescents

Nancy Doda and Mark Springer, Alliance for Powerful Learning

Have you ever become lost on your way to an important destination? Have you ever experienced that unsettling sense of apprehension as you realize that you made wrong turns somewhere along the way, and now you have little idea of how to get back on course? Fortunately, in this age of GPS, few of us experience that any longer while traveling, but those of us born before the GPS or smart phones certainly remember it. All of us, though, can imagine how similar that feeling is to the angst we felt as novice middle level teachers. Bewildered by the myriad of unique developmental needs of our young adolescents, newly learned pedagogy, unfamiliar curriculum plans, and a lengthy list of extra responsibilities, we stood without a GPS or even a map in front of a class of young adolescents who looked to us to guide them safely along an extremely vital path in life. We felt lost; but then again, we could see they felt lost, too. Perhaps it was this mutual floundering that fueled an emerging respect and admiration for these young people. Whatever the cause, we could see that we were needed, and that compelled us to find our way.

In today's educational world, we face new and complex challenges in the work of educating young adolescents. Business and legislative groups at times erect roadblocks or generate new obstacles that seem to toss aside the very needs of young adolescents. Today, many middle grades educators feel so pressed to ensure their students master standardized tests that they can hardly breathe, let alone breathe life into student learning. Faced with overwhelming accountability pressures, many administrators and, in turn, their teachers are reticent to experiment with more ambitious and progressive practices fearing that test results will not follow. At the same time, the fast-paced and ever-changing world calls for students to acquire new and more sophisticated capacities in critical thinking, problem solving, teamwork, creativity, literacy, and communication. So many of us fear, as we did at the start of our careers, that we are once again lost. With so many competing voices lobbying to determine the focus for middle grades education, it seems fitting to ask once again, "What matters most in educating today's young adolescents?"

We believe we need a new map—or better yet, a new GPS, one that accounts for the latest research on how young adolescents best learn, addresses the challenges we face in preparing our students for today's complex world, and helps us clarify which changes are most needed in how we teach. Here, in the pages that follow, you can find your way anew, not only through the many voices of students who speak from the pages, but through the wealth of knowledge, research, examples, and models that illuminate what practices and perspectives best serve the needs of this extraordinary age group. Whether you are new to the field or an experienced middle grades educator, this book will inspire and support you as you encounter steady challenges in developing a healthy understanding of and relationship with your young adolescents. Moreover, you'll receive practical guidance on effective teaming, student-centered planning, curriculum development, and effective advocacy for best middle level practice and more.

As the next generation of middle grades teachers rallies to shape the next generation of middle level practice, this book promises not only to guide us toward a more comprehensive understanding of our young adolescents, but to offer sorely needed attention to issues that have for too long remained below the radar. In spite of decades of discussion in the field regarding meaningful and relevant curriculum, middle schools still find this an area of change too often beyond reach. With its emphasis on twenty-first century learning, project-based learning, and flipped classrooms, this book brings our attention once again to the critical importance of a student-centered curriculum and to the power of student voice in classroom life. Changing instructional methodology is vital to teaching young adolescents, but it is not sufficient if we hope to develop enduring understanding, hardy intellectual investment, active curiosity, and a commitment to lifelong learning. To that end, the authors have clarified the rationale and dividends for developing more meaningful curriculum, partnering with our young people, and placing student questions and concerns front and center in our planning. Further, they share with us numerous pathways we can explore in designing such student-centered curriculum and instruction.

> In spite of decades of discussion in the field regarding meaningful and relevant curriculum, middle schools still find this an area of change too often beyond reach.

We believe we need this new GPS now more than ever. With such a guide pointing us in a true direction, backed by effective practices and visible evidence of success, we will be ready to sustain what matters most for the next generation of young adolescents. Thanks to Dave and Trudy, you have that guide in your hands. For the sake of all our young adolescents, please use it wisely.

◆▌ Foreword (2nd Edition)

We Really Should Know This

James A. Beane

As anyone who's ever done it can tell you, teaching middle school is a very tricky business. Whether it's good or bad depends largely on how you see things. Young adolescents are in a real serious life transition, and they bring the ups and downs of that to every teacher they meet. If teachers see those ups and downs as a problem or inconvenience, middle school teaching can be very frustrating.

Worse yet, as parents and guardians see the dependence of childhood slip away and the press for independence get under way, they often expect teachers to influence their children's lives in ways they cannot seem to themselves. Thus the so-called "problems" posed by young adolescence end up compounded by their family's expectations that teachers can do what they can't. Meanwhile, education authorities and policy makers who may never have actually taught middle school make demands about what and how to teach. Too often those demands assume young adolescents have nothing but schoolwork on their minds and can't wait to move from one piece of content to the next. Now the whole business of teaching is buried under the weight of being expected to teach a group of "up and down" young people things they do not want to know, as prescribed by authorities who never tried to do it themselves.

On the other hand, if you see what young adolescents bring to your classroom as a promise rather than a problem, middle school teaching can be one of the most exciting and satisfying things you will ever do. The fact is that young adolescents have tons of questions and concerns about themselves and their world, and their imagination and curiosity work around the clock. They love new ideas if those ideas shed some light on topics that are personally and socially significant. They love to explore and debate issues of fairness and justice. They love to learn new skills that will help them do something they want to do or think is worth doing. They love to dig deep into projects that are about big ideas or problems. And if you see young adolescents this way and learn how to teach in a manner that reveals their promise, along the way they will learn more and learn better than if you see who they are as a problem to be solved in order to teach them abstract content that they, and maybe even you, don't really care about. When this happens you really see that young adolescents can do well, and you put yourself in a position to help parents and guardians see the same.

There is a world of difference between seeing the promise in young adolescents and seeing them as problematic. Seeing the "promise" is at the center of *What Every Middle School Teacher Should Know*. From start to finish, young adolescents are treated with dignity and respect, and their education is more an adventure worth having than a trial to be endured. In a way, saying what every middle school teacher should know may seem pretty pretentious, but what is offered here really does make sense. How can you be a good middle school teacher if you don't know something about young adolescence, or effective curriculum and teaching approaches, or what middle schools are for, or how middle schools ought to be organized? And how can you be really good if you don't see yourself as an advocate for the young adolescents you work with?

Teachers seem to work with one of two general theories. Some hold to the idea that "if only the kids were different, we could do a great job." But because young adolescents are who they are and cannot be someone or something else, this theory can only lead to frustration for both teachers and students, and more than a little conflict between them. Others believe that "if only we did things differently, the kids could do a great job." In the end, it is this second theory that leads toward worthwhile experiences for teachers and students because teachers can shape and reshape classroom life so that young adolescents can do great work. *What Every Middle School Teacher Should Know* is full of ideas and information to support that second theory. And this is why every middle school teacher really should know what's in this book.

◆❚ **Preface**

Young adolescents now reaching the ages of eleven through fifteen have much different lives, in some respects, than those who reached their middle school years seven years ago when we wrote the second edition of this book. Their lives have been heavily influenced by technology in ways that no one could have predicted. The new technology is as natural to teens as breathing. But to the adults in their lives, the uncensored access—a mere finger touch away—to every imaginable event, piece of information, and photo is cause for concern.

That concern is warranted because the social, emotional, physical, and intellectual growth processes of young adolescents are always filled with excitement and unpredictable volatility. Technology has not eliminated those growing pains. Instead, it has created greater dilemmas and stress for any adolescent generation and their families since the opportunities afforded teens with second family cars in the late 1950s—an event that coincided with the highest teenage pregnancy rate in the past seventy years.

Middle level teachers are perhaps also feeling more stress today than when we wrote the previous edition of this book because states have been forced to adopt federal education guidelines requiring teachers be evaluated using students' test scores. The testing industry has shamelessly caused the elimination of many teachers' research-based developmental practices, as educators grapple with how to ensure student-test success rather than choosing innovative pedagogical strategies that excite and promote young adolescents' comprehensive growth. The NCLB era is over, but the replacement federal education department policy du jour is creating more ineffective teaching, and is based on another set of content standards that provide a false sense of learning and limited cognitive growth.

In this new edition, we address this latest external assault on our profession, but include suggestions for folding these lists of facts and behaviors into the middle level philosophy and practices that best meet the needs of young adolescents. Teachers don't have to adopt an either/or perspective—either they prepare students for tests or use developmentally appropriate practices. The middle level teachers' voices within and most recent research demonstrate how to serve both masters.

Our intent in this third edition is similar to the first two editions: to guide preservice and inservice middle level educators in comprehending and responding to the unique growth processes of young adolescents. This edition contains more student voices than the first two, as well as additional teachers' comments on how to guide young adolescents through these challenging times with compassion informed by research-based knowledge. We know that we, teacher educators, and teachers cannot ignore the heavy hand of federal, state, or the testing industry's misguided influence on teachers' thought processes as they design and deliver lessons. But the student voices within and the accompanying research we provide are stark reminders of what young adolescents need teachers to do each day to reach them and help them actually grow during this time of their lives.

We divided the previous edition's Chapters 2 and 3 into four smaller chapters on developmental processes. Adolescent developmental researchers reveal the latest findings on how adolescents respond to their personal challenges, and we provide critical information in Chapter 2 on updated physical growth patterns. Chapter 3 is a look at neuroscience perspectives on cognitive processes and accompanying brain growth, and their effects on young adolescents' unpredictable behaviors and learning characteristics.

In Chapters 4 and 5, among the topics that students and former students describe are their challenges in fitting in socially and finding an ethnic identity, and they describe how these journeys impact their path to social and emotional homeostasis. We would be remiss to ignore the history of the middle level movement, which we describe in Chapter 6, and we include recent suggestions from the Association for Middle Level Education and the National Forum to Accelerate Middle Grades Reform, organizations that prompt middle level schools to adopt the full range of middle school structures that support young adolescents' needs. A recurring topic, initially addressed in Chapter 6, is our concern and suggestions for addressing content standards while continuing to meet students' needs and provide effective learning environments.

We chose to combine the last two chapters from the second edition into the new Chapter 7, which now provides the most recent researched-based positive effects of implementing all of the essential structures of genuine middle level schools. Understanding young adolescent development is a feckless venture unless teachers implement advisories, teaming, common planning time, curriculum integration, and student self-assessment into their school design.

We provide more student voice in this edition in Chapter 8 on why and how teachers can create the environment for learning that young adolescents need. Research clearly supports the power of individual teachers in positively influencing student learning, and we address this with specific teacher behaviors in Chapter 8. Engaging young adolescents in designing curriculum around their questions is an essential component of genuine middle level schools. Addressing new content standards while implementing true curriculum integration is the crux of Chapter 9. We specify how you can accomplish your goals for higher student test scores via student-designed curriculum integration with hard data that support the viability and advantages of implementing this democratic approach to learning.

We devote Chapter 10 to teacher voices on the development of curriculum integration. They explain how to make curriculum integration work and the advantageous journeys that result for their students when in control of curricular decisions. Both experienced teachers and teachers new to curriculum integration describe how and why curriculum integration is so beneficial for students' comprehensive developmental growth.

We replaced earlier descriptions of brain-based learning with recent discoveries in neuroscience, the study of brain functions that inform practical strategies for improving student learning. With that premise, in Chapter 11 we describe several innovative processes—including a new approach to the traditional KWL chart, called KiNL, and Universal Design for Learning—which are other strategies for meeting the needs of diverse learners. New information on culturally responsive teaching also appears in Chapter 11, as do ideas for infusing technology into learning. Chapter 11 ends with advice on how to address content standards while simultaneously helping students grow cognitively by following the middle school philosophy.

Ensuring student growth is the essential message of Chapter 12, in which we describe how to fuse state content standards with assessment—a means of determining what students can or can't do. No appraisal of student learning at the middle level is complete unless it encourages student self-assessment and the accompanying development of metacognitive skills, leading to student-led conferences and personal goal setting.

The Epilogue is new to this edition, and it contains some significant quotes from notable middle level researchers who summarize the essence of a well-prepared middle level educator. It is a "call to arms" to all middle level professionals to embrace middle level philosophies as they continue to make a difference in young adolescents' lives.

If you're wondering if there's anything new in this third edition, consider how the past seven years have changed for young adolescents: the impact of technology and accompanying influence on their lives, the emphases and new information from the Association for Middle Level Education on preserving the mission of genuine middle level schools, the effects of neuroscience on educational practices, the pressure of content standards and teacher evaluation mandates, and the latest middle level education research supporting the middle level concept. These topics are all addressed in this edition. In this time of intense teacher dissatisfaction, we need the middle school philosophy and the innovative practices that accompany it to preserve the joy of being with students and to protect the professionalism that is critical to meeting young adolescents' needs. We urge you to become an advocate and continue your support for the middle level philosophy and design by reading this new edition. Share it with colleagues and caregivers as the rationale for your professional decisions and actions.

PART I:

WHO ARE MIDDLE LEVEL TEACHERS?

For successful middle level educators, teaching is an explicit response to their students' social demeanors and emotional states each day rather than an unyielding determination to get through the next few pages of the book.

CHAPTER 1

You Want to Be a *What*?

One of the biggest challenges of our age is school and the mixture of social life and grades. We are at the age where teachers are trying to get us ready for high school and loading us with work. This can be extremely stressful, especially if you don't know how to manage it. Also, because a lot of us are still immature and are trying to figure out who we are—social life, drama, and fitting in can be a problem. However, because we still need to deal with the stress of grades and homework, the social part of school can be hard to manage. Some people focus more on school and not on social life, and have no friends. On the other hand, others focus only on social life, but are producing bad grades. The most important thing is finding a balance between the two, and we are at the age where we are figuring out where our balance is.

—**ALEX**, AGE FOURTEEN

Imagine that you are a new skier standing on the top of a mountain. You look down with fear. The only way to get to the bottom is to ski down, so you push your poles into the snow and begin. Suddenly you hit full speed. You are flying. You've never felt such exhilaration. Just as quickly, you lose control and fall down, not once, but again and again and again. You are ready to quit, but you are only halfway down the mountain, so you stand up one more time and promise yourself that if you just make it down in one piece, you'll never attempt to ski again. You dig in your poles, take off, and soar to the bottom. Before you know it, you're on the ski lift again. You are halfway up the mountain before you realize you'll have to go down again. You know you'll fall, but you also know you'll fly. It's that one brief moment of flying that makes it all worthwhile.

You are about to take a ride as a middle school teacher. Going to school each day is exhilarating because you love your students. Sometimes you realize, however, that your emotional state matches that of your students, with all the ups and downs. You fall and get up again and again and again. You go home exhausted, wondering why you ever chose teaching as a career. The next day you're back in the classroom and you're soaring. You feel that you could teach forever. Teaching middle schoolers is not an easy trip, but the ride is exhilarating.

◆❙❙ Who Are Young Adolescents?

Adolescence is a stage of development that everyone identifies with and recognizes as a challenging, yet exciting time in life. It would be a mistake, however, to label students from the ages of ten to fifteen as *adolescents*. The unique growth processes in every domain of development—physical, social, emotional, cognitive, and identity—overwhelmingly affect the behaviors, attitudes, and thinking of students in this age range thereby justifying its own label: *young adolescence*.

WHAT ARE THEY LIKE?

What are they like, these young adolescents attending middle school? You've seen them. They're everywhere—walking in the mall, hanging out on street corners, living in your house. In fact, you were one, perhaps not so long ago. You know what they're like.

- They eat all the time.
- Their music is too loud.
- They take social issues very seriously.
- They frequently exclaim, "You don't understand."
- They cry a lot.
- They laugh a lot.
- They're sure that nobody has ever felt what they are feeling.
- They like hanging out at home and being with their parents.
- They hate hanging out at home or being seen with their parents.
- They have difficulty focusing on something for more than a minute at a time.
- They will spend hours texting or playing electronic games.
- They care passionately about the world, and want to save everyone in it.
- They are plagued with acne.
- They are seldom satisfied with the way they look.
- They're loyal to their friends.
- They talk behind their friends' backs.
- They outgrow their clothes every few months.

> Middle school is very complicated.
> —**ROBERT**,
> AGE THIRTEEN

> Not trusting a fourteen-year-old because he is "just fourteen" is silly and stupid. Alexander the Great took the throne before he was sixteen, so why can't I think for myself?
> —**GRANT**,
> AGE FOURTEEN

- Their voices crack when they sing in mixed chorus.
- They want to be independent.
- They don't want to let go of their childhood.

This time of vast emotional, social, physical, and cognitive change has been called *pubescence, transescence, emergent adolescence, early adolescence,* and *young adolescence.* Students at this stage are often called *difficult, obnoxious, hard to handle, impossible,* and *hormonally driven.* We would like to characterize this stage positively.

What should we call this time of change? *Transescence* is out. It is hard to say and sounds like a form of alien abduction. *Pubescence* suggests that the only significant aspect of this age is emerging sexuality. *Emergent adolescence* focuses too much on the future—on what will be instead of what is. What's left is *early* or *young adolescence;* these are the terms we will use in this book.

HOW DO WE DEFINE YOUNG ADOLESCENCE?

Should we define *young adolescence* according to age? Grade level? Physical attributes? Behaviors? Family or peer interactions? Emotions? Cognitive abilities? All of the above?

This period of time is characterized by vast developmental changes. Physical changes are more dramatic than at any other time in life except *in utero* and early infancy. Cognitive changes create vast leaps in thinking ability. Social and emotional changes result in a move from dependence to independence. The development of various identities, from personal to ethnic to sexual, occupies young adolescents' minds as they search for a persona that fits who they want to be. Some children begin these developmental changes at age ten, some not until fifteen. Most are somewhere in between. The definition of *young adolescence* is as complex as the people we are attempting to define.

Perhaps, for purposes of this book, it is better to define *young adolescence* as the time a child spends in middle school. But that definition can also be complicated. Middle level grade configurations are not consistent. The most common grouping is sixth through eighth grade. You will also find middle schools that contain the fifth and/or ninth grades, and some only have seventh and eighth grades. Grade configurations in most circumstances generally don't affect students' social, emotional, or cognitive development. Definitions, however, are not what the young adolescent is all about. Perhaps descriptions are a more appropriate way of explaining this age.

Kevin, a middle level assistant principal, provided this description of an eighth-grade male in his building: "He was carrying around a Build-A-Bear one day he had recently 'built.' Middle level students frequently act like children, but they want to be adults. They look like adults—their bodies are fully developed; some have tattoos—then they forget to wear deodorant." The fluidity of movement that young adolescents experience daily from childlike characteristics to adult behaviors reveals the challenges that accompany being in their presence.

Effective middle level educators respond to students' social and emotional states with acceptance and empathy. For successful middle level educators, teaching is an explicit response to their students' social demeanors and emotional states each day rather than an unyielding determination to get through the next few pages of the book.

TIME FOR REFLECTION

Why do you or did you want to be a middle level teacher? What characteristics do you think a middle level schoolteacher needs to have? How will or do you weigh the urge to complete lessons and ready students for tests with your students' needs for more socialization? How can or do you balance assertiveness with care?

◆❙❙ Becoming a Middle Level Teacher

If students aged ten to fifteen are unique in their developmental growth processes, it follows that their needs differ from elementary students and high schoolers. Teacher training and certification ensure greater opportunities for educators to design learning experiences that match the developmental needs of their students. The distinct differences in the design of certification programs for elementary versus high school teachers are related to students' needs at each of those levels. Young adolescents deserve professional preparation programs for their teachers that prepare middle level educators to respond appropriately to the unique developmental processes that define young adolescence.

MIDDLE LEVEL CERTIFICATION

Some teachers seem to be born to teach in the middle. That's where they want to be and that's where they belong. Some middle level teachers come from the ranks of elementary-certified faculty. Teachers might explain, "I really wanted to teach second grade but this was the only job I could get." Others come from the ranks of certified high school educators: "I really wanted to teach eleventh grade American history and government, but this was the only job I could get."

One elementary certified teacher, Kristi, reported as she started her first experience with middle school, "I was nervous, and every day I came home with a new story of their unexpected behaviors. It's an amazing job, though; every day I get hugs from some kids and mature lectures from other students." Tim, who thought he'd land a job in high school following graduation from college, revealed, "You have no idea what to expect when you get to middle school—I wasn't prepared as a secondary education major for these kids."

McEwin and Greene (2013) reported that forty-five states offer middle level teacher certification, licensure, or endorsement, but many of these states do not *require* teachers to be certified at this level. Twenty-eight states offer the option to be licensed specifically for middle level only, while eighteen states have an endorsement for teaching at the middle level (Mee, Rogers Haverback, and Passe 2012). Most states offer a standard 7–12 content area certificate instead, that many teachers obtain before being hired at the middle level. The "highly qualified" requirements from NCLB only mandated that states ensure that middle level teachers receive content area emphases in their teacher training rather than specific young adolescent development information or specific pedagogical strategies for working with middle level students. However, a national survey of middle level principals revealed that 84 percent believe that it is very important or important for teachers entering the middle school to obtain specific middle level certificates (McEwin and Greene 2011).

Understanding content is one criterion for successful teaching—but only one. Outstanding educators at all grade levels possess something more significant than content knowledge: a deep understanding of their students. Comer (2005) noted the following in studying over a thousand schools across the United States:

> [I]t became clearer that both academic and behavioral success were more likely in places where teachers and administrators bought into the value of basing their work on the principles of child and adolescent development. The focus on child development that is largely missing from the preparation of educators probably contributes more to creating dysfunctional and underperforming schools than anything else. (757–58)

The developmental characteristics of young adolescents are unique. Knowledge of these traits is imperative for you to experience the success you expect to have as a middle level teacher. We fear, as Comer (2005) has discovered, that those teachers who become middle level educators without proper course work on effective middle school practice and young adolescent development will focus on content while ignoring the developmental and academic needs of their students. The result may be student and teacher dissatisfaction and may be detrimental to the success of many students at this crucial period. Middle level teacher, Heather, suggested, "Teaching middle level is all about relationships. The curricula take a back seat to their lives. What's ever on their minds is what teachers must respond to at that moment. Their emotions are a giant shield that gets in the way of the curriculum. The task of the middle school teacher is to develop the middle school child." Effective middle level educators find ways to customize their content so that it complements the developmental traits of their students. Each grade at the middle level requires a different set of strategies to help students connect to the curricula.

So, what should you know before you become a teacher of young adolescents? For beginners, we suggest that you consider young adolescent behaviors that you'll frequently experience. Students will

- ask personal questions about your life and family
- question the way you dress
- surprise you with their sophisticated questions that demonstrate their deep concern about the world
- wonder about the type of car you drive
- ask about how much money you make
- swear at you occasionally
- ask you if you've considered plastic surgery or a makeover
- act completely socially inappropriate on occasion, yet surprise you with their social graces at other times
- experiment with their personality
- fall "in love" and "out of love" weekly
- pass notes
- text message one another during class
- act emotionally out of control one day and completely mature the next
- completely depend on you some days but act totally independent on others.

We consider these behaviors demonstrations of growth. Teaching middle school is not a job for those whose primary aspiration as an educator is the transmission of content. Unless you become knowledgeable of and responsive to the lives of young adolescents, you'll be a frustrated teacher. McEwin and Dickinson (2001) clearly described the value of knowing young adolescents:

Teaching middle level is all about relationships. The curricula take a back seat to their lives.

The most important quality that middle school teachers bring to their classrooms is their commitment to the young adolescents they teach. Without this commitment, there is little substantive progress for either party, and teaching and learning is reduced to some mechanical act, the consequences of which fall most heavily on the young adolescents, their families, and ultimately the nation. (11)

Tim, a middle level social studies teacher, emphasized the importance of teacher/student relationships at the middle level: "You have to be a people person—the kind who can easily form relationships with your students." Middle level assistant principal, Kevin, described the kind of teachers he hires: "I hire the interviewees who do the best job answering questions about the way middle level kids would react in certain situations. The teachers in this building know how to develop students' academic skills using knowledge of kids; and they have strong personalities that fit well with their students' unpredictable social and emotional behaviors." Heather described the uniqueness of middle level teachers noting, "If you like to be the master of your domain, like some high school or elementary teachers, the middle level isn't the right place for you. Middle school teachers are team players—a must in the middle level."

CHARACTERISTICS OF EFFECTIVE MIDDLE LEVEL TEACHERS

If you are in a middle level certification program or hold a middle level teaching certificate, consider yourself fortunate. Being enrolled in a specific middle grades certification program and getting your teaching certificate, however, is not enough. Passing content area tests will also leave you searching for answers for how to succeed with young adolescents. You will need several personal and professional characteristics that you demonstrate daily as a classroom teacher. How does your list of characteristics match ours?

As a middle level teacher you will need

- a sense of humor that you share with students regularly
- flexibility that you demonstrate in your instructional and curricular planning and delivery
- the ability to actively listen to your students
- the ability to show unconditional caring for your students
- a contagious passion for learning
- a willingness to move beyond the boundaries of your subject area
- a philosophy and action plan that places students at the center of the learning process

- a belief in the process of collaborating with students regarding instruction and curriculum
- the confidence to guide students on their path to learning
- an awareness of adolescent health issues and a willingness to address these issues with students
- a strong sense of your own identity
- a wealth of knowledge about young adolescent development
- a belief in all students' ability to succeed
- knowledge and skills to help all students achieve success.

Naturally, the list could go on. The one trait, however, that your students will notice clearly each day they see you is a positive attitude. Nechochea et al. (2001) described its importance:

A positive attitude for teaching adolescents is a necessary element for becoming an effective middle level teacher. Because of its elusive nature, teacher attitude is difficult to teach, but by all means needs to be incorporated into teacher education programs to instill a sense that middle school teachers can make a significant difference in the lives of young adolescents. (176–77)

As you read through this book, ask yourself whether your personality and educational philosophies match the characteristics necessary to be an effective middle school teacher.

TIME FOR REFLECTION

What questions or concerns do you have about young adolescents or the structure of middle school?
What questions or concerns do you have about being a middle school teacher?
What do you think is the most important thing a middle school student can do or learn in school?

Your answers to the first two questions will become the basis for your inquiry into middle level education. Your answer to the third will develop into your philosophy of learning at the middle level. This book will enable you to explore your questions concerning middle level education.

We hope that you will find the answers to many of your questions in this book. We suspect that as you read it you will generate additional questions. In fact, we hope this is the case. Learning begins with asking questions, and the most effective teachers are inspired by their own quest for learning. So hold onto your hat. We believe working with young adolescents will be the most exhilarating ride you will ever take.

Adolescence is one of the most fascinating and complex transitions in the life span: a time of accelerated growth and change second only to infancy; a time of expanding horizons, self-discovery, and emerging independence; a time of metamorphosis from childhood to adulthood.

PART 2:

WHO ARE YOUR STUDENTS?

CHAPTER 2

Understanding

Young Adolescents'

Physical Development

Being a young adolescent is very cool because you're going through lots of changes—like, your body is changing and your voice is cracking and it's a new environment. And I'm meeting lots of people I never met before and switching class. I don't have recess anymore.

—**ERIC**, AGE THIRTEEN

This awkward transition phase from child to adult is difficult mentally, emotionally, and socially, which ultimately leaves us as the tired and cranky "young adults" that we are said to be.

—**MAIA**, AGE FOURTEEN

Your success as a middle level teacher will be determined by both your comprehensive knowledge of young adolescents and your ability to respond to their varied needs. Their bodies and minds are changing, creating a preoccupation with self-examination as they strive to discover and craft a personality. As the young adolescent begins to foster independence from the family, social interaction with peers becomes very important. It's not always easy to cope with such rapid and dramatic changes. One thirteen-year-old, Evan, described the difficulty he experienced: "It's a really tough time. You're not a teenager but you're not a baby. I think it would be easier if you were an adult or younger."

Creating a school environment that is responsive to the changing needs of young adolescents requires an understanding of their developmental changes. More importantly, however, it requires an understanding of how young adolescents perceive those changes. Their perceptions become their reality.

Figure 2.1 shows how Lindsay, an eighth grader, describes herself in both poetry and art.

What's on the Inside

I am an artist,

who draws what she feels, sees, and encounters,

I need love from my friends and family,

I need affection to help me be successful in life,

I want to be all I can be,

To do this I will work hard to achieve,

I am human,

I make mistakes and learn from them,

I will not give up and therefore,

I will be the best by being me.

—Lindsay Hamilton

Figure 2.1 Lindsay's Self-Description

TIME FOR REFLECTION

Dig through some old pictures of yourself and find one from your middle school years. Write a few thoughts about how you felt about yourself during that time of your life.

Photo day arrives at Smith Middle School. Students line up from shortest to tallest and march into the gym to have their pictures taken. There they stand: from four feet nine inches to six feet two inches. Six months ago, they were much more similar in size. What is happening to these kids?

It's *puberty*—a word that strikes fear in the hearts of parents and confusion in the hearts of young adolescents. When does it start? When does it end? Does puberty

> The greatest problem for middle schoolers is growing up too fast.
> —**BESSIE**, AGE THIRTEEN

> I've changed physically. I've gotten so out of shape. I come home so tired every day. All I want to do is eat. I gained twenty pounds this year.
> —**DAN**, AGE TWELVE

start when the physical changes begin? For some of your students that may be as early as ten or as late as fifteen. Does it start when the child goes to middle school? That may be fifth, sixth, or seventh grade. If we can't even identify when it starts, how will we know how to address it? How do these changes affect our students? How do these physical changes affect our attitudes and expectations toward our students?

Physical development is an overriding concern of young adolescents. Looking at themselves in every mirror they can find, they will often see an alien body staring back. Whether it's the reflection in the bathroom mirror at home or the one hung in their locker, in the window of a car, the doorknob to their classroom, or a cafeteria spoon, middle level students watch themselves, convinced that everyone else is watching them too. They want to know, "Am I normal?"

A former school administrator tells a story that emphasizes the need young adolescents have for self-examination (Blackburn 1999). A middle school principal was receiving complaints from teachers in the building that students were constantly going to the restroom during class. Annoyed by the students' need to leave during lessons, the teachers were looking for solutions. The perceptive principal asked the central office administrator to purchase mirrors for every classroom. The mirrors were placed strategically inside the door of each classroom. The result was an amazing drop in the number of student requests for restroom breaks.

◆❘❘ The Growth Spurt

The first physical change in young adolescents is a growth spurt of the skeletal and muscular systems that begins at about age ten for girls and twelve for boys and lasts for two to three years. The sequences of the changes tend to be somewhat consistent, although individual variations occur. What is less standardized is the age and speed at which the changes happen (Rice and Dolgin 2005).

Height gain may be as much as four or more inches a year in young adolescents, with usually two years of fast growth followed by three years of slow, steady growth. That could mean the addition of ten to twenty inches in just five years. Average height gain during adolescence for females is seven inches; for males, it is nine to ten inches.

Weight gains amount to eight to ten pounds a year. Many young adolescents gain as much as forty to fifty pounds before it's all over. One middle schooler told us, "I

Theory into Practice

Young adolescents' concerns about their bodies are manifested in social and emotional reactions that may affect their ability to learn. Understanding physical development is vital in creating an environment conducive to learning.

gained ten pounds in six months. I'm not too proud of that." Another student added, "In the last year I've grown a lot—four or five inches."

Girls' growth spurts peak about two years earlier than boys'. Attend a middle school dance, and you will observe this phenomenon firsthand: five-foot-five-inch girls dancing with five-foot-one-inch boys. Suddenly girls are taller, stronger, and more mature than most of the boys their age.

◆‖ Skeletal and Muscular Changes

A defining characteristic of the physical development of young adolescents is rapid and uneven skeletal change. The bones in the legs may grow when nothing else seems to be growing, giving young adolescents the appearance of being all legs. The feet may grow while height remains constant. Arms may lengthen while the torso stays the same. The hands may seem disproportionately large. The result is "the awkward stage." In June of one year, the body is well proportioned; the student is an exceptional athlete. The following June, the child is lanky and graceless. What happened to the physical coordination of just a year before?

To complicate matters further, bone growth tends to surpass muscle growth (Sheehy et al. 1999). This variable development is significant, particularly in physical education and sports programs: Kids are often encouraged to lift heavier weights, jump higher, throw curve balls, and run faster when their muscles cannot sustain the effort. This information is something male and female athletes need to understand, but it's probably more critical information for their coaches.

Van Hoose and Strahan (1988) reported that another result of the changing skeletal structure of young adolescents is that the three tailbones fuse and harden into their final adult form. It is a process that can cause pain and discomfort. Eric told us, "Sometimes when the teachers are not looking, I need to stand." When Tom, age thirteen, was asked what he would change about school, he commented, "I would change the chairs. We have rock-hard chairs and it hurts after a while."

Long bones, awkwardness, underdeveloped muscles, pain in the tailbone, huge feet, long hands—no wonder the young adolescent is concerned. Despite these uncomfortable growing pains, we put them in a setting where they have to sit for most of the day.

**Theory into
Practice**

What are some of the strategies teachers can use to address the physical needs of middle level students? Describe ways that teachers can help students manage in a room for 45+ minutes with traditional classroom furniture. When you're feeling physically spent, how do you find comfort? And how can you transfer your solutions for comfort into your classroom?

◆‖ **Hormones**

Scientists have identified almost fifty different types of human hormones. They are essential to everyday life, and they are at play every moment of our lives, every year of our life. So, if hormones regulate all sorts of bodily functions for all ages of people, why would we blame hormones for the teenage daughter's sudden [emotional] outburst? (Walsh 2004, 61)

Hormones have gotten a bad rap in discussions about young adolescents; they are often blamed for behaviors that many adults don't seem to understand. Hormones play a powerful role in development. If we understand their role, we can better understand young adolescent behaviors.

The body begins preparing for full sexual maturity during early adolescence. Males and females experience increased amounts of the hormones testosterone and estradiol that affect sexual development.

The most dramatic increase for males is in testosterone. Walsh (2004) reported that testosterone affects the male brain as well as sexual characteristics: "While testosterone does all sorts of good things, it is also likely to trigger surges of anger, aggression, sexual interest, dominance, and territoriality" (62).

The primary increase for females is in the hormone estradiol, or estrogen; levels are approximately eight times what they were before puberty (Nottelmann et al. 1987). Estrogen along with progesterone "[H]ave a powerful influence over neurotransmitters. The main neurotransmitters that are active in the adolescent brain are norepinephrine, dopamine, and serotonin. All three have a big influence on mood" (Walsh 2004, 63).

Hormonal secretions dictated by the pituitary gland also increase, often in an irregular way. For example, sudden secretions of adrenaline into the body from the adrenal gland could make the young adolescent want to run around the school building ten times just when asked to sit and do a worksheet. At other times, the gland is underactive, resulting in lethargy (Association for Middle Level Education [AMLE] 2010). Peter, a sixth grader, describes the result of these physical changes: "One of the hardest things for me is just waking up in the morning and going through the day without pulses of tiredness. Sometimes I get real restless because I get really tired."

Sweat glands also become very active, explaining why classroom windows are frequently open even in the dead of winter. Active sweat glands contribute to oily hair and the development of that scourge of adolescence—acne. One middle school language arts teacher describes how she insists on giving her eighth graders the "deodor-ant talk" each year in late October, explaining that although they may not notice their body odor, she and others do. She continues to explain how their bodies are changing and the need to address those changes with proper hygiene.

◆❚ Female Physical Changes

In addition to the growth spurt, during young adolescence the female body prepares for full reproductive capability. The major benchmark is menstruation, accompanied by the fear in girls that they'll be the last in their peer group to experience it.

Along with menstruation, girls experience breast development—often accompa-nied by behavioral changes such as the wearing of baggy shirts; the adoption of an erect, proud walk or a slumping of the shoulders in an effort to conceal development; the growth of pubic and underarm hair; and rounding of the hips.

The beginning of menstruation creates challenges for many females. Many girls have a negative view of it, particularly those who mature before the age of twelve (Rice and Dolgin 2005). Medical research reveals that puberty and physical sexual maturity are occurring earlier for males and females than they did a century ago (Berk 2012; Walsh 2004). Researchers have noted that African American females reach puberty about six months earlier on average than Caucasian females (Anderson, Dallal, and Must 2003). Researchers also discovered that girls from families in conflict are more likely to reach menarche earlier (Bogaert 2005; Tremblay and Frigon 2005).

Several researchers report that early developing females may be at greater risk of developing mental health issues because they are not prepared for the physical, psy-chological, and social challenges brought on by puberty (Ge et al. 2003; Graber 2003). For instance, girls who are early maturers "are more likely than other girls to exhibit depressive, eating, and delinquent symptoms as well as general behavior prob-lems" (Graber et al. 2002, 40).

Early physically maturing females may experience low self-esteem because they are so different from their peers: they're heavier, taller, and more developed sexually. Berk (2012) reported that "(E)arly physical maturers of both sexes more often report feeling emotionally stressed and show declines in academic performance" (542).

In her study of 335 adolescents over a three-year period from sixth through eighth grade and during their last year of high school, Petersen (1987) found that late or early maturation affected individual satisfaction with appearance. The girls Petersen studied

Theory into Practice

Young adolescents need frequent physical activity despite often being tired during the day. Provide stretching exercises, two-minute dance periods, or a walk or run up the nearest stairwell during each class you teach. Insist that your school provide a time for an unstructured recess period at all middle grade levels.

Theory into Practice

*We believe every middle
school teacher is a
health teacher because
young adolescents have
a constant stream of
questions about their
health, questions that may
never be asked of parents.
Discussions about
physical growth concerns
can be uncomfortable
for many teachers who
aren't certified as health
teachers, nurses, or
counselors. When teachers
are uncomfortable, they
should guide students to
appropriate personnel
and/or encourage them to
hold conversations with
their parents.*

"

I know everything I
need to know about
being an adolescent.
You grow hair on your
chin and want to have
sex all the time.
—ROBERT,
AGE TEN

in the seventh and eighth grades seemed less satisfied if they were early maturers. Although these girls were seen as more popular, at a personal level they were often self-conscious and insecure.

An adolescent's physical maturity is no guarantee of simultaneous social or emotional maturity. Adults' unrealistic expectations of mature social and emotional behaviors can add to the undue pressure that physically early-maturing young adolescents may already experience. We hope that every middle level school provides a health education curriculum that addresses these issues and encourages all teachers to help students find the appropriate adult to address sensitive physical growth issues.

◆❙ Male Physical Changes

Males generally begin the physical maturation process later than females. The growth spurt begins between the ages of eleven and a half and thirteen. Most males don't reach their full height until age seventeen. The greater physical changes for most males occur between the ages of thirteen and sixteen. The voice deepens because of the rapid growth of the larynx (Adam's apple) and a lengthening of the vocal cords across it (Archibald, Graber, and Brooks-Gunn 2006).

A primary physical maturational characteristic for males is testicular and penile growth. Frequent erections are common during adolescence and may cause a lot of embarrassment (Rice and Dolgin 2005). Most young adolescent males experience nocturnal emissions, also called "wet dreams." The first ejaculation, called "semenarche" or "spermarche," occurs for most males before their thirteenth birthday. This event, unlike females' first menses, is usually hidden from others, since many males have no knowledge that this is going to happen. Paddack (1987) reported that boys who are taught about these physical changes have more positive feelings about their occurrence. We hope, once again, that as a middle school teacher you can understand the importance of finding appropriate health teachers to disseminate information to young adolescents about these changes.

Other later physical signs of male physical maturity include a broadening of the shoulders, facial hair growth, and muscular development. While some young adolescents experience these changes by eighth grade, others may be far from any need to shave.

Males who don't begin to mature physically by age fifteen are more likely to suffer negative effects than on-time or early-maturing males. The first challenge is what

Rice and Dolgin (2005) refer to as "locker-room syndrome": In the locker room, some males begin to notice that they have less hair in places, have an underdeveloped penis, are considerably shorter, and have less-developed muscles (91). Males who reach puberty much later than their counterparts may experience feelings of inferiority due to poorer athletic skills and a less mature appearance, and they reported being more anxious and depressed than early maturing males (Graber et al. 2002; Huddleson and Ge 2003). Graber et al. also noted in their study that "late-maturing boys reported more self-consciousness, more conflict with parents, and more trouble in school" (47).

Early maturers enjoy many social advantages because their superior height and advanced muscle development often provide success in athletics, greater leadership roles, and more popularity among peers and adults (Berk 2012). Rice and Dolgin (2005) noted that early-maturing males generally have greater expectations for mature behavior and responsibility placed on them from adults in their lives and are often given greater freedom with less supervision. Early maturers may then be expected to participate in activities that are more appropriate for older adolescents. For instance, one of us taught an eighth-grade male who was six feet four inches tall and an accomplished player on the school's basketball team. He enjoyed skateboarding with friends, but when he got hurt doing that the coach was upset by his participating in a "childish" activity.

◆▌▌ The Appetite: Insatiable and Peculiar

Young adolescents require a wide variety of nutrients because of the rapid growth of the skeletal system and other physical changes. It is common for young adolescents to eat continuously from the time they get home from school until bedtime. Active young adolescents need anywhere from two to three thousand calories a day. Females generally need fewer calories due to a smaller stature and a lower metabolic rate (Berk 2012).

Physical type and size as well as activity levels should determine how many calories an adolescent needs. Unfortunately, given the cultural prevalence of fast food in this country, many of these kids are not eating foods that give them the maximum benefit.

Several factors exist that prevent adolescents from eating well. Young adolescents often choose snacks high in fat and sugar while eating only small quantities of nutritious foods. Rice and Dolgin (2005) reported, "One quarter of all vegetables eaten by teens are french fries" (114). Adolescents often don't eat regular healthy

**Theory into
Practice**

*Males receive less support
and guidance during
puberty than females,
from both parents and
educators. Early physically
maturing males need to
be able to act their age—
not be treated as adults.
Be sure you hold realistic
expectations for behavior
rather than expecting them
to act more mature socially
and emotionally. Be careful
not to assign too much
responsibility to them, thus
creating undue stress.*

meals with their families. Social pressures may also affect eating habits, particularly among females.

The structure of the middle school day can also contribute to poor nutrition. Imagine your students catching the bus at 7:00 a.m. but not having a lunch period until 12:45. That span of time without food can have an impact on learning. In addition, students who eat lunch at 10:30 may not be getting the appropriate nutrition they need for effective learning later in the day. Most schools prohibit any eating in the halls or classrooms, meaning that many students are going through their busy days without eating for as long as five hours. Add an extracurricular activity to that after school and students extend their time without food even longer.

Despite their needs for more caloric intake, many young adolescents make poor dietary decisions. Adolescents are the most likely age group to skip breakfast and eat between meals (Ritchie et al. 2007). Vending machines at school and school lunch choices can contribute to unhealthy eating habits, as well as daily influences of peers.

Childhood obesity rates have increased since the mid-1970s, and currently approximately one third of school-age children and adolescents are overweight (Flegal et al. 2010). The trend during the past few years is a leveling off of the percentage of overweight youth, but childhood obesity remains a health concern in the United States (Santrock 2013). A greater percentage of ethnic minorities are overweight and obese than Caucasian youth (Ogden et al. 2010). There are many health risks associated with obesity, but among adolescents, issues of social rejection and low self-esteem also affect their lives (Berk 2012). Rimm (2005) noted that both males and females who were overweight had considerably less confidence and generally didn't believe they were above average intelligence. Rimm's story of an overweight female's description of how her eighth-grade teacher encouraged her is something that every middle school teacher should hear:

Ever since I was a little kid, I was fat, and that made me feel different from other kids. Kids left me out of their groups. A wall kept going up separating me from everyone. This year my teacher liked me. She told me I was good at writing, math, and music and that I had a good personality. Her confidence made me feel different, but in a good way. I started making friends and felt smart and better about myself. (205)

The other side of unhealthy adolescent eating behaviors is that the ideal American body image leads some adolescents to deny even minimal nutritional needs. Researchers note that about one percent of female adolescents have anorexia (Anorexia Nervosa and Related Eating Disorders [ANRED] 2008). Anorexia nervosa afflicts all socioeconomic levels and is more common among Asian, Caucasian, and Hispanic American females than African American females (Berk 2012). Approximately 10 to 15 percent of those diagnosed with anorexia are boys, and about half of those are homosexual or bisexual (Raevuori et al. 2009).

This want for the perfect body image influences some young adolescents to seek an easy path to male physical dominance, so some males succumb to a habit of taking steroids to develop what they believe is an appropriate body type. Although high school males are more likely to use steroids, use among younger males during middle level years does occur.

◆❚ Adolescents' Sleep Needs

Ask middle school teachers about their class schedules and some will tell you that they despise teaching first period because their students are so tired they appear comatose or close to it. Young adolescents of this generation receive less sleep than those from previous years because they have so many additional stimuli to keep them awake for hours in the evening: cell phones, computers, electronic games, and, often, televisions in their rooms (Carskadon, Acebo, and Jenni 2004).

The expectation to communicate almost entirely by texting or with social media such as Facebook has increased social demands on adolescents. To ignore responding to friends electronically in the evening is unthinkable to anyone who wants to be in, or become a member of, a peer group. Evidence of less adolescent sleep is indicated in a study of 600 thirteen- to eighteen-year-olds in which 54 percent revealed receiving less than six to eight hours of sleep a night during school evenings (Chen, Wang, and Jeng 2006). Less sleep among these adolescents led to reduced exercise, an inability to manage stress well, and poor eating habits.

Carskadon (1999), a sleep researcher, explained that the hormone melatonin that regulates sleep is secreted later at night as teens progress through puberty. This translates into teens' inability to go to sleep early at night and wake early in the morning. In addition, teens need approximately nine and a half hours of sleep to function effectively during the day (Crowley and Carskadon 2010). Telling them to go to sleep earlier isn't necessarily the solution since the delayed release of melatonin prevents them from feeling tired.

Sleep aids in the release of hormones needed by adolescents for growth and sexual maturation (Wolfe 2005). Adequate sleep is also necessary for the brain to regenerate

Theory into Practice

Teachable moments occur often in middle school classrooms as students discuss their favorite music groups, actors, or athletes. These are prime opportunities to talk about cultural influences on body images versus realistic physical appearance. Teachers' familiarity with all their students provides opportunities to notice weight challenges among certain students and when severe weight changes occur for others. Conversations with nurses and parents can help all the adults who know these adolescents address sudden changes.

and operate efficiently during the day. Sleep deprivation causes numerous problems for adolescents:

- contributes to poor reasoning
- causes difficulty focusing
- impairs functioning memory
- increases the stress hormone cortisol that compromises the immune system
- affects alertness
- impairs the ability to process glucose, which contributes to excess weight. (Walsh 2004, 182)

Sleep deprivation may also lead to mood disorders in which feelings are more intense, which may lead to difficulty controlling emotions. Armed with this information as a middle school teacher, your reaction to students' emotional outbursts must be more tolerant.

Wolfson and Carskadon (1998) studied sleep patterns among adolescents and found that students earning C and D grades were getting about forty minutes less sleep per night and stayed up later on weekends than students receiving A's and B's.

◆❙❙ Concluding Reflections

Not surprisingly, young adolescents' self-esteems are strongly associated with their acceptance and perceptions of their body images (Harter 2006). When teachers notice that students are rude to one another, seem irritated, and lash out at adults, these behaviors can often be attributed to the uncertainty about their bodies.

Effective middle level teachers recognize their frustration and address the unruly behaviors with an understanding of what students are experiencing. Empathy is needed to assure students that variations in growth during their middle level years is normal and that negative feelings associated with their growth are common. Helping students focus on their other strengths and having appropriate personnel provide factual information on what they are experiencing may stem the frustration. Just listening to them may be the most meaningful action teachers can take.

**Theory into
Practice**

*Teachers can't control
when students go to bed
at night or the habits that
exist in their students'
homes. They can, however,
advise adolescents and
their caregivers that
middle level students
need a great deal of sleep
and that there are serious
consequences to their
ability to learn when
they ignore those needs.
Teachers should not
embarrass students who
fall asleep in class, but
instead should speak to
them privately about their
sleep habits and educate
them about the value of
sleep to their academic
success and overall health.*

CHAPTER 3

Understanding Young Adolescents' Unique Brain Growth and Cognitive Development

I don't have good time management and decision-making skills, so it makes it extremely hard to juggle everything in middle school.

—**JAY**, EIGHTH GRADER

I think my biggest challenge is getting all the kids in the class to reach the same conclusions and the same level of thinking—which I can't do. So, when I ask why something happens, I have some kids who are wondering what's happened.

—EIGHTH-GRADE TEACHER

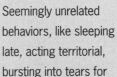

Seemingly unrelated behaviors, like sleeping late, acting territorial, bursting into tears for no reason, and taking risks, make much more sense when you know what's happening inside the adolescent brain.

—**WALSH**
(2004, 12)

The term *developmentally appropriate practice* has been used for well over thirty years in educational research and literature as a defining description of teaching young children—especially during primary school. This same term is used in the research on teaching young adolescents, although the emphasis on raising test scores and meeting content standards often erases this essential guiding instructional and curricular principle from middle schools. Teaching to the cognitive needs of young adolescents in some way defines the difference between the original junior highs and genuine middle schools; but more importantly, responding appropriately to their cognitive needs leads to genuine learning.

◆▌▌ The Effects of Blossoming, Pruning, and Myelination

Although the brain of an adolescent is fully grown if one is measuring its physical size, it's what's going on inside that heavily influences the behaviors, attitudes, and learning capabilities of young adolescents. Using new medical technology for the past decade, medical scientists have been able to peer inside adolescents' brains (Giedd et al. 2006).

Of particular importance to teachers are the continued "blossoming" and "pruning" of brain connections and the myelination of brain cells that are especially prevalent during growth spurts. Blossoming occurs when dendrites in the brain go through hypergrowth—that is, more brain connections are being made. This hypergrowth peaks for females around age eleven and for males around twelve and a half.

All these new brain cells don't survive; those that are not regularly used shrink and eventually disappear. This is called *pruning*, but it is a positive rather than a negative process. Walsh (2004) stated, "The periods of blossoming and pruning are critical in brain development. Experiences during these periods, more than any other time, physically shape the brain's neural networks and have a huge influence on how the brain gets wired" (34). Walsh added that critical areas of the brain undergo blossoming and pruning *only* during adolescence. Young adolescents also begin to process information more effectively than before due also to the thickening of the corpus callosum in the center of the brain that contains fibers connecting the right and left hemispheres (Gilliam et al. 2011).

Myelin is a white fatty substance, an insulator, that covers the main cable of the neuron—the axon—making nerve-signal transmissions faster and more efficient. Walsh (2004) reported that the myelination process in certain parts of the adolescent brain "actually increase[s] by 100 percent from the beginning to the end of adolescence" (37). The result of pruning and myelination is fewer but faster connections in the brain, making it more efficient. More myelination improves short-term memory, which may in turn lead to better reasoning and problem solving (Lenroot and Giedd 2011). These cognitive changes are revealed in young adolescents' intense curiosity, varying intellectual development, ability to think abstractly in more situations, and greater need for active versus passive learning (AMLE 2010).

Cognitive processing will improve if students are given powerful learning experiences with opportunities to make genuine connections between content and their experiences. Traditional instructional approaches involving lectures, note taking, or copying from a book will not improve middle school students' cognitive growth.

**Theory into
Practice**

*More efficient processing
takes time to develop in
middle school students—
they're not yet adults.
Young adolescents need
meaningful, challenging
learning experiences in
order to develop and
sustain cognitive growth
processes.*

◆❙❙ The Effects on the Brain of Multitasking with Technology

The influence of technology on students' lives heavily influences the minds of young adolescents. Despite young adolescents' growing cognitive skills, they are not immune to the distractions caused by the allure of socializing via their latest electronic device. The term *multitasking* has often been used as if it's akin to intellectual superiority. That belief is based on several *fallacies* about learning.

The complexity of the brain reveals that certain kinds of meaningful learning are actually linear processes. The brains of those who multitask are actually only performing one task at a time—although they may be switching back and forth quickly, only one cognitive task is being completed at a time. Imagine reading a book, then texting, then returning to the book—are you actually reading and texting simultaneously? Or does it take time to return to the correct passage in the book? Three researchers discovered that those who multitask are much more inefficient than they would be if they merely focused on one task at a time (Rubenstein, Meyer, and Evans 2001).

The type of learning that should occur in school and while completing assignments is called *declarative* learning—higher-level learning that leads to greater applicability and is deeply embedded in long-term memory so that one may use the information again when needed in novel situations. If students want to create permanent memories, they need to ensure that they are singularly focused while reading or completing computations, or learning new principles. Completing assignments while texting or emailing friends, watching videos for entertainment, or snapping pictures to share on social media obliterates any opportunities for meaningful and sustained learning due the brain's inability to simultaneously or efficiently conduct both activities.

◆❙❙ The Prefrontal Cortex: Its Effects on Behavior

Some of the most significant changes occurring during young adolescence are changes to the prefrontal cortex (PFC) of the brain. The PFC is the CEO of the brain, influencing one's abilities and skills in making appropriate decisions, considering the impact of certain behaviors, planning for the future, and organizing materials. Walsh (2004) described it as a major "construction site," noting that it is far from being fully developed throughout all of adolescence (43). Since the PFC is far from mature during

Theory into Practice

Teachers and parents can and should explain the perils of multitasking to their adolescent charges. Demonstrating this in class with students would clarify the fallacy that multitasking is a productive manner to learn. We suggest explaining to parents and students that unless they are legitimately using technology in their schoolwork, leaving electronic devices in a remote location while completing assignments will lead to a much better understanding of new principles in that latest homework assignment, and ultimately more long-term meaningful learning.

Theory into Practice

It is critical for educators to challenge students with meaningful learning opportunities that match their interests while helping them acquire the cognitive strategies needed to organize, prioritize, and take responsibility for their learning. Many middle level students need assistance in developing organizational strategies. Time must be provided each class period to show students how to organize class materials and content. Teachers should explicitly describe how they organize their work space and content knowledge as a way to encourage students to think about organizing their own thinking and materials.

young adolescence, middle school students may lack many of the organizational and social skills that teachers expect.

When we asked experienced middle level teachers, "What are the most important concepts and principles for students to learn during their middle school years?" one of their frequent responses was, "To learn how to be organized." Given young adolescents' developing PFC and teachers' learning priorities, it's easy to see how teachers might become frustrated with their efforts to help students gain such skills as writing assignments in notebooks, organizing their lockers, prioritizing after-school activities, choosing the appropriate books and materials for class, organizing an essay, or choosing the right strategies for solving problems.

◆❚ Piaget's Findings

Jean Piaget (1977a) provided the first distinct description of the stages of intellectual development. Of the four cognitive stages identified by Piaget, the final two, concrete operations and formal operations, describe what is happening intellectually to young adolescents.

CONCRETE OPERATIONAL THOUGHT

In the concrete stage, students can do the following:
- classify and order objects into hierarchical relationships
- understand reverse processes (comprehend that all actions, even mental actions, have an opposite)
- think logically about concrete objects
- arrange objects in order from large to small or small to large
- conceptually combine objects to form categories, for example, "boxes" and "jars" into "container." (Rice and Dolgin 2005, 124–25)

Elkind (1970) warned, however, that the learner in the concrete stage of cognitive development can understand only two classes or relationships at the same time. Elkind also noted that those children in the concrete stage "can only reason about those things for which they have had direct, personal experience" (Rice and Dolgin 2005, 125).

It is clear then that students who process information at the concrete stage need direct experiences and do better with real as opposed to abstract objects or thought. Middle level students in this concrete stage are better able to cognitively grasp higher-level principles when ideas are taught with the use of hands-on activities and real materials rather than presented in a lecture or by reading a textbook. Teachers must be aware that most middle school students remain in this concrete operational stage through eighth grade (Newman, Spalding, and Yezzi 2000; Muuss 1988; Piaget 1977a).

FORMAL OPERATIONAL THOUGHT

In the formal operational stage, students develop the capability to think in hypothetical ways about abstract ideas as well as to generate and test hypotheses systematically. When asked how his thinking had changed, Rob (age fourteen) responded, "I think I examine problems more and try to put the problem with something else I already know." Formal operational thought implies that students can understand the multidimensional nature of problems.

Another formal operations skill is the ability to think about the future and therefore to plan and explore, often with an extremely idealistic perspective—hence middle school students' sudden preoccupation with life plans and their concern for the world around them.

Another trait of formal thought is an ability to expand one's thinking. The middle school student's mind is suddenly open to a myriad of ideas, solutions, and imaginings. The ability to think hypothetically produces unconstrained thoughts and a sense of unlimited possibilities. "Reality" is no longer the benchmark of thought, having been overtaken instead by "what is possible."

METACOGNITION

One of the most powerful growth processes during this stage is the development of metacognition, or the ability to reflect on one's thoughts. Caine and Caine (1994) describe *metacognition* as "thinking about the way we think, feel and act" (160). When a seventh grader doesn't understand something, he or she can suddenly think about not understanding. Such thinking may not lead to understanding and may in fact lead to frustration. They may even worry about why they are thinking about their thinking.

For the early adolescent, the growth of metacognitive abilities generates greater understanding of abstract principles and results in more meaningful learning. Metacognitive growth includes the ability to monitor and reflect on on-task academic behavior. Another essential aspect of metacognition is the realization that students must take responsibility for their academic effort. Students tap into their metacognitive skills when they choose among a set of strategies to use to solve problems or

Theory into Practice

Students often misunderstand lessons when teachers "cover" vocabulary words too quickly for them to understand the new concepts and principles associated with these words. Some teachers believe that their students can absorb a long list of 20 to 25 vocabulary words a week, meaning they completely comprehend their meanings and will know how to use these words later. Teachers attempting to disseminate this much information in short time periods fail to help many middle schoolers genuinely understand new content.

> The middle school
> student's mind is
> suddenly open to
> a myriad of ideas,
> solutions, and
> imaginings.

**Theory into
Practice**

*Teachers can help students
develop these strategies by
explicitly modeling them—
literally saying out loud,
"When I can't solve the
problem this way, I think,
'Maybe I'll try reversing
those numbers to see what
effect that has on solving
this problem.'" Teachers
can also help students
identify their preferred
learning style and explain
to students that they are
personally in control of
their attitudes and effort
toward learning.*

complete assignments. A final aspect of metacognition is an awareness of their personal learning profile: "I know I will understand this better if I draw a picture."

MOVING FROM CONCRETE TO FORMAL THOUGHT

Most students will be in the concrete operational stage as they enter middle school and experience periods of formal operational thought by the time they leave. Middle school is a period of cognitive transition where students move back and forth between concrete and formal operational thought. Many students remain primarily in the concrete operational stage of development throughout their middle school careers, with only about one third of eighth graders consistently demonstrating an ability to use formal operations (Newman, Spaulding, and Yezzi 2000; Piaget 1977b). Lounsbury and Clark (1990) indicated that academically talented eighth graders often experience confusion because they are adjusting to and accommodating more powerful cognitive strategies.

When young adolescents use their formal operational thinking abilities, they begin demonstrating traits of intellectual growth in the following ways:

- persevering when the solution to a problem is not immediately apparent
- decreasing impulsivity and deferring judgment until adequate information is available
- using flexibility in thinking and sustaining problem-solving skills until an answer is found
- checking the accuracy of their work
- initiating questions themselves instead of relying on teachers to ask questions
- transferring knowledge beyond the classroom to real life
- using more precise language in speech and writing
- enjoying problem solving on their own. (adapted from Forte and Schurr 1993, 201, and Schurr and Forte 2009, 31)

Teachers must cognitively challenge young adolescents to help them take advantage of their intense brain growth. We don't want teachers to believe that because most middle level students haven't reached formal operations that the curricula must be "dumbed down." Young adolescents are ready for many intellectual challenges that lead them to capitalize on their cognitive potential. It is the manner in which lessons are presented and the opportunities students have to interact intellectually with new concepts, principles, ideas, and theories that determine whether your lessons will contribute to their movement from concrete to formal operational thought. As Rice and Dolgin (2005) noted: "The highest levels of reasoning are attained when individuals are given the chance to discuss, argue, and debate with people whose views are different from their own" (137). Using interactive learning and engaging students in the process of curriculum decision making are significant strategies for effecting cognitive change.

Middle school students are learners in the purest sense of the word. With their developing capacity for abstract thinking, middle level students are curious about life and highly inquisitive about everything life has to offer. They challenge principles that don't fit their view of the way things work. This curiosity leads to the desire to participate in practical problem solving and activities that reflect real issues.

◆❚❚ Adolescent Risk-Taking

Even the meekest, smartest, most obedient, and sensible teenager will, at some point or another, find himself or herself facing the angry, disbelieving face of an adult who shouts, "What were you thinking?" (Walsh 2004, 55)

All these cognitive changes among young adolescents create another challenge in their lives: a desire to engage in risky behaviors; that is, a time of physical, social, and emotional excitement and impulsivity beyond the daily routine.

A result of expanding thought processes is the sense of personal uniqueness and infallibility. Middle level students are certain that no one has ever thought the thoughts they are thinking or felt the feelings they are feeling. As they get caught up in their personal worlds, young adolescents can begin to feel indestructible. The belief that "it won't happen to me" contributes to risk-taking and impulsive behaviors. The imbalance caused by adolescent brain development translates into a desire for novel experiences often driven by over-emotional behaviors, including the possibility of experimenting with drugs and alcohol, sexual encounters, and other delinquent activities (Berk 2012). Santrock (2013) reported that, "A longitudinal study (Schofield et al. 2008) revealed that attention problems and high rates of aggressive disruptive behavior at school entry increased the risk of multiple problem behaviors in middle school, which in turn was linked to early initiation of sexual activity" (437).

At school, middle school students might suddenly

- say something completely inappropriate to fellow students, teachers, or visiting adults in the school
- begin crying over something that appears minor to adults
- physically and verbally bully other students
- try physical stunts that are incredibly dangerous.

Studies reveal the value and significance of strong relationships between adolescents and caring adults to reduce risk-taking behaviors (Markham et al. 2010; Schofield et al. 2008). Middle level educators can have a positive impact on young adolescents' behaviors by encouraging and developing caring relationships with their students.

◆❚❚ Concluding Reflections

Medical research indicates that young adolescents experience a critical period of brain growth. Learning experiences must be vibrant and exciting to promote the greatest intellectual development. All of the developmental processes in young adolescence are intertwined. Changing bodies and advancing intellectual capacity create more than just larger, smarter children. Cognitive changes also impact young adolescents' social and emotional processes.

CHAPTER 4

Understanding Young Adolescents' Social Development

The fact is that teens sometimes have a tough time getting along with themselves, let alone with their parents and family.

—**WALSH** (2004, 17)

Although the growth of abstract thinking allows early adolescents to revisit their self-systems, early adolescents' self-theories are not very coherent.

—**AZMITIA** (2002, 170)

Physical and cognitive changes create a challenge for the young adolescent's search for identity. Every young adolescent at some time from sixth through eighth grade questions who they are and how they fit in with their peers, teachers, family members, and other adults in their lives. They might ask: Are my current friendships appropriate? Should I find new friends? What about having a girl or boyfriend? Should I join that particular peer group? Who do I sit with at lunch? Should I text that person? Should I accept a "friend" request from those two on Facebook? Would it be a good idea to attempt to "friend" that guy I saw in school today, or should I take a selfie, send an Instagram pic, and see if he'll "like" me?

Young adolescence sets into motion a search for identities: social, sexual, gender, ethnic, cultural, familial, socioeconomic, and spiritual, all related to who they think they are and who they want to become. Their future lives seem more immediate to them, although they are years from taking on the responsibilities of mature adults.

School, a corrupt environment filled with all sorts of pubescent adolescents, can be a living nightmare for some kids. Drama, sarcastic teachers, excessive amounts of homework, being judged, grades, balancing after-school activities, and finding yourself are just a few of the challenges of being this age. All of this is A LOT to handle.

—**CAROLYN**, AN EIGHTH GRADER

Beliefs related to their own maturity lead to many assumptions and much confusion about how much independence they have, are entitled to, and desire. Their constant search for a persona often leaves the adults in their lives confused. Teachers need to address young adolescents' social and emotional concerns and identity issues through curriculum, school programs, and the development of a personal healthy relationship with each student.

◆❙ Developing Interpersonal Relationships

Although family, church, and community are important sources for developing friendships, for most students school is a primary place to acquire a sense of social group belonging and to practice skills necessary for making and keeping friends. (Sheets 2005, 71)

At a time when dramatic physical and intellectual changes are occurring, children are taken from the safety and security of the self-contained elementary school and put in an alien environment. They often go to larger schools with students they've never met before. They change classes and are responsible for being at certain places at certain times. As frightening as this new setting appears, it also provides the exciting and challenging prospect of meeting new people and gaining increased control of their lives. Bordeaux (1992–1994) reflected on this prospect in the following poem.

Finding a Place in the Group

Alone

In the back of the room

with this growing sense of doom

Laughter to the left of me

Smiling to the right.

Alone in the middle

No land in sight

Drowning in fright

Hey, somebody

Anybody

throw me a line

and I'll be fine

I'll pull myself in

Show you what's within

Give you the straight poop

And maybe

Just maybe

Find my place in the group.

One eighth grader provided Doda and Knowles (2008) with these comments about friendships and peers in middle school:

I think every middle school teacher should know, or try to understand, the social whirlwind of statuses that forms and so quickly hardens with every student in their place. What may seem, to a teacher, a classroom full of students peacefully working, may be exactly the opposite to a student. It becomes a room full of pitfalls, danger signs, and safe havens situated carefully in familiar territory. Every student, throughout the day, moves cautiously on "safe" paths from room to room. They will not read in another level's territory. They will not mix; everyone knows their place. Only a teacher or a student from a higher level will cause them to mix.

The separation between boys and girls is even more pronounced. Boys have territory separate from girls, and their own divisions in that. Boys and girls will absolutely not mix, except in the rare groups of girls and boys that are friends; these groups are either absolute highest status or the very bottom. Every student, boy or girl, has their place, their territory, their paths, the people they can stay with on their level. I think middle school teachers should know of, and try to understand, this code of the students. This network of statuses and levels is ever present in middle schools. While some students may not be directly aware of it, they always have a subconscious understanding of where they fit. (29)

Asked about the most important thing a middle school student should do or learn in school, teachers have surprisingly similar responses to their students: "how to get along"; "social interactions along with social responsibility"; "socialization"; "social interaction with fellow peers and adults." Although academics remain important in preparing these students for life, teachers acknowledge the vital role that socialization plays during the middle school years.

Sheets (2005) reported that young adolescents begin to understand "the need to be satisfied by friendships and to value the importance of sustained relationships. Mutual aid, intimate self-disclosure, trust, commitment, and loyalty become important functions of friendship in adolescence" (71). As students age from 11 to 15, they rely more on friends than parents for companionship, personal worth, and significant relationships (Santrock 2013).

Theory into Practice

Young adolescents frequently need guidance in their social interactions with both friends and teachers. School is their training ground, and they're going to make mistakes. Wise teachers purposely plan lessons that offer social opportunities: collaborative research projects, debates, readers' theatre, writing workshop, simulation games, and role-playing activities. Placing students in mixed social groups in academic situations during adolescence may help them better develop their social skills (Sprenger 2005). Socializing can boost self-esteem, reduce anxiety, and help young adolescents develop their sense of identity as they learn skills important for future relationships (Manning 1993).

Females' friendship needs differ from males' during this stage of development, as they seek intimacy and emotional support from their female friends. Males seek friends who can provide material support and who will stand by them in times of trouble. Berk (2012) noted that friendships contribute to several aspects of psychological health, such as:

- providing opportunities to explore the self and develop a deep understanding of others
- promoting a foundation for future intimate relationships
- enhancing sensitivity for and concern for one another by promoting empathy, sympathy, and prosocial behaviors
- improving attitudes toward and involvement in school. (625–626)

Friendships influence adolescents in many ways, as researchers discovered in a study in which young females' depression and anger were affected more by social factors than hormones (Brooks-Gunn and Warren 1989). The Association for Middle Level Education (AMLE 2010) noted that young adolescents "are psychologically vulnerable, because at no other stage in development are they more likely to encounter and be aware of so many differences between themselves and others" (60). Ally, an eighth grader, revealed her feelings on developing friendships: "There is so much pressure on popularity and being perfect in middle school, and it's hard to recognize your 'real' from 'fake' friends."

Socialization skills, however, do not always come easily to young adolescents. An underdeveloped prefrontal cortex (PFC) of the brain may cause young adolescents to completely ignore or misread facial expressions of others (Brownlee 2005). Adolescents may interpret messages of surprise or concern as anger, threats, or insults. Misreading these messages may lead them to exaggerate their intensity and intention: for example, saying, "Ms. Green yelled at me today when I wasn't doing anything wrong!" when the teacher calmly and politely asked the student to stop talking.

◆|| The Role of Peers

Young adolescents experience different points of view, try out new ideas, and experiment with different ways of thinking and behaving as they search for personal identity as part of a group. Peers offer feedback on clothes, appearance, behavior, and every other significant issue. Peer feedback permits young adolescents to gauge their new patterns of behavior in search of what fits.

This expanding social landscape creates questions in young adolescents' minds about how to get peers to like them. They begin to see that some kids are popular while others aren't. They question where they stand and wonder what their peers think of them (Santrock 2013).

Middle school students' perceptions of popularity are often based on who they think is the most well-known (Eder 2002). In some schools "being known" is associated with athletic success. In other schools, popularity may be associated with other activities, such as being in the band or in the drama club. In addition, males found "physical and verbal fighting skills, use of humor, and willingness to be daring" instrumental in determining social status (Eder 2002, 154). For females, appearance, particularly the clothes they wear, was critical to being accepted. The idea that popularity even matters is a testament to the changing social landscape for young adolescents.

Researchers make a distinction between *cliques* and *crowds* that are common in middle schools (Berk 2012; Santrock 2013). Cliques are groups of five-to-eight students who are friends that often share values, family backgrounds, and attitudes (Brown & Dietz 2009). Crowds are larger groups usually made up of several cliques in which membership is based on reputation and traditional stereotypes such as "jocks (athletes), populars (class leaders who are highly social), brains (academically successful), nonconformists (no need to fit in socially), and normals (academically average who fit in with other social groups)" (Berk 2012, 626). Students' affiliations within cliques or crowds often reflect their self-concepts and feed into their personal belief systems.

Cliques and crowds assist in overall adolescent development, providing a context for " . . . [E]xperimenting with values and roles and offering the security of a temporary identity as adolescents separate from the family and construct a coherent sense of self" (Berk 2012, 627).

Although feelings of sexuality emerge, often in the form of "puppy love," same-sex affiliation remains dominant and is preferred by the middle school student (Berk 2012). Sex roles begin to change, but it is often parents, teachers, other adults, or the media that encourage that change and stress opposite-sex relationships. Informal and sometimes formal dances encourage young adolescents to form relationships at a time when they may prefer friendly interactions, text or email exchanges, mixed-group activities, and casual flirting.

Peer pressure is real to the young adolescent. As young adolescents try to fit in, they become sensitive to what other people have to say about them, particularly if it is negative. One student, when asked about peer pressure, said, "You gotta fit in so you get good friends."

Middle school teachers need to know that middle school students are under a lot of stress. We are constantly being judged and bullied by our peers.
—**SARAH**, GRADE 8

Every middle school teacher should know that as students we come to school to learn. But we also come to make friends and build relationships that could be very valuable to our future. We don't always have the best days because there are some pretty mean kids who try to bring you down. So those friendships we build help us get through the day and enjoy learning which is what we should do.
—**GRACIE**, GRADE 8

**Theory into
Practice**

*The influence of peers
follows students as they
leave for home each
afternoon. The ubiquity
of cell phones, texting,
and email leads to
continued "conversations"
for hours after leaving
school. Teachers must
recognize their students'
social needs and provide
opportunities for students
to develop social skills
during learning activities.
Appropriately designed
middle level schools
also provide advisories
that offer students
opportunities to discuss
social challenges and
relieve some of the
pressures associated with
socialization.*

When asked what the greatest problem is for middle school students, Celeste, an eighth grader, responded, "Smoking, peer pressure, and trying to fit in." Her friend Melissa continued, "A few [students] got caught with marijuana; someone got suspended for carrying a pack of cigarettes; I also think graffiti—people draw on the walls. People were dyeing their hair with markers." Parents may not approve, but middle schoolers are more encouraged by the approval of their peers than discouraged by the disapproval of their parents.

◆▌ The Role of the Family

As young adolescents attempt to move from dependence to independence, their social affiliations broaden, with allegiance split between the family and the peer group. Although authority remains primarily with the family, young adolescents want to begin making their own choices about what to do and with whom.

Parents begin to lose their omnipotence and are no longer viewed as infallible. Suddenly the parents don't know all the answers to the homework questions. Parents may eventually become an embarrassment to young adolescents.

Early adolescents struggle with the conflict inherent in the need to depend on parents for support as they move toward independence. The seventh grader who occasionally asks her parents for assistance with homework may ask her father to drop her off a block from school to ensure that he doesn't embarrass her in front of her friends. Later that day, when the father returns to the same intersection to pick his daughter up, she might chastise him for not driving right up to the school building.

Although young adolescents may challenge their parents' beliefs and appear to reject suggestions from them, parents continue to play a primary role in the young adolescent's life. When asked who the most important person was in their life, young adolescents we interviewed almost universally picked one or both of their parents:

> "I'd say my dad. He always helps me. He'll help me understand things better, like in school."

> "My parents. They pretty much make you the person you are. If you're little, they guide you. They teach you your manners, they teach you what to do."

> "I think my parents. I have a really close relationship with them. I definitely think they help me a lot. I really look up to them."

> "My mother, because two years ago my dad died, and my mother had to take over two parts of the family."

◆‖ The Role of the Community

Along with the need for successful peer interaction comes an increased awareness of the broader social world with an accompanying concern for social justice. Young adolescents' sense of right and wrong is intense. If you want to find a solution to a social problem, give it to a group of middle level students. Their new awareness of the world around them, a need to be involved with their peers, and a mind that is open to all possibilities allow them to seek and act on solutions that are seemingly out of the realm of adult thought. Their new cognitive thinking skills come unimpaired by experiences of failure, which often impedes adults in devising solutions.

Although parents may be relegated to a lesser role in the influence they hold over their young adolescent children, these same children will listen to and emulate other adults. Whether teachers, parents of their friends, or community members, adults have the opportunity to influence and lead the young adolescent in positive directions. AMLE (2010) noted, "Young adolescents increasingly welcome and benefit from positive relationships with adults outside their families, such as coaches, teachers, spiritual leaders, and neighbors, especially when these adults encourage, support, and nurture young adolescents' pursuit of their sparks or passionate interests" (61).

Students' letter-writing campaigns, recycling programs, volunteering, and political activism provide a wide range of experiences and a sense of empowerment and meaning within the group—all essential elements in young adolescent growth.

Theory into Practice

Young adolescents need stability and security in a world that sometimes seems upside down and confusing. Although parents may be equally confused, they can provide the stability and security that the child needs. We encourage teachers to mention to parents and caretakers during beginning-of-the-year open houses and in parent-teacher conferences that they should continue to provide support and guidance even when their children appear to want to distance themselves.

◆‖ The Role of Technology

Technology has a dramatic impact on the young adolescent in both positive and negative ways. Young adolescents have immediate and constant access to the world through technology. Their phones provide instant access to personal, local, and international information: photos, videos, and messages that travel from person-to-person in seconds via social media.

These electronic interactions are more commonly used and preferred for most adolescents over face-to-face exchanges or phone calls. Taylor, a sixteen-year-old, noted, "Phone calls have a much deeper meaning; we only call to clarify misunderstandings in text or Facebook messages and Tweets." Researchers (Madden et al. 2013) with the Pew Research Center's Internet & American Life Project conducted surveys with 802 teens between the ages of twelve and seventeen and their parents on their use of social media. Most of teens' social activities are conducted online or via texting.

Eighty-one percent of adolescents surveyed in the Pew study reported having Facebook accounts, each with an average of 300 "friends."

Madden et al. (2013) reported that adolescents are quite aware of their online "reputations" (8) and regularly spend time managing their content to ensure that it represents them well in an attempt to garner "Likes" from their "friends" when thoughts or pictures are posted. Facebook profiles are an extension of their social personas, so adolescents are careful to ensure a positive representation of themselves (Madden et al.). Most of the youth in the Pew survey reported that they posted photos, their real names, their addresses, their birthdates, and their school names in their Facebook profiles (3). Such common use of social media can and often does create safety issues for young adolescents, who are often incapable of recognizing the dangers of placing personal information online. One-third of teens surveyed admitted, for example, that they have online "friends" who they have not met in person (Madden et al. 2013).

All of this social networking is time consuming, as two-thirds of those teens surveyed reported visiting their accounts several times a day (Madden et al.). It may be challenging for young adolescents to ignore these social opportunities, thereby preventing them from attending to both academic and personal responsibilities. Multitasking is common among adolescents; one survey showed that 39 percent of them admitted almost constantly using at least two media concurrently (Brown and Bobkowski 2011).

Respondents from the Pew study provided remarks on emotional drama that often erupt on social media sites. One fourteen-year-old female revealed, "On Facebook, people imply things and say things, even just by a Like, that they wouldn't say in real life" (26). A thirteen-year-old female remarked, "I feel like on Facebook people can say whatever they want to . . . [and] if they say something mean, it hurts more" (27).

Just as face-to-face social interactions can be challenging for young adolescents, so can social media experiences. Because online interactions are not face-to-face, young adolescents develop a false sense of security and engage in more risk-taking in the form of inappropriate comments, posted pictures, and responses to and from one another. Young adolescents are ill-prepared to think critically about their reactions on social media sites.

"Teaching" young adolescents how to manage their time and social interactions online is a new responsibility for parents and teachers—yet a critical lesson for teens. Young adolescents' immaturity also ensures that their impulsiveness may result in instant social miscues, from inappropriate words to the most embarrassing photos that often breech recently enacted laws to protect youth.

> Social media has a big impact on our lives. Kids can get bullied on social media over every little thing, like hair or clothes. They can get depressed as a result.
> —**SARAH**, GRADE 8

> Facebook is really about popularity. And the popularity you have on Facebook transmits into the popularity you have in life. (fifteen-year-old female)
> —**MADDEN ET AL.**
> (2013, 36)

Every new technological device and process brings exciting changes to societies, as well as challenges. Adolescents are naturally drawn to technological advances if they help them to be entertained, provide information to satisfy their own curiosity, and lead to more control over their lives. Today's immediate electronic access via smart phones and computers makes it almost impossible to prevent children and adolescents from directly witnessing any event or story that occurs, including many events that they are incapable of processing in a mature manner. Much like the age-old concerns about television and traditional media, social media and technology can offer a steady diet of unhealthy role models for growing adolescents.

◆❙❙ Moral Development

Moral development is an ongoing process throughout everyone's life. It is generally believed that as one matures cognitively, moral development advances as well (Kohlberg and Gilligan 1971). As young adolescents experience social interactions, process more cognitively, and develop relationships, they simultaneously experience moral dilemmas that they never before considered. They are capable of more complex moral reasoning and begin to see things from various perspectives and viewpoints (AMLE 2010).

Adolescents' skills in moral reasoning improve when they are able to reflect successfully on their behaviors and ascertain the effects on others and themselves (Berk 2012). The traditional elementary school mantra that each situation is as simple as making a "good choice" or "bad choice" doesn't fit the more advanced moral reasoning of young adolescents. They begin to see other possibilities they previously weren't able to imagine. They may initiate arguments about rules or policies, attempting to get to the root of the reasoning behind them and the application of rules to them personally.

As young adolescents respond to peer influence and pressure, they may act "so as to gain others' approval and do what others think is right" (Rice and Dolgin, 335). Deciding what is "right" is often a murky process for young adolescents, depending on the situations that arise in their lives and from whom they seek approval. Disagreements about morals between adults and adolescents occur when adolescents believe that adults have interfered with some of their personal choices regarding fashion, style, friends, constant focus on social media, or activities.

Young adolescents explore and examine their own moral behavior and ultimately develop their own personal values. Despite the disagreements they have with parents,

> A challenge of being a young adolescent is that we are basically too young, but also too old to do many activities. We are too old to go to a "Chucky Cheese," but too young to go to an "R"-rated movie alone. We have to act mature in order to be treated older, or act less mature if for some reason we wanted to be treated as a younger child.
>
> **—CASSIDY**,
> AN EIGHTH GRADER

Theory into Practice

*Any typical middle
school day presents
many opportunities for
conversations centered
around "teachable
moments" that involve
moral decision making.
Events reported by the
media give teachers
a chance to initiate
meaningful conversations
about how to act in
specific situations that
occur locally or nationally.
Teachers should embrace
the ever-present moral
development of young
adolescents as an
opportunity to guide
them to further maturity.
Taking time to meet with
students privately when
they act inappropriately
and helping them think
through their actions
aids in their moral
development.*

the values they choose often parallel their parents' values (AMLE 2010). Middle school teachers need to know that young adolescents may disagree with adults about moral issues yet clearly need (and may seek) the assistance of parents and other adults in deciding how to act in certain moral situations.

The developing moral maturity among young adolescents is a positive thing. Young adolescents have a strong desire for justice and are interested in idealistic plans for making the world a better place (AMLE 2010). They are frequently concerned about how to ensure worldwide peace, contribute to environmental issues, and create safe environments for animals. Young adolescents "believe that if they can conceive and express high moral principles, then they have attained them, and nothing concrete need be done" (Rice and Dolgin 2005, 130). By developing curriculum based on students' questions and concerns, teachers can provide an environment in which students can explore these issues and act on their beliefs.

◆❚❚ Concluding Reflections

Middle school provides an opportunity for young adolescents to explore their social world and try to find their place in it. While dependence on the family decreases and the need for peer approval increases, young adolescents attempt to navigate an increasingly complex social milieu in order to find a place where they can be themselves. Gentle and tactful adult guidance is necessary while permitting young adolescents to explore and expand their social worlds. In the next chapter we will explore their personal journey and look at emotional development and the search for identity in young adolescents.

CHAPTER 5

Understanding Young Adolescents' Emotional Development and Search for Identity

Cultural competence refers to the ability of students to grow in understanding and respect for their culture of origin. Rather than experiencing the alienating effects of education where school-based learning detaches students from their home culture, cultural competence is a way for students to be bicultural and facile in the ability to move between school and home cultures.

—**LADSON-BILLINGS** (2002, 111)

I believe that there are many challenges to being this age. The first one is finding who we are. We need to start evaluating who our true friends are, and what our personality is.

—**HOPE**, EIGHTH GRADER

One of the primary jobs of adolescence, in my view, is to find something that you spontaneously love and are good at.

—**HINSHAW** (2009, 63)

◆❙❙ Emotional Unrest

The middle school student confronts a number of diverse changes all at one time:

- accepting physical changes
- experiencing new modes of intellectual functioning
- striving for independence from the family
- establishing a unique identity
- adjusting to a new school setting
- relating to new friends.

This period of transition between dependence and independence results in a multitude of needs and a dramatic change in self-concept. Physical changes and the hormones that cause them often trigger emotions that are variable and little understood.

**Theory into
Practice**

*Teachers who explicitly
design time during
class periods to listen to
students' personal stories,
concerns, or fears provide
a forum for healthy
conversations and increase
the likelihood of positive
student decision making
when critical issues
arise. They help students
develop strategies for
taking responsibility for
their actions and finding
creative and appropriate
ways to handle their
excessive emotions.
Conversations can occur
privately or become a
whole class problem-
solving experience about
how to handle a common
dilemma that might
occur. These situations
are common activities for
advisory sessions.*

MOOD SWINGS

Eric, a thirteen-year-old seventh grader, was having a particularly rough evening. He had gone to school that morning his typical bouncy self. That evening, he lay around on the couch with his dog at his side, staring into space. Questions by his mom brought monosyllabic responses, "Yes," "No," "Nothing." When she didn't let up, he finally said (thanks to his school's comprehensive health curriculum and class unit on self-esteem), "Don't worry, Mom. I'm an adolescent now. I'm supposed to have mood swings."

Mood swings are a quintessential characteristic of young adolescence. Emotions change rapidly. Students are happy one moment and angry or sad the next, quiet one day and loud and boisterous the next, apprehensive about one issue and overconfident about another, anxious on Monday and self-assured on Tuesday.

Too often mood swings are blamed on hormones and discounted as temporary aberrations. Although we can attribute some mood swings to chemical imbalances or rapid hormonal fluctuations, that's only part of it. If we consider the wide social and intellectual changes young adolescents are experiencing, as well as their continued brain development, their emotional variability seems understandable.

EGOCENTRISM

One aspect of young adolescents' thinking is a new form of egocentrism. Unlike the egocentrism of younger children, who assume that others think the same way they do about everything, young adolescents begin to understand that people have different beliefs and attitudes. They become immersed in their own thinking. They reflect on and analyze their thoughts and assume that everyone is as interested in their ideas as they are. A typical thought process is, "Because I am thinking about me, then everyone must be thinking about me. Because I notice my hair, everyone else must be looking at it. Because I pay attention to myself, everyone else must be paying attention to me."

Much of young adolescents' emotional energy is expended in responding to this *imaginary audience* (Buis and Thompson 1989). Since adolescents believe they are constantly being watched, they often react by being loud or acting provocatively, wanting to appear cool. Or, to avoid standing out from others they may try to fit in, to conform. Adolescents' beliefs that others care so much about their appearance also helps them to embrace friends and family members who provide support and thus enhance self-esteem (Bell and Bromnick 2003). Because of their imaginary audience, young adolescents also have an increased need for privacy: When they are alone, they can relax. Self-consciousness is at its highest levels from the ages of fourteen to nineteen (Tice, Buder, and Baumeister 1985).

Young adolescents believe that their feelings and emotions are indeed unique— that no one has ever experienced what they have experienced. Elkind (1967) referred to this as *personal fable*. In addition, they are convinced that they will live forever and that the horrible things that happen to others will not affect them. They'll never have an unwanted pregnancy, be in a car accident, or get a sexually transmitted infection. As irritating as personal fable can be to adults, researchers reveal that the sense of omnipotence associated with personal fable often predicts an enhanced self-esteem and positive adjustment that helps adolescents cope with the emotional and social challenges of this age (Aalsma, Lapsley, and Flannery 2006).

◆▌ The Search for Identity

The middle school years are marked by an almost constant search for an identity in many areas: gender, ethnic, cultural, relational (friendships), socioeconomic, sexual, spiritual, physical, academic, and concerns about one's future life (which job will I have, how much money will I make, will I marry and have children?). Discovering *who* one is may be the most challenging and elusive journey for young adolescents; and although it is just beginning, identity development is critically affected by middle school experiences. Young adolescents' *academic identity* may impact the effort they put into learning, and it affects their self-esteem related to academic success; thus educators can't ignore their students' identity searches.

Young adolescents frequently experiment with some social identities and sexual identities, and they may try to demonstrate different academic identities. Experimenting with who they are is generally a healthy process (joining the school band, trying out for an extracurricular activity, running for student council). Young adolescents may also seek and engage in dangerous identity search activities such as alcohol, tobacco, or drug abuse; sexual encounters; or gang activity. Such activities reveal a need for adult guidance during their searches.

Young adolescents who are from diverse ethnic backgrounds and/or English Language Leaners (ELLs) have a greater challenge than European American Whites in finding a healthy identity in a majority White world. In the "Ethnic Identity" section of this chapter, we provide a separate section on identity challenges for these youth, to emphasize the differences between them and their White European American classmates.

The search for identity is almost continuous as young adolescents try on different personas through the planned and unplanned events and activities that

Identity is a patchwork of flesh, feelings, and ideas held together by the string of the moment.

—BORDEAUX
(1993–1994)

occur during this time in their lives. Young adolescents can learn much about their interests and themselves by participating in extracurricular activities in school or in their communities.

◆❚ Identity Search Begins

The first comprehensive look at identity during early adolescence was done by Erik Erikson during the 1950s and 1960s (Erikson 1950, 1968). According to Erikson, during adolescence individuals struggle to find out who they are and where they are going in life. Young adolescents are just beginning this struggle, trying to integrate their childhood experiences with their developing bodies and biological drives, their new thinking capacities, and their ever expanding social roles. This search for identity doesn't begin and end during early adolescence. It involves a slow search for a lifestyle that is compatible with physical changes, intellectual understandings, and social interactions.

Despite interest in conforming and belonging to a social group, young adolescents still want individuality. The need for confirmation by a social group is really a need for personal validation. Learning to understand the self, however, is an important part of the successful transition to independence. When Rob, a fourteen-year-old eighth grader, was asked what the most important thing to learn at school was, he commented, "Not caring what other people think. Most people, if they get made fun of, they'd take it personally. I've learned, and a lot of people make fun of me, that if you don't care, you have a lot more fun because you're not trying to impress people. It's getting your own style." According to Rob the biggest problem facing middle school students is "making your presence known." Rob appears to be socially well adjusted yet feels the need to develop a strong sense of identity and begs for personal acceptance as well as the acknowledgment of himself apart from the group—as an individual.

The search for identity often revolves around trying out new ideas and behaviors that would have seemed incomprehensible only a year before. It involves looking at situations through different points of view and making decisions about how to act in a given situation, all in an attempt to develop a public self that is congruent with the inner self and is validated by peers and society. Those decisions, never etched in stone, become the foundation of an identity that is ever changing throughout life.

◆‖ Experimenting with Identity

Young adolescents are a paradox—always trying something new because they want to become someone different, but often not following through because it's not "cool" or interesting anymore, saying "It's too difficult" or "It'll take too long for me to become famous doing this." They start guitar lessons hoping to become a musical icon; go out for cheerleading to be one of the "most popular"; or try out for the basketball team because their favorite professional athlete is the person they most want to be like. Parents agonize over their adolescent's indecision, as the guitar sits untouched in the corner of the room for months, and wonder why they were "talked into" purchasing it.

These "Walter Mitty" moments, however, are critical to the identity development of young adolescents. Too often we push students into making choices. We limit opportunities rather than encourage dreaming and risk-taking. Schools let only the "best" be part of the jazz band or choral group. Only those who demonstrate acting ability can be in the play. When we limit opportunities, we pass on the message that a certain student is not capable enough, good enough, strong enough, or smart enough to make a contribution or to develop skills in something they've never been good at before. Our job at the middle level is to provide opportunities, not deny them.

Few, if any, students develop their full identity during young adolescence, nor should they. Young adolescence should be preserved as a time of identity exploration. Throughout high school, college, and into early adulthood, opportunities should exist for people to explore options and make decisions and choices about their futures.

◆‖ Ethnic Identity

Many First Nation Peoples, African, Hispanic, and Asian American as well as recent immigrant students experience an additional challenge during adolescence in developing a personal identity that recognizes that they are not White European Americans whose primary language is English (Hurd 2012; Umana-Taylor, Updegraff, and Gonzales-Bracken 2011; Brown and Leaman 2007; Gay 1994; Ogbu 1991). As children, these students are cognizant of their ethnic diversity. As adolescents, however, they become acutely aware of the differences between their White classmates and

> Generations of children are disenfranchised because the relationship between their ethnic background, cultural histories, and knowledge of their human developmental process has not been adequately addressed.
> —SHEETS (2005, 52)

> Researchers are increasingly finding that a positive ethnic identity is linked to positive outcomes for ethnic minority adolescents . . . [for instance, a healthy] ethnic identity was related to higher school engagement and lower aggression.
> —SANTROCK (2013, 488)

themselves as they experience the challenges of meeting parental needs of maintaining their cultural heritage while simultaneously wanting to join their peers—embracing U.S. teen culture with the behaviors, dress, and traditions that accompany it.

Not only do students from diverse ethnic backgrounds have to go through a process of self-identification, they also have to develop a cultural identity (Gay 1994). Gay describes their identity development stages during adolescence as:

1. Identity diffusion—minimal exploration of ethnicity
2. Foreclosure—no exploration of ethnic identity
3. Moratorium—active exploration of ethnicity
4. Achievement—the understanding of and contentment with one's ethnic identity.

These ethnic identity development stages are similar and experienced by all ethnically diverse groups. The order in which adolescents experience the stages is fairly consistent, but the amount of time that adolescents spend in each stage is dependent on many environmental factors and the amount and quality of familial support. Ethnically diverse adolescents who are able to assimilate comfortably into their White communities often have the support of their families to reinforce the value of their cultural heritage while they find a relaxed crossing in and out of their majority White world. White adolescents have identity stages, too, but don't struggle with ethnic identity.

Movement through the ethnic identity stages is a lengthy journey in which students of diverse backgrounds are influenced by the way they are treated in their schools and communities. Because of their heightened self-consciousness, young adolescents are particularly aware of being treated differently. A barrage of media images also influences how ethnically different students perceive their place in society. Adolescents of diverse ethnic backgrounds can't escape the stereotypes that exist and are likely to hear comments from classmates or adults that reveal negative attitudes, prejudice, and discrimination. Teachers must recognize, though, that these categories of "Hispanic," "Latino," or "Chicano"; "Native American" or "First Nation Peoples"; and "Asian American" are far too broad to define the ethnic characteristics of many of their students from Hispanic or Asian countries or varied Native American tribes (D. Brown 2002b). Biracial students, whose parents are from separate ethnicities, also experience identity challenges that exceed those of White students. Part-Black biracial teens reported as much discrimination as those who were Black, but they were not as concerned about their identities (Berk 2012). Hurd (2012) describes the identity challenges for one middle school student, given the pseudonym Nick, whose ethnicity is French-Canadian Honduran-American—known as *Mestizo*, a Spanish word "created to designate peoples of mixed European and Native American ancestry"—and who is now living in Iowa (113). For Nick, both "Hispanic" and "biracial" labels for his ethnicity are grossly inaccurate and misleading, and neither tells anything about his family's cultural experiences or their journey. Hurd (2012) noted,

---

Nick's mixed identity was exemplified in his navigation between worlds. He negotiated not only as an adolescent caught between childhood and adulthood but as one of mixed heritage between two worlds of race, culture, and class. Therefore, Nick was caught in the middle: leaving childhood and striving toward adulthood. (117)

Because 87 percent of U.S. teachers are White European American, many may be curious about how they can positively affect the ethnic or cultural identity development of students of diverse backgrounds. Ethnically diverse students expect teachers to recognize their heritage via personal conversations during the school day. Teachers should inquire about their language, families' country of origin, or cultural celebrations. Strickland (2012) suggests that connecting with ethnically diverse immigrant students requires that teachers refrain from judging their students based on initial English language abilities, and instead take time to listen to their personal "storylines" in an effort to find ways to "bridge" their cultural experiences with daily classroom events (89).

Teachers must go further though by honoring all voices as they create lessons. All students must see themselves in the curriculum and be a vital part of the discourse. Researchers have reported that a healthy "ethnic identity is associated with higher self-esteem, optimism, a sense of mastery over the environment, and more positive attitudes toward one's ethnicity" (Umana-Taylor and Updegraff 2007; Worrell and Gardner-Kitt 2006—cited in Berk 2012, 607).

Ewing Flynn (2012) investigated middle level students and their teachers while studying racism and White privilege. She suggested, as did the respondents in her study, "that teachers should not be afraid to bring up race in the classroom; that most students—even middle school students—can and do want to talk about racism" (108). Ewing Flynn added that making students aware of the stages of ethnic identity development may significantly benefit them.

◆❙ Identity Challenges for Diverse Language Learners

Language also plays a crucial role in identity development, particularly for those students whose primary language is not English. The core of one's identity is language, and the significance of honoring students' languages is summarized by Lisa Delpit: "Our language embraces us long before we are defined by any other medium of identity. If school considers someone's language inadequate, they'll probably fail" (Delpit and Kilgour Dowdy 2002, xix).

The number of students in U.S. public schools receiving services as English Language learners (ELLs) has grown to almost five million and multiplies daily as immigrant families continue to arrive. Not only must teachers be responsive to how we teach these students, but we must also be aware of how their culture and language impact their identity development. Young adolescents have to learn English while trying to manipulate the middle level years, adding additional cognitive challenges to already overwhelming developmental changes.

Much of the discussion on ELLs focuses on achievement. Many ELLs must take high-stakes achievement tests before they have a thorough grasp of the English language, resulting in lower achievement levels. We know, however, that the achievement and intelligence of ELL students is not the primary reason for these low achievement scores—language is! And yet it is easy to understand how issues of self-confidence and identity can be tied to those achievement tests.

Wilma Ortiz, a second language learner herself, taught middle school for many years and was the 2011 Massachusetts Teacher of the Year. She had this to say about early adolescents and language development:

> Language in general is intrinsic in the development and construction of one's identity. Language carries a world of history, beliefs, values—all that it means to be human within sociocultural and political contexts. As a result, the language and words chosen to communicate with purpose and intentions impact how we see ourselves and the world around us. Language defines and redefines identity. When teachers support students' primary language in meaningful ways, students feel recognized and validated in the classroom, which results in a stronger sense of self.

Learning techniques to effectively teach content to English Language Learners should be part of your teacher education program. But learning those teaching techniques is only a small part of the work necessary to help these students navigate the middle level years.

One of the authors (Trudy) embarked on a journey to Honduras to teach English to students there. She remarks,

I learned some valuable lessons in Honduras. The lessons had less to do with how to teach than with how to get into the minds and hearts of those you are working with.

First: It is frightening, demoralizing and, at times, humiliating to not understand. . . .

Second: It is frightening, demoralizing and, at times, humiliating to not be understood. . . .

Third: It's hard and sometimes frightening to live in a different culture. (Knowles 2007)

Teaching young adolescents who are ELLs requires sensitivity to their culture, their language, and their struggle for identity. Researchers Sumaryono and Ortiz (2004) described teachers' responsibilities:

English Language Learners could become invisible in the mainstream classroom or even disconnect from the learning process if teachers do not display sensitivity toward their cultural identity. Moreover, if our energy is concentrated on mainstreaming students at any cost, we run the risk of placing little value on the students' ability to speak two languages. Recognizing and validating multiple cultural identities in the classroom community and developing positive student-teacher relationships strengthen individuals' sense of worth and, ultimately, their academic performance. (16)

Oppositional Identity

The behaviors of African, Hispanic, Native, and Asian American students may lead to what is described as *oppositional identity* (Ogbu 1991). Finn (2009) noted, "Members of the oppressed group come to regard certain beliefs, skills, tastes, values, attitudes, and behaviors as not appropriate for them since they are associated with the dominant culture" (42). Students who take this viewpoint may refuse to participate in the traditional teaching/learning rituals that are a part of classrooms across the United States.

Students from many backgrounds may develop an oppositional identity attitude if they believe that their opportunities for educational advancement, better jobs, and a higher quality of life are not possible because of their oppression by the majority culture. Demonstrations of oppositional identity include a Chicano student who refuses to speak English in school when addressing teachers and an African American student who refuses to do any academic work at school or at home since he/she doesn't want to fit into a "White" world. Young adolescents who have been affected by racism, prejudice, and discrimination are very aware of these forces (Howard 2013). White

Theory into Practice

Teachers can initiate conversations with ethnically diverse students by inquiring about their families, personal interests, or countries of origin if they're immigrants. Middle level students are ready for conversations about racism—both nationally and even within their own schools—which teachers can start through teachable moments such as the Travon Martin situation. Ethnically diverse students can share their feelings about how their families have responded to prejudice, and many of these conversations can take place within the context of the curricula they study.

Theory into Practice

*The middle level years
are critical for providing
support for ethnically
diverse youth to help them
maintain their ethnic
identity and prevent
them from experiencing
academic failure.
Educators must develop a
positive culture of respect
and trust for all students
that explicitly addresses
negative perceptions
and provides strategies
for reversing attitudes
among both educators
and students about their
academic potential. Nasir
(2012) believes that
"learning and identity
are social and cultural
processes that influence the
manner in which students
experience schools" (cited
in Howard 2013, 73).*

European American adolescents may also experience oppositional identity, believing that their futures are predetermined thus preventing them from being motivated by academic opportunities.

Oppositional identity is most often provided as a reason by many educators that African American males don't succeed (Howard 2013). The academic challenges that exist for African American males is clear in the data on their school performance, as Howard reveals:

Approximately 47% of Black males graduated within 4 years from U.S. high schools in 2008, compared with 78% for White males. Although reading scores of Black males in Grades 4 and 8 have increased over the past decade, they still trail behind White, Latino, and Asian males, and a large majority fall short of grade-level proficiency. In many large urban districts across the country, the reading achievement scores for eighth-grade Black males are consistent with the reading scores for fourth-grade Asian American and White males. (60)

In addition to academic underperformance, African American males experience different treatment at school for their behaviors. Researchers reported that Black males were three times more likely than Latino and Asian males to be suspended from school (Aud, Fox, and Kewal Ramani 2010). Students may choose to ignore school responsibilities when they are treated unfairly or when educators have lower expectations for performance, so they choose behaviors consistent with oppositional identity.

Teachers may inadvertently be responsible for students choosing oppositional identity by sending messages consciously or unconsciously that they don't believe these students can succeed academically. Howard (2013) describes the problem: "Many of the challenges that confront Black males in education go beyond their communities and their social class status and is directly located in classrooms, the lack of racial awareness and cultural ignorance among school personnel, apathetic teacher attitudes, and poor quality instruction that they receive, be it in urban, rural, or suburban schools" (61–62).

Gay (1994) indicated, "A clarified ethnic identity is central to the psycho-social well-being and educational success of youth of color" (151). She goes on to say, "If ethnic identity development is understood as part of the natural 'coming of age' process during early adolescence, and if middle level education is to be genuinely client-centered for students of color, then ethnic sensitivity must be incorporated into school policies, programs, and practices" (153).

◆❙❙ Developing Sexual and Gender Identities

Young adolescence is a developmental time period during which an increase in gender stereotyping via attitudes and behaviors occurs, called *gender intensification* (Berk 2012). Biological, social, and cognitive factors all affect one's gender identity development, and parents and peers have the greatest impact on how adolescents view their gender roles. For young adolescent females, media images influence their perceptions of what it means to be *female* (Bentley 2002). From television advertisements, MTV videos, and Internet ads to storefront mannequins, young adolescent females are bombarded with "perfect image" messages that also affect their definitions of gender. These images portray a narrow path to gender identity that is highly accepted by most young adolescents searching for a mature gender identity beyond their childhoods (Ward and Benjamin 2004).

Researchers reported decades ago that females often experienced an overwhelming decline in confidence and self-esteem during the middle school years (Ornstein 1994; Brown and Gilligan 1992). Zittleman (2007) found that a percentage of adolescent females continued to doubt themselves, reporting that approximately 18 percent of 223 middle school females surveyed from five separate middle schools in several states revealed that the "best thing about being a girl" was "nothing." Almost 25 percent of males in this same study used the word *nothing* when asked what the best thing about being a girl might be. The same percentage (18%) of 217 males surveyed noted that the best thing about being a boy was "entitlement" (Zittleman 73–79). These findings reveal that gender identity issues need to be addressed in schools.

Decades of greater opportunities, changes in societal expectations, and successful adult role models have led to higher goal setting and greater confidence for adolescent females. Kindlon (2006) studied the successes of many adolescent females and reported heightened levels of self-esteem, successful college careers, strongly defined sense of self, and satisfying personal and professional lives following college. Hinshaw (2009) revealed, however, that the pressure created by equal opportunities caused mental health difficulties for some adolescent females through increased pressure to achieve at high levels in every aspect of their lives.

Although women are the majority in the United States, and also among college students, they are still discriminated against in not receiving equal wages, health benefits, pensions, and social security compared to men. These statistics reveal that adolescent females need equal opportunities to reach their potential needs for happy and healthy lives, and a supportive journey through middle school is an essential component.

Theory into Practice

*Teachers must assist
students in understanding
how they are affected
by family, community,
and media in choosing
a gender identity and
judging others' gender
identities. Teachable
moments via national
news are daily fodder for
gender roles, expectations,
and how those match
familial perspectives.
The 2008 Democratic
presidential primary race
between Senators Obama
and Clinton was one such
opportunity to discuss
gender, ethnicity, and
equity among groups of
U.S. citizens. A national
news story of a college
football player announcing
he's gay before entering
the NFL draft provides yet
another chance to address
identity issues.*

Traditionally, males have been able to choose from a variety of interests, whether academically or in extracurricular activities, without limitations. Gender identity for males, however, is also based on traditional male roles and usually defined by one's masculinity, as reflected in participating in athletics, demonstrating physical strength, and acting aggressively when confronted by others. Males who choose more diverse behaviors and interests are often confronted and accused of not being "man enough." These types of stereotypes are demeaning to many males and deny them the opportunity to develop healthy gender identities that counter traditional roles.

Perhaps one of the most damaging attacks on male identities is the use of the word *gay* to embarrass and harass students. Many middle school halls and classrooms are filled with students using that word to demean and bully both males and females. When teachers ignore students who publicly use the word, they are sanctioning their behaviors and promoting the bullying that goes with it. The message for those students being bullied is that their teachers aren't willing to protect them from bullying, and also may not be willing to support and protect students who may be homosexual.

Middle schools are powerful training grounds for the development of sexual and gender identity. School personnel and extracurricular opportunities influence how males and females view their gender roles. As Berk (2012) reported,

> Teenagers who are encouraged to explore non-gender-typed options and to question the value of gender stereotypes for themselves and society are more likely to build an androgynous gender identity. Overall, androgynous adolescents, particularly girls, tend to be psychologically healthier—more willing to speak their own mind, higher in self-confidence and self-esteem, better liked by peers, and identity-achieved. (618–19)

Many may think most teachers are cognizant of gender equity concerns; research indicates, however, that these views are inaccurate. When almost 100 teachers were asked whether any gender issues existed in school, the overwhelming response was that none exists (Zittleman 2004).

SEXUAL IDENTITY

Sexual identity differs from *gender* identity in that sexual identity is a persona adopted by adolescents that defines how they want to be perceived sexually. Sexual identity may be exhibited by flirting, choice of clothing, wearing make-up, sending written sexual messages, splashing on cologne, and demonstrating either heterosexual or homosexual interests. Students who exhibit signs of sexual diversity by identifying as gay, lesbian, bisexual, or transgender are also displaying sexual identity.

Sexual orientation describes a preference for sexual partners and is a central aspect of adolescent development. A large majority of adolescents identify as heterosexual. Sexual orientation, whether heterosexual or homosexual, originates in the brain, and geneticists believe that it is determined by a combination of genes affecting concentrations of sex hormones in the brain when it is forming prior to birth (Walsh 2004). Berk (2012) noted that heredity is the most important contributor to homosexuality as evidenced by the fact that homosexual identical twins are more likely to share that sexual orientation than fraternal twins. Savin-Williams and Diamond (2004) reported that as many as 50 to 60 percent of adolescents who identify as heterosexual have admitted engaging in homosexual acts.

Berk (2012) described three phases of homosexual identity formation. In the first, gays and lesbians described *feeling different* from other children when they were between the ages of 6 and 12: Boys preferred quiet activities and were more emotionally sensitive than other males, and girls preferred being engaged in more athletic activities than other females. Many of these adolescents reported questioning their sexual orientation by the age of ten.

The second phase of homosexual identity development occurs between ages 11 and 12 for boys and between 14 and 15 for girls. It is known as *confusion*, where adolescents begin to recognize a physical attraction for the same sex. During these middle level years, gay and lesbian students struggle emotionally and feel isolated, lacking adult guidance, family support, or peer acceptance. The final stage is *self-acceptance*, which occurs in late adolescence. At this stage, the challenge is in determining whether to tell others and predicting hostile reactions, from peers to parents. Parental acceptance is the strongest predictor of healthy homosexual adjustment (D'Augelli, Grossman, and Starks 2008).

Most middle school students are aware of the labels, views, and attitudes associated with homosexuality, although they may not fully understand the characteristics of gays and lesbians, or the reasons why one identifies as homosexual. Middle schools are breeding grounds for attacks on those students who appear to be different from mainstream social attitudes or behaviors. Walsh (2004) described gay and lesbian students' concerns:

It can be difficult for an adolescent to deal with his or her homosexuality at the very time in life when it is so important to fit in and be accepted. The emotional and psychological torture that many gay and lesbian adolescents experience can be overwhelming. Studies suggest that one third of all teens who commit suicide are gay or lesbian. For them death can seem preferable to the pain of accepting a sexual identity that their friends or family or culture find perverted, sinful, or shameful. (109)

Theory into Practice

Teachers must provide a caring and supportive environment for all of their students, listening to them, protecting them from sexual harassment, and providing them with the resources and appropriate contacts to discuss their specific sexual concerns.

Theory into Practice

*Teachers are responsible
for every student feeling
welcome, psychologically
safe, and supported in
their classrooms and
throughout the building.
Middle level educators
must be psychologically
healthy so that they can
respond with maturity
and provide guidance to
students when they act
inappropriately, rather
than lash out against them
to "get even" or "make an
example" of them. Zero
tolerance policies are poor
remedies for students'
glib comments, angry
reactions, and physical
confrontations. Instead,
students need explicit
demonstrations of care,
respect, and guidance
to help them see their
mistakes and improve on
future behaviors.*

Transgender adolescents feel they are trapped in the wrong body. Young adolescent males who prefer to look and behave feminine are frequently teased and bullied. Although cross-gender behavior is somewhat more acceptable for females, they too experience instances of verbal abuse. Transgender students generally have a life history of being bullied that seriously affects the development of healthy self-esteem (deVries, Cohen-Kettenis, Delemarre-Vander Waal 2006). These students need accurate information about their sexuality. Unfortunately though, transgender issues are often forbidden topics in school, and parents are just as likely to ignore or refuse to address these issues.

Young adolescents should clearly understand that it is normal to have questions about their sexual orientation. If adolescents don't receive accurate information about their concerns about sex from adults—parents, counselors, and teachers—they'll instead ask peers and risk receiving flawed information and perhaps little support (Pollock 2006).

BEHAVIORAL ISSUES

The search for meaning and identity can be a difficult—even traumatic—experience. Young adolescents face a constant concern about whether they are normal; a dissatisfaction with who they are, how they look, what they believe; a belief that something is wrong with their physical development. It's no wonder that at times young adolescents exhibit behaviors that are bizarre, dangerous, and mercilessly cruel. Sensitive to criticism and easily offended, young adolescents may take their frustrations out on family members, teachers, and especially their classmates with behaviors such as insults, name calling, and pejorative labeling.

Young adolescents' feelings of inadequacy and attempts to gain control over their constantly changing environments prompt much of their inappropriate behavior. Lashing out against others is often the chosen path of self-protection. Asked about problems for their age group, Sarah, a seventh grader, reported, "People take [their frustrations] out on school, their friends, their school life . . . They make their lives miserable for themselves instead of making them better."

On the other hand, middle schoolers can be intensely loyal to their peers, team, parents, and family. They can be kind, compassionate, and deeply concerned about others. Behavior is subject to wild fluctuation. One never quite knows what to expect—except that if we wait a while, it will change. Danielle, an eighth-grade teacher, describes a sound philosophy and appropriate ways of responding to young adolescents' needs:

These students are in so many places developmentally. I have a background in psychology, and I can use every aspect of that education with these students. They want to talk about so many things, but they get into these situations where they don't think they can talk to anyone. They're asking questions they've never thought of before. In an environment like this, we're not the "givers of knowledge"—they need to see us as humans instead.

—*Danelle, eighth-grade teacher*

◆ ▌ Self-Esteem

The self-evaluative nature of young adolescence produces many questions and doubts in middle schoolers' minds. This questioning persona leads to lower self-esteem in many young adolescents who begin to see flaws in their academic, social, and physical traits that were never noticed before reaching this age.

The level of self-esteem students have depends on their perceptions of four central issues that affect their feelings of self worth:

1. the amount of perceived control over their circumstances
2. the degree to which they are accepted by those from whom they desire acceptance (peers, teachers, parents)
3. a need to be competent in what they attempt and wish to accomplish
4. a sense of being virtuous to others.

The self-consciousness that accompanies this stage of growth originates in the young person's perceived loss of control over his or her environment. Body image has perhaps the most powerful influence on and predicts young adolescents' levels of self-esteem (Berk 2012). When *control* is a need, the inability of young adolescents to control their changing bodies affects perceived worth. Higher academic expectations, a greater emphasis on evaluation and academic performance, and increased comparisons among students create another layer of frustration as students lose the confidence that accompanied their elementary academic successes.

Berk (2008) stated that middle school transitions "disrupt close relationships with teachers at a time when adolescents need adult support" (580). Middle level teachers often "emphasize competition during a period of heightened self-focusing; reduce decision making and choice as the desire for autonomy is increasing; and interfere with peer networks as young people become more concerned with peer acceptance" (580).

Early and middle adolescence are characterized by the elaboration and differentiation of social-related roles and self-attributes. These developments are accompanied by a susceptibility to all-or-none thinking, inaccurate over-generalizations, and instability and conflict regarding one's self-perceptions and self-evaluations. Based on these changes and issues, it would seem that early adolescence is a crucial time for schools and teachers to provide self-perception guidance to their students.

—BRINTHAUPT
(2013, 4)

Bessie, a seventh grader, stated the needs of young adolescents quite clearly: "My least favorite thing about school is being told what to do. I think that if you're going to find out what it means to grow up, you need to make your own decisions."

Young adolescents' abilities to establish positive feelings about themselves, have some control over their learning, and develop healthy relationships with peers are key to successfully developing positive self-esteem. Rob, age fourteen, jokingly tells his friends, teachers, and family, "Seventy percent of middle school kids suffer from low self-esteem and you're contributing to the problem." Rob acknowledges that his statistics may be in error but senses the need among his peers for affirmation and success.

Young adolescence brings with it life's first identity crisis. Students attempt to project an image consistent with the inner self that they hope will be accepted by others who make up their world. Young adolescents' concerns are real, their problems are unique to them, and their bravado often masks fear and anxiety.

◆❚❚ Concluding Reflections

Cameron et al. (2012) describe adolescents' lives with these comments:

Adolescence is a remarkably difficult time under the best of circumstances. Authentic thrusts toward exploration and independence are too often met with treatment befitting a very young child. Adolescents are told to "behave like an adult," but what this too often means is "comply like a child." The best school environment is one that is flexible and forgiving, one that understands that young people are not *made* but *in the making*. (24)

Young adolescents face a multitude of changes throughout their middle school years, changes that have a significant impact on their lives. Keith recalled his middle school experience in a statement he wrote as a college junior: "Every aspect—my friends, family, school, emotional and physical changes—all greatly affected me while I was growing up."

As we work with young adolescents, we must be aware of these changes. It is a time of transition between dependence and independence, a time to explore new alternatives and try out new identities, a time to experiment with new points of view, and a time to learn how to interact with others.

Think about these possibilities:

- What if we supported young adolescents in their quest to develop a "self"?
- What if we based schooling on respect for their development?
- What if we developed a curriculum that responded to their changing worlds?
- What if we provided an environment that supported their physical, cognitive, social, and emotional needs?
- What if we listened to what they said?
- What if their questions became our questions?
- What if . . . ?

Theory into Practice

Middle schools must provide opportunities for students to understand the growth they are experiencing and exercise their independence in supportive ways. Researchers revealed "that a strong, positive attachment to an adult, such as a teacher, is associated with more favorable development, self-esteem, and greater resilience among adolescents." (Brinthaupt, Lipka, and Wallace 2007, 211)

PART 3:

WHAT RESEARCH TELLS US ABOUT EFFECTIVE MIDDLE LEVEL SCHOOLS

Middle level schools should be designed to fit adolescents' unique developmental traits. Schools that implement teams, common planning time, challenging curricula, varied learning opportunities, advisories, and exploratories create greater opportunities for student success than those schools that only employ one or two of these structures.

CHAPTER 6

The True Middle School: More Than a Sign on a Building

> *You wake up early, you work all day at school, and then, they expect you to do homework.*
>
> —**ELIZABETH**, SEVENTH GRADER
>
> *Middle school is like a prison.*
>
> —**RYAN**, SIXTH GRADER

> *Advocates for the middle school concept see less value in a national- or state-dominated curriculum, preferring one that begins with the needs and interests of students.*
>
> —**GEORGE** (2011, 48)

Now that you know about young adolescent development, imagine a school where curricular or instructional decisions are made without considering their characteristics and without input from them. Although progressive administrators and teachers have always considered young adolescents when making curricular or instructional decisions, the demands of policies such as No Child Left Behind and Race to the Top have made it increasingly rare. Instead of considering the overwhelming changes middle level students are experiencing, many administrators persist in maintaining traditional structures that are inappropriate for young adolescents. In a country that values democracy, there seems to be very little of it in many of our schools—for either students or teachers.

◆ ❙❙ A Typical Day

It's 8:15 a.m. Three hundred students enter a long hallway filled with lockers that are too small, standing only inches apart. Classes begin and students sit passively for forty-two minutes as they listen to a lecture with little relevance to their lives, complete worksheets, answer questions in the back of a textbook chapter, or take written tests. When the bell rings at the end of each period, students file into the crowded hallway and play the locker game again, jostling for position with only three or four minutes to get to their next class. Finally, after three hours of classes, they have a lunch period.

The lunch line is long. Lunch periods are short, twenty to twenty-five minutes. The lunch menu is determined by administrators and does not allow for student choice. Lunchtime is the only opportunity for students to socialize until after school on the bus ride home, despite their urgent need to communicate with one another. By denying adequate socialization opportunities for students, the frustration and anxiety they feel prevents them from focusing on academics.

Students head back to class after lunch without any opportunity for physical exercise, except an occasional dash down the long hallway if there are no teachers in sight. They return to the classrooms for three more 42-minute classes—with hour-long homework assigned in each one.

Finally, students board the bus for a forty-five-minute trip home. If they begin their homework soon after they arrive home, they may complete it by 10:00 p.m., provided they don't spend any time texting friends, exercising, or just hanging out for an hour or so.

> I feel like a cow. They herd us in the building in the morning trying to fit a thousand kids in two doors. Then they make us get into our stalls. Then they make us get into line and serve us all the same food. Then they give us fifteen minutes of pasture time after lunch, then herd us back into the classroom.
>
> **—ROB**,
> EIGHTH GRADER

A visit to most middle level schools would reveal the reality of the aforementioned description. Is this an appropriate way to educate young adolescents? Who designed such a stifling environment for students, and why?

◆▌ Emulating the Factory

The development of the factory assembly line in the early 1900s had an enormous impact on the structure of education. Factories were designed so that each person had a specific job to do and performed the same task all day long. Work started and ended with the blast of a horn or a bell. Breaks were granted to workers on a set timetable. Work was evaluated by the amount of time on task and the number of items produced each day. The boss' job was to keep the employees on task. Reflective thinking was not required or valued. Bosses wanted compliant employees who were highly productive during long hours on the job. They did not expect employees to question the work they were responsible for completing or how it was done.

During the early 1900s, schools were "concerned with producing a workforce to staff and operate the factories" (Caine and Caine 1994, 13). Hence, school structure was based on the factory model. Schools contrived a seven- or eight-period day, with classes lasting approximately forty to forty-five minutes, ending with a bell. Students filed out into the halls for four minutes, and then into another classroom. Subjects were taught separately, and the learning outcomes were predetermined by textbook design or pre-structured curricula chosen by central office administrators. Every student learned the same curriculum at the same pace, and all students were taught in the same way. Compliant behavior was rewarded; creative and critical thinking were discouraged.

INFLUENCE ON TEACHING

When education is designed according to the factory model, students are treated as raw materials to be molded and polished into something new without regard to the needs or variations of the original material. Numerous assumptions are implicit in this design:

1. All students have similar learning characteristics.
2. Teaching is a simple process whereby one style fits the needs of all students.
3. The information students need to learn is unilaterally predetermined, involves a fixed set of concepts and principles, and has an established limit.

4. Content can only be accessed from textbooks or experts.
5. All students are expected to perform similar responsibilities after they graduate.
6. Learning means memorization of facts.
7. Every student will learn the content at the exact same pace. Creative and critical thinking are not valued.
8. Connections do not exist among subjects.
9. Teachers are unilateral decision makers in the classroom.

These assumptions ignore what researchers know about neuroscience, the learning process, young adolescent development, and changing technology. Adopting any of the faulty logic above denies the existence of computers, the Internet, and smartphones. And yet schools are still designed in this model, with the day divided into six or seven periods of forty-minute segments.

Federal and state education policies have helped to promote factory model teaching and learning with testing mandates, performance standards, Common Core standards, and by labeling students as "proficient." Many professional educators struggle daily with choosing to either use research-based, developmentally appropriate teaching strategies or accept a philosophy that pedagogically sound teaching can't be used because the consequence for doing so negatively impacts their students' test scores and teachers' performance evaluations. In addition, for many this is the only school model that has been experienced, so it becomes difficult to envision a different school structure.

It's faulty thinking to believe that teacher-directed lessons, lock-step daily curricula delivery, and "back-to-basics" instructional and curricular emphases will improve middle level students' cognitive growth. Yet, teacher fear associated with the Federal Department of Education's "Race to the Top" program, which requires teachers' evaluations to be based partially on students' test scores, wreaks havoc on effective teaching (D. Brown 2013b). One middle level teacher interviewed in Brown's recent study revealed the following frustration as a result of the implementation of NCLB policies:

In the beginning I was so disappointed. We used to teach trade books, and we could be creative; but then we were told to go back to the textbooks. All the teachers from different language arts classes were teaching the same lessons the same week, and some lessons had to be taught on the same day in each classroom. Newer teachers who were hired following NCLB weren't comfortable with the flexibility of using different curricula to excite students or match their needs. And the testing caused a lot of stress for students. They had practice tests in January before the official tests in April, and the students got sick of writing the five-paragraph essay.

This story mirrors the frustrations of many educators who feel intense pressure to raise students' test scores by any means necessary. Those *means*, however, don't generally reflect developmentally appropriate practices for young adolescents, and consequently deny young adolescents opportunities to maximize their constantly growing brain potential with cognitively challenging thinking processes.

INFLUENCE ON TEACHER BEHAVIORS

The factory approach and erroneously designed teacher accountability systems not only affect educators' choice of instructional strategies but also student socialization, student–teacher relationships, and the general quality of the school day. The factory model, amplified by the inappropriate invasion of the testing culture, makes it more difficult for teachers to develop the kind of caring relationships with students that are required as a basis for learning. In a study in which researchers asked young adolescents what they wanted their middle school teachers to know about them, it became clear that students wanted strong personal relationships with their teachers (Doda and Knowles 2008). One student responded,

> The key to being a good teacher is to know the kids. You have to know every single one and have a relationship with every single one. I think that one thing that really allows me to work hard is knowing that my teacher knows where I am in life at that moment. (28)

When the focus is primarily on the structure of the school and on the content of the classes, these warm relationships are more difficult to establish.

Researchers who study the relationship between emotion and cognitive processing (Sousa 2010; MacLaury 2002) have warned us of the negative effects of a sterile learning environment. Forty-two minutes is not sufficient time for teachers to develop the kind of healthy, caring relationships with students that are necessary to promote meaningful learning (D. Brown 2013a). Adam, an eighth grader, describes one aspect of his "perfect" middle school: "Teachers would be friendly with the kids. Some are okay, but the teachers aren't close enough to kids." When students and teachers have opportunities and time to communicate with one other, they begin to care about each other in ways that make meaningful learning possible. Edith, a sixth-grade teacher, explained, "I definitely think the middle school should be more nurturing. I find my role as a teacher is just one part of it. I feel like I am a counselor, a grandmother; it's much more than just teaching."

> When students and teachers have opportunities and time to communicate with one another, they begin to care about each other in ways that make meaningful learning possible.

Similarly, forty-two-minute periods prevent teachers from designing lessons that ensure optimal learning for all students, which limits opportunities to complete curricula in a meaningful manner. Instead, teachers are encouraged to cover topics briefly, move on to another topic, and complete the book—a book that has information in it that students can access 24/7 on devices that fit into their skinny jeans pockets.

STUDENTS REVEAL THEIR NEEDS

Young adolescents have wise advice for middle level teachers about their learning needs. Sheila, a seventh grader, had this to say about the traditional lecture-style classroom: "Civics is so boring. We read our book and we do these answer-and-question pages. We never do anything as a whole class—we just read and take notes the whole time." If this civics class represents a typical middle school classroom, then young adolescents aren't going to grow cognitively. They need and want meaningful learning—learning that engages them socially, emotionally, and is intellectually challenging. This isn't merely a distant philosophical statement meant to be uttered during a teaching interview. Ten- to fifteen-year-olds are emotional machines, and they want their teachers to tap that emotional vein in classroom lessons every day of the week!

You may recall in Chapter 3 our description of how to help young adolescents move from the concrete operational stage cognitively into formal operations—the last stage of cognitive development. Data-gathering from a multiple-guess test is an unlikely match for what students learn during a 180-day school year and is minimally capable of improving students' abilities to think more abstractly. D. Brown and Canniff (2007) noted, "The developing cognitive processes of young adolescents are enhanced when they are engaged as active participants in their own learning" (22). The act of changing instruction to improve students' test scores should never be associated with improving students' cognitive growth.

In addition to the lack of cognitive growth in the factory model, the abandonment of developmentally appropriate teaching that prepares students for standardized tests limits quality socialization among students. Short periods, four minutes between classes, large class size, and predetermined curricular guidelines are a few of the structures that discourage teachers from using collaborative learning experiences in their lesson design. Collaborative learning strategies take more time to implement initially, and short class periods may discourage teachers from using them (D. Brown 2001). Edith, a sixth-grade teacher, was in a middle school that moved to longer blocks of time for each period. She commented, "This year I started a double whole language period and then math—it was fabulous. From 8:15 until 9:45 I have the same children. This is really advantageous to the students." Longer class periods have created much more teacher–student interaction, thus meeting young adolescents' social and emotional needs while simultaneously promoting intellectual growth (D. Brown 2001; D. Brown and Canniff 2007).

Based on what is now known about how learning occurs, the developmental abilities and needs of young adolescents, and the proliferation of easily accessible information on every topic via electronic devices; middle schools must abandon the factory approach to schooling, focus less on test-score data and content standards, attend to the developmental needs of young adolescents, and evolve into more effective centers of learning. The middle school movement was borne from these simple courses of action—knowing who young adolescents are, listening to them, and responding to their needs. Paul George (2011), an internationally renowned middle level researcher, describes the mission of every teacher and the foundation for designing effective middle level schools:

Trust, meaningful relationships, freedom, empowerment, equity, optimism, diversity, complexity, tolerance, child-centeredness—these are the core components of the alternative, progressive worldview in education. They are also the core components of the middle level concept, one of today's clearest manifestations of that worldview. (48)

Some schools have recognized the needs of young adolescents by replacing the factory model with more developmentally appropriate structures. These structural and philosophical changes began to be incorporated thirty years ago.

◆❙❙ The First Junior High Schools

Until 1893, the most common organizational pattern of education was eight years at an elementary school and, if students were continuing their education past that, high school. Concern about the inconsistencies in college preparation resulted in a division into six years of elementary school and six years of high school that lasted until 1909, when concern about the immaturity of sixth-grade students and overcrowding of high schools led to the development of the first seventh- through ninth-grade school in

Columbus, Ohio. This school was recognized as a junior high school: "a school in which the seventh, eighth, and ninth grades are segregated in a building (or portion of a building) by themselves; possess an organization and administration of their own that is distinct from the grades above and below; and are taught by a separate corps of teachers" (North Central Association 1919, 4).

The junior high was originally designed to provide a program that would respond to the uniqueness of this developmental stage and offer a practical and active curriculum that would engage the young adolescent mind (Tye 1985). However, junior high school educators were concerned that students needed to be prepared for high school. Therefore, they chose the Carnegie Unit structure, whereby completing courses gained students credits required to graduate, in an effort to bolster junior high school students' academic preparedness for high school.

FALSE HOPE

Approximately sixty-five hundred junior high schools existed across the country by the 1950s. Despite its popularity and the rhetoric of developmental appropriateness that accompanied its initiation, the junior high school never quite lived up to its promise of providing a distinct experience for young adolescents. Many junior highs were staffed by teachers with little or no knowledge of young adolescent development who lacked the strategies needed for meeting students' cognitive, social, and emotional needs (McEwin, Dickinson, and Jenkins 1996). Instead of developing practical and active curricula, junior high schools maintained traditional content-specific curricula and a factory design of six forty-two-minute periods throughout the day.

Throughout the 1940s and 1950s, the need for a distinct educational experience for young adolescents remained in the forefront of the minds of many educators and developmentalists. These educators suggested that junior high schools provide curricula designed for student exploration and integration of knowledge and also offer many opportunities for socialization. It was the Association for Supervision and Curriculum Development (ASCD) that responded to these calls for change in 1961 with the publication of *The Junior High School We Need* (Grantes et al. 1961). The authors envisioned a school in which educators were specifically trained to use appropriate instructional strategies to teach young adolescents. They recommended smaller schools with flexible schedules. The authors' suggestions, unfortunately, were not implemented widely until the 1990s.

◆❙ The Promise of a New Design

"What if we attempted to respond to the needs of young adolescents? What if we developed a school with the characteristics proposed by the ASCD?" some educators were asking. Fueled by such powerful convictions, the middle school movement was born. In his edited collection of writing and reflections by early middle school visionaries, Robert David (1998) wrote,

> The middle school concept did not spring from sterile, educational thought. It was the result of the work of dedicated and inspired leaders who recognized that traditional secondary practices did not meet the needs of emerging adolescents. William Alexander, Donald Eichhorn, John Lounsbury, Conrad Toepfer, and Gordon Vars, identified as founding fathers of middle level education, . . . had the vision and determination to create a new and powerful educational reform effort for the 11- to 14-year-old child. . . . Each focused on a vision regarding the programming and educational needs of the young adolescent. And they articulated a philosophy born out of the awareness that the middle level learner is a unique individual with special needs that call for a distinctive educational program. (ix)

William Alexander, often referred to as the "father of the middle school," first coined the phrase *middle school* in a speech, "The Junior High School: A Changing View," given at Cornell University in 1963 (David 1998). Alexander argued that junior high school should not simply be an extension of elementary school or a preparation for high school but that schools in the middle needed validity in and of themselves as places that met the needs of a unique age group. He called for one institution with three distinct parts designed to meet the developmental needs of students at those levels: the "lower, middle and upper level or a primary, middle and high school" (5).

Alexander called for a strong general education for all students, with project-based instruction that allowed students to answer real questions through hands-on investigations. He stressed the need for a flexible curriculum that differentiated instruction based on individual student needs. In addition, he cited the importance of a comprehensive health, physical education, and guidance program to help students cope with their rapid physical changes as well as an exploratory curriculum that would expose students to new topics and ideas. One of Alexander's most important recommendations was the call for teacher education programs to prepare teachers to work with the unique needs of the young adolescent. Alexander also called for changes in the organization of the school: The best structure would be teams of from three to five teachers who would be responsible for a heterogeneous group of students. Each student would be in a small homeroom class with a teacher who knew him or her well.

The vision of a unique school for young adolescents began to take form and would become the core of the middle school concept. In the mid-1960s Upper St. Clair, Pennsylvania; Centerville, Ohio; and Barrington, Illinois were three of the first communities to implement this new middle school concept (George et al. 1992).

In Upper St. Clair, assistant superintendent Donald Eichhorn not only talked about the need for reform, he was instrumental in creating a new middle school structure. As such, "he shook not only Upper St. Clair; he shook the nation's middle level schools and put into motion a process in Pennsylvania which led to the recognition of the middle grades as a distinctive level in K–12 education" (Brough 1994, 19). Eichhorn redefined instructional practice, established advisory programs to meet students' emotional needs, and developed multi-age grouping. Perhaps his greatest accomplishment was his courageous willingness to question the validity of the existing traditional curricular structure. Although more middle schools were created throughout the United States shortly after the Upper St. Clair innovation, most of these were middle schools in name only and did not implement the innovations suggested by Alexander, Eichhorn, and the other educators who were working on true middle level reform.

DEMOGRAPHIC INFLUENCES ON MIDDLE SCHOOL DEVELOPMENT

Many junior highs that changed their names to "middle school" did so because of demographic factors: The baby boomers completed high school, and a small "baby boomlet" flooded the elementary grades with overwhelming numbers of new students (George et al. 1992). Suddenly classrooms were available in high school buildings, and a shortage of classrooms existed in kindergarten through sixth-grade buildings. The school board's solution was to move the ninth graders into the high school, move the sixth and sometimes fifth graders into the junior high, and rename the junior high the "middle school." In response to the mandates of Brown v. Board of Education, other school districts moved to the middle school design in order to desegregate schools (George et al.).

Often these were middle schools in name only—not in their design or in the ways in which students' developmental needs were addressed. Middle schools of the 1960s and 1970s frequently utilized features common to high schools, such as departmentalized instruction, forty-two-minute periods, and students tracked according to ability—in essence, the factory approach to educating students.

◆‖ Support for Genuine Middle Schools

As more districts began to develop sixth- through eighth-grade schools, educators realized the need for a national organization to advocate for young adolescents. Research on adolescent development soon followed from various organizations and educational researchers supporting the developmental perspective that defined and justified genuine middle level school design.

THE NATIONAL MIDDLE SCHOOL ASSOCIATION

As a result of educators' growing concerns, National Middle School Association (NMSA) was founded. In 1982, NMSA published the first comprehensive position paper outlining the role of the middle school in meeting the unique developmental needs of the young adolescent. The authors of this report asserted that simply designating an institution a "middle school" did not mean that it met the needs of young adolescents; schools must also be responsive to developmental issues. Entitled *This We Believe*, the work outlined the essential elements present in a true middle school and set the standard for middle school reform. Revised in 1995, 2003, and 2010, *This We Believe* is an important statement about the vision of a middle school that fulfills its promises to young adolescents.

THE CARNEGIE COUNCIL ON ADOLESCENT DEVELOPMENT

The Carnegie Corporation of New York established the Carnegie Council on Adolescent Development in 1986 out of concern for the high risks for drug and alcohol abuse, early pregnancy, school failure, and violence that adolescents faced. This group's task was to develop strategies to meet the needs of adolescents in a rapidly changing environment. Education became a central focus of the Carnegie Council with the establishment of the Task Force on the Education of Young Adolescents. One role of the task force members was to determine why middle and junior high schools were not meeting the needs of young adolescents. The group reported the following:

- Middle and junior high schools contained large enrollments.
- The students had developed few meaningful relationships with the adults in the schools.
- The chosen curricula were irrelevant to students.
- The majority of instructional strategies used were better suited for specialized classes in high school or college.

The task force developed a proposal for educators and parents to suggest the design of a school that would better meet the needs of middle level students. The group's report, published in 1989, was titled *Turning Points: Preparing Youth for the 21st Century* (Carnegie Council on Adolescent Development 1989). David Hamburg, chair of the council, provided this comment about young adolescents and the responsibility that schools had to these students:

> The emerging adolescent is caught in turbulence, a fascinated but perplexed observer of the biological, psychological, and social changes swirling all around. In groping for a solid path toward a worthwhile adult life, adolescents can grasp the middle grade school as the crucial and reliable handle. Now, the middle grade school must change, and change substantially, to cope with the requirements of a new era—to give students a decent chance in life and to help them fulfill their youthful promise. (14)

The Carnegie Task Force members provided eight recommendations that became basic guidelines for developing an appropriate educational setting for young adolescents. These recommendations are the core of the middle school concept. They clearly reflected the earlier work of Alexander, Eichhorn, and other educators who had called for middle level reform for more than two decades. Here is the executive summary of the task force's recommendations (1989):

1. *Create small communities for learning* where stable, close, mutually respectful relationships with adults and peers are considered fundamental for intellectual development and personal growth. The key elements of these communities are schools-within-schools or houses, students and teachers grouped together as teams, and small group advisories that ensure that every student is well known by at least one adult.

2. *Teach a core academic program* that results in students who are literate, including in the sciences, and who know how to think critically, lead a healthy life, behave ethically, and assume the responsibilities of citizenship in a pluralistic society. Youth service to promote values for citizenship is an essential part of the core academic program.

3. *Ensure success for all students* through the elimination of tracking by achievement level and promotion of cooperative learning, flexibility in arranging instructional time, and adequate resources (time, space, equipment, and materials) for teachers.

4. *Empower teachers and administrators to make decisions about the experiences of middle grade students* through creative control by teachers over

the instructional program linked to greater responsibilities for students' performance, governance committees that assist the principal in designing and coordinating schoolwide programs, and autonomy and leadership within subschools or houses to create environments tailored to enhance the intellectual and emotional development of all youth.

5. *Staff middle grade schools with teachers who are expert at teaching young adolescents* and who have been specifically prepared for assignment to the middle grades.

6. *Improve academic performance through fostering the health and fitness* of young adolescents by providing a health coordinator in every middle grade school, access to health care and counseling services, and a health-promoting school environment.

7. *Reengage families in the education of young adolescents* by giving families meaningful roles in school governance, communicating with families about the school program and students' progress, and offering families opportunities to support the learning process at home and at the school.

8. *Connect schools with communities*, which together share responsibilities for each middle grade student's success, through identifying service opportunities in the community, establishing partnerships and collaborations to ensure students' access to health and social services, and using community resources to enrich the instructional program and opportunities for constructive after-school activities. (9–10)

After the report was published, some middle schools began to implement the core recommendations, developing team structures and creating smaller communities for learning. Advisory programs were developed in some schools. Tracking was eliminated and instruction was designed to better meet the unique needs of the young adolescent.

◆❚❚ Support for Genuine Middle Level Schools Today

NMSA changed its name in 2011 to the *Association for Middle Level Education* (AMLE) to represent middle level schools internationally rather than merely within the United States, and to clarify that the words *middle level* represent any school educating students between the ages of 10 and 15 in any configuration—not merely those housing sixth through eighth grades.

In the latest version of *This We Believe: Keys to Educating Young Adolescents* (2010), the AMLE authors provide four essential attributes, noting: "An education for young adolescents must be"

- developmentally responsive—using the nature of young adolescents as the foundation on which all decisions are made
- challenging—recognizing that every student can learn, and everyone is held to high [reasonable] expectations
- empowering—providing all students with the knowledge and skills they need to take control of their lives
- equitable—advocating for every student's right to learn and providing challenging, relevant learning opportunities. (adapted from 14)

Some of the specific characteristics of effective middle level schools that the authors note include:

- Educators value working with this age group and are prepared to teach them.
- Students and teachers are engaged in active, purposeful learning.
- Curriculum is challenging, exploratory, integrative, and relevant.
- A shared vision that is developed by all stakeholders guides every decision.
- Leaders are committed to and knowledgeable about this age group, educational research, and best practices.
- The school environment is inviting, safe, inclusive, and supportive of all.
- Health and wellness is supported in curricula, school-wide programs, and related policies. (adapted from 14)

This We Believe authors provide research in the field of young adolescent development, instructional practices, curricular design, and assessment processes that specifically describe how middle level schools should be designed. Any mandated policies that affect how young adolescents are taught must refer to and reflect the recommendations of AMLE.

◆❚❚ Content Standards Influence Middle Level Schools

The standards era was introduced and thrust upon schools during the 1990s, partly because the business community and legislative bodies were determined to influence education. Broad content standards related to what students should know or should be able to do when they graduated from high school were developed by most state departments of education as well as many school districts. The standards developed related to problem solving, communication skills, and being a participating member of society, and they gave schools broad latitude in designing curricula.

The federal government's reauthorization of the long-established policies for funding schools through the Elementary and Secondary Education Act under the new name of No Child Left Behind (NCLB) in 2001 changed the way standards were designed. Broad goals were quickly replaced by specific content standards mandating what students should know as a result of studying specifically designated topics.

Perhaps no single event had a greater impact on the structure, organization, curriculum, instruction, and assessment practices of the middle school than the focus on content-standards-based teaching, coupled with high-stakes tests associated with the No Child Left Behind Act of 2001. NCLB policy required that each state develop benchmarks (minimum test scores) for student performance. Each school was required to meet an established level of "adequate yearly progress" (AYP). In most states, AYP was determined by the percentage of students reaching a certain performance level, called *proficiency*, on a standardized test. Schools, primarily in urban areas, had a high enough percentage of students who were "not proficient," providing ammunition for their state departments of education to close those schools but then reopen them the next year as for-profit charter schools frequently staffed by a percentage of uncertified teachers, led by unlicensed and nonprofessional administrators, and unaware of educationally sound instructional or curricular practices and adolescent development (D. Brown 2012; Saltman 2005). The effect of closing the original middle level schools in many of these situations has been the eradication of middle level philosophies and practices within their classrooms.

With the influence of NCLB policies, teacher accountability in the eyes of many administrators and legislators quickly became synonymous with acceptable student test scores. If students achieved test-score proficiency, according to popular belief, teachers had done their jobs.

Even teacher certification programs began to focus more on content knowledge at the expense of pedagogical expertise. NCLB policy defined "highly qualified teachers" at the middle level as those who received heavy doses of content knowledge, rather than those with pedagogical or adolescent development research-based expertise. Content-area standardized teacher tests were developed by outside agencies and used as a primary criterion for receiving middle level certification. Even experienced middle level teachers' content knowledge became the primary criterion for them to maintain their current teaching positions despite years of excellent teaching, their

> With the influence of NCLB policies, teacher accountability in the eyes of many administrators and legislators quickly became synonymous with acceptable student test scores. If students achieved test-score proficiency, according to popular belief, teachers had done their jobs.

knowledge of young adolescent development, and implementation of appropriate middle level philosophy, practice, and curriculum. Many highly effective middle level teachers were forced to suddenly take a subject area content test that would allegedly determine that they were "highly qualified" to remain in the profession.

As a result of the standards-based movement bolstered by NCLB policies, many middle schools returned to the factory model. Teachers felt pressure to abandon innovative teaching and become transmitters of information to prepare students to reach proficiency on high-stakes tests. Some of these teachers still used developmentally appropriate practices, yet felt compelled to fill students with facts because their administration feared being declared a school "in need of improvement." Take note of these words from William Alexander's speech in 1963:

There seems little disagreement that the youngster of twelve and above needs many and varied opportunities to identify and/or deepen worthwhile interests, and all of us would applaud what junior high schools have done to this end. However, the recent pressures on schools to give greater emphasis to the academic subject may be curtailing the exploratory feature. Earlier languages, more mathematics and science, more homework, may mean for many pupils less time and energy for the fine arts, for homemaking and industrial arts, and for such special interests as dramatics, journalism, musical performance, scouting, camping, outside jobs, and general reading. (David 1998, 5)

Alexander's quote was a response to another time, among several over the past fifty years in our educational history, when rigorous academics became the focus of education at the expense of the individual needs of students. It is as relevant today as it was then.

RESPONDING TO PROPOSED CONTENT STANDARDS AND FALSE ACCOUNTABILITY MEASURES

As a result of overbearing government oversight, some districts reverted to the junior high model with the belief that they must prepare students for high-stakes tests through traditional curricula that simulate high schools. Other districts, particularly in large urban areas, replaced middle schools with K–8 schools because administrators wanted to raise test scores and believed that K–8 buildings would accomplish this— although no evidence exists of this positive effect (George 2005).

The danger in reverting to the junior high model or changing to K–8 schools is that schools will likely be based more on an elementary rather than a middle school concept. In a 2005 analysis of K–8 schools throughout the country, researchers discovered that only a third of the schools reported using interdisciplinary teacher teams compared with 77 percent of the middle schools at that time. K–8 schools offered fewer exploratory and extracurricular programs to young adolescents (McEwin, Dickinson, and Jacobson 2005). Teachers in K–8 schools also had less common planning time, an important element for middle school success (Mertens et al. 2013).

As 2014 neared, the Federal Department of Education (ED) and the Secretary of Education realized that 100 percent of U.S. students would not be *proficient*, as NCLB policy mandated. Rather than claim that all public schools were inadequate if all schools didn't meet AYP, the ED proposed another strategy for providing money for Title I funding, called *Race to the Top* (RTTT). RTTT was designed unilaterally by ED personnel and funded by Congress as part of the American Recovery and Reinvestment Act of 2009. The federal government relied on the ED to "reward" those states that would adopt ED's un-researched guidelines.

Rather than approved by legislative means, RTTT is a federal grant program in which $5 billion dollars was to be evenly distributed in the first year of the program among those states that agreed to pass/mandate new statewide education policies in lieu of schools not making AYP. States that enacted new federal education policies had an opportunity to "win" the federal dollars needed to sustain their diminishing education budgets. Since the original rollout of RTTT, almost all states have adopted proposed ED education policies as a requirement for receiving needed federal funding.

RTTT proposed the adoption of un-researched policies to evaluate teachers, adding more charter schools, approving school choice policies, and adopting new curricula content standards called the Common Core State Standards (CCSS). The RTTT guidelines are questionable, unfounded educational mandates. The most egregious policy that accompanied the RTTT money was tying teachers' evaluations to their students' test scores via the *value added model* (VAM). The VAM theory for evaluating teachers is based on limited, faulty research of economists, spurred on by the advice of Bill Gates about strategies for connecting students' test scores to teachers' evaluations (D. Brown 2012). The CCSS were designed by alleged "reformers," yet few, if any, of those who advocated for these content standards or teacher performance evaluations were certified teachers, educational researchers, or administrators.

RTTT's adoption has created stressful school environments as teachers rush to learn the new content standards so that they can have an impact on their students' test scores since teacher evaluations will be partially based on their students' test score successes (D. Brown 2013b). As with the initial implementation of NCLB, RTTT reduced the creative, innovative, student-driven instruction and curricular emphases to a mere infusion of facts for students to memorize, regurgitate like owl pellets for the state tests, and forget shortly after. George (2011) summarized the dangers of NCLB, RTTT, and CCSS to the middle level philosophy:

> Accountability measures have, for example, insured that millions of dollars have been shifted from instruction to assessment. Ability grouping has seen an upsurge. Passive learning of scripted curriculum seems recommended as standard classroom fare. Curriculum alignment and pacing are common test-preparation activities. (46)

One Pennsylvania middle level social studies teacher revealed the new challenges since the adoption of CCSS:

> These new social studies standards are mostly on Western Civilization. None of the content reflected many of my students' lives: I have Chinese, Indian, and African American students, so I want to implement integrated curricula, but I can't because there isn't enough time. I used to also do much more hands-on activities; but now I do less especially because of all the writing we have to do.

In their attempt to raise test scores, school districts must be careful about creating learning environments that ignore the unique needs of the young adolescent.

Middle schools continue to proliferate nationally despite the return by some districts to K–8 buildings or junior highs during the mid-2000s. There were over 15,000 public middle schools in 2013 compared to 13,227 in 2008. A 2009 nation-wide survey of 827 public middle schools revealed the 6–8 grade configuration to be the most common grade-level pattern (McEwin and Greene 2011). Schools with the "middle school" sign on the building, however, don't necessarily reflect the tenets of genuine middle level schools.

McEwin and Greene (2013) reported, "Data from the HSMS (highly successful middle schools) survey, along with other research results, confirm that middle grades schools authentically following the middle school concept/philosophy are more likely to be associated with higher scores on achievement tests and other positive student outcomes" (79). The HSMS study was conducted with 101 middle level schools that were recognized for their excellence in middle level design by the *Schools to Watch* (STW) program, sponsored by the National Forum to Accelerate Middle-Grades Reform that was developed to identify exemplary middle level schools based on academic excellence, developmental responsiveness, organizational structure, and social equity.

Ultimately it is the
implementation of
effective middle level
practices that provides
young adolescents with
a meaningful learning
environment.

To receive recognition from STW, schools must follow the guidelines of AMLE in designing and delivering genuine middle level principles and programs to their students. The STW program is a critical component of encouraging middle schools to adopt a middle level philosophy and design the school along those developmental guidelines.

Whether a district keeps their middle schools, returns to a junior high format, or moves young adolescents into a K–8 setting, what is important is that an intentional effort is made to develop curriculum, instruction, assessment, and a school environment appropriate for young adolescents. As Erb (2005b) noted, "The middle school concept is about organizing and delivering developmentally appropriate programs for young adolescents—not about what grades may or may not be housed in the school building" (3). School districts can change the name of the school, restructure the configuration of the classes, or move students into another building, but ultimately it is the implementation of effective middle level practices that provides young adolescents with a meaningful learning environment.

TIME FOR REFLECTION

- *Return to the middle school design you devised at the start of this chapter. Compare your group's design with the thoughts put forth by AMLE and the Carnegie Report.*
- *Decide as a group how you would alter your design or change the design suggested by the AMLE and the Carnegie Report.*
- *Describe how "teaching to the test" isn't actually promoting cognitive growth.*
- *How does designing a genuine middle level school help students grow more than using primarily teacher-directed lessons to improve student test scores?*
- *Discuss how your school can meet content and performance standards while still meeting the learning needs of young adolescents.*

◆▮ Concluding Reflections

Until No Child Left Behind, the original recommendations of *This We Believe* and *Turning Points* drove the middle school movement. Now increasing accountability and high-stakes testing fueled by the Common Core standards and teacher evaluation based on student test scores influence educators' decisions about middle level practices. The idea of a middle level school responding to the needs of young adolescents must be honored despite the focus on rigid content standards and teacher accountability. McEwin's and Greene's (2013) study of highly successful middle schools demonstrates how designing genuine middle level schools creates academic success *and* meets the developmental needs of young adolescents. The Schools to Watch (STW) program, with its focus on several outcomes rather than mere test data, has the potential to encourage middle schools nationwide to implement research-based middle level programs.

Pedagogy and the field of young adolescent development are research-based disciplines that provide scientific guidance for designing programs that meet the needs of young adolescents. Middle level educators will receive the most recent reliable research on what works in middle level education from the Middle Level Education Research (MLER) Special Interest Group (SIG) of the American Educational Research Association (AERA). The education researchers who are members of the MLER SIG produce peer-reviewed studies that provide evidence for successful middle level practices based on sound theories and educational practices.

National news networks often interview high-profile people who have been called "education reformers" on television, and these persons believe that they are education "experts." Unfortunately for students throughout the United States, they *are not* from the education profession, *do not* hold teaching certificates, most *have never taught*, and they lack the knowledge and experience to access quality research in the field of pedagogy and adolescent development to positively influence the lives of young adolescents. It is unprofessional for educators at any level to develop policy or practices provided by non-education "reformers." We advise teachers, administrators, and policy makers searching for reliable research to inform appropriate middle level practices to go directly to the resources available from AMLE and the MLER SIG of AERA.

In attempting to respond to accountability concerns, we must not forget the inherent curiosity; the desire for curricular relevance; and the social, emotional, and physical needs of the young adolescent in designing their school day. Genuine accountability for middle school teachers occurs when they respond to the specific needs of each young adolescent they teach. Fear of accountability based on narrow student assessment measures and unfounded teacher evaluation systems should not result in knee-jerk reactions to bureaucratic mandates at the expense of meeting every student's needs.

We sincerely hope that preservice and inservice teachers will continue to work to develop middle schools that are sensitive to the developmental stages and needs of young adolescents and also implement democratic principles in classroom practice. The courage and actions of teachers change schooling more than the efforts of administrators or professors who write books! It is imperative that teachers comprehend their role and assume responsibility for improving middle level education. Rhetoric and policy decisions are not on the minds of young adolescents, who seek adventure, excitement, and motivation each day they enter your classroom. That's what we are accountable for, meeting their needs—that's what *accountability* actually means.

CHAPTER 7

School Structures
That Support
Young Adolescents

"[I]t is [critical] to implement multiple elements of middle grades reform and maintain those elements over time in order to see positive outcomes for students. Which of the systems of the human body could you eliminate that would not be debilitating if not fatal? Amputations and organ removals may leave a body living, but they leave a body with a diminished capacity. So it is with middle grades reform. Flexible structures and a shared vision are important, but without a challenging curriculum, varied learning approaches, and programs for health and wellness, the middle grades school will function with diminished capacity.

—**ERB** (2005a, 3)

◆❚❚ Misunderstanding the Middle School Concept

The middle school concept is not always supported by those outside education or those associated with education through political appointments. Despite years of research supporting the components of true middle level schools, often the public hears a negative report that is unsubstantiated by research. A *Time* magazine reporter, for instance, claimed: "A series of studies depict U.S. middle schools as the 'Bermuda Triangle of education'" (Wallis 2005, 50–51). George (2011) described our frustration as educators: "Even with less compelling evidence, the drumbeat of destructive disinformation about the supposed failure of public education, and middle level schools in particular, has not diminished" (45).

Those who make unsupported claims that misguide the public about the value of middle level schools usually lack any knowledge of the developmental traits of young adolescents. School districts that drop their middle school arrangements may attempt to justify their change based on these erroneous claims, thereby creating schools that ignore the needs of young adolescents.

Unfortunately, the public doesn't generally access professional educational journals and encounters only the erroneous (and unsupported) perspectives that are often publicized. Fortunately, professional educators, you among them, have many opportunities to promote the middle school concept based on reading valid research and other accurate accounts of effective middle level practices. Erb (2005b), in a *Middle School Journal* editorial, called the attacks on middle schools "The Making of a New Urban Myth"; he cited numerous studies in support of schools that implement a true middle school concept. Recognizing the research of Brown, Roney, and Anfara (2003), he stated, "The evidential base supports the middle school concept as a means to improve student behavior and achievement when it is implemented in healthy schools" (3). Researchers from the American Educational Research Association (AERA) through the Middle Level Education Research (MLER) Special Interest Group continue to conduct research on and provide evidence for implementing the middle level concept. Numerous studies are conducted monthly and yield favorable results for students who attend genuine middle level schools.

Another organization that is contributing to the development of genuine middle level schools is the National Forum to Accelerate Middle-Grades Reform, a group of practitioners and researchers who evaluate and honor middle level schools that follow the recommendations of MLER researchers and AMLE personnel. The National Forum describes high-performing middle level schools based on three components: academic excellence, developmental responsiveness, and social equity. The Forum established the *Schools to Watch* (STW) designation for schools that create exceptional programs reflecting the Forum's list of research-based quality guidelines. Many middle level schools across the nation have been designated as STW schools, and many others are currently attempting to receive the STW label through the implementation of exceptional programs for their students.

Based on the level and volume of high-quality research, the middle school concept is not an educational "fad" that is doomed for a short shelf life. The middle school concept developed during the 1960s and has been supported by continued research, and more middle schools open each year, many motivated by the latest research and others by the National Forum's identification as a Schools to Watch school (McEwin and Greene 2013). The middle school concept exists primarily because of specific needs of young adolescents.

Lounsbury and Brazee (2004), in an attempt to dispel misunderstandings associated with the design of the middle level concept, noted the following typical *myths* about the purposes of middle schools:

- The middle level school is a "feel good" school.
- The middle level school exists to prepare students for high school.
- The middle level school is "fun time."
- Middle level schools have "failed." (38)

None of these statements about the true purpose or successes of middle schools is accurate. In fact, effective middle schools, through their specific design and implementation, respond to the needs of young adolescents to ensure their success during these critical years of growth. In our work as middle level researchers, teachers, and teachers of practitioners, we find that schools with the name "middle school" face the most difficulty when they lose sight of the goals of true middle level education.

◆❙❙ The Core Elements of Effective Middle Level Schools

If middle schools are to survive, we have to hold on to the core elements of the middle level concept as described by the Carnegie Council (1989) and listed in Chapter 6, which describe middle school as a place that values community, a core academic program that promotes citizenship, equity, empowerment, teaching expertise, and family and community involvement.

The Carnegie Council's initial recommendations, provided decades ago, spurred the development of middle level schools across the United States. Since these recommendations, many other research-based organizations have provided additional support for the value of these suggestions. As middle level educators, we need to support and advocate for these continued recommendations.

◆❙❙ Teaming: The Heart and Soul of the Middle School Concept

Teaming is the most vital aspect of the middle school structural design and an identifying feature of true middle level schools. From the Carnegie Council's (1989) original *Turning Points* first recommendation—"School should be a place where close,

Teaming is the most vital aspect of the middle school structural design and an identifying feature of true middle level schools.

trusting relationships with adults and peers create a climate for personal growth and intellectual development" (37)—came two specific suggestions that advocate the use of teams to transform middle level education.

First, the enormous middle grade school must be restructured in a more human scale. The student should, upon entering middle grade school, join a small community in which people—students and adults—get to know each other well to create a climate for intellectual development. Students should feel that they are part of a community of shared educational purpose.

Second, the discontinuity in expectations and practices among teachers, the lack of integration of subject matter, and the instability of peer groups must be reduced. Every student must be able to rely on a small, caring group of adults who work closely with each other to provide coordinated, meaningful, and challenging educational experiences. In turn, teachers must have the opportunity to get to know every one of their students well enough to understand and teach them as individuals. Every student must have the opportunity to know a variety of peers, some of them well. (37)

AMLE (2010) reinforces the use of teaming as a way to support young adolescents: "Effective middle grades schools develop structures that ensure students will be known as individuals and feel cared for and valued. Instructional teams are essential to the process of creating learning communities. The team is a home away from home—the place where students work and learn together with teachers and classmates with whom they identify" (34).

The rationale for the development of teams focused on the problems inherent in the traditional structure of middle level schools—a departmentalized system based on the factory model (see Chapter 6). When students change classes every forty-two minutes for six to eight periods a day and are continually confronted with a new teacher and a new group of students, the close relationships that are so important for the young adolescent are more difficult to develop. The departmentalized, separate-subject model also provides little opportunity for students to make sense of the curricular material or to integrate knowledge across subject boundaries.

The most predominant team structure consists of four teachers from the four major content areas (math, science, language arts, and social studies) who have shared responsibility for 100 to 125 students and are empowered to make decisions about what is best for these students. The students move from teacher to teacher with the same group of peers throughout the school day.

Some middle schools use teams comprising two teachers and a smaller number of students. Others add a fifth member to the four-person teams, such as a reading teacher or special-subject instructor (for example, music, art, physical education). In some schools, multi-grade teams are developed, with seventh and eighth graders on the same team and often in the same classes. Team structures can be as varied as the students they serve. Decisions about teaming should be made after considering space, time, staffing, and student demographic issues.

Despite numerous research reports validating the advantages of students that are a part of teams, the level of support among middle level schools is waning (Mertens et al. 2013). A surge in the implementation of teaming occurred during the 1980s, 1990s, and into the 2000s. In a 2009 survey, though, of more than 800 middle level schools, the percentage of schools using teaming dropped to 72 percent from a reported percentage of 79 percent a little less than a decade earlier (McEwin and Greene 2011). It's unfortunate to see this drop when the advantages for students are clearly delineated.

BENEFITS OF TEAMING

A genuine *team* includes characteristics such as support for one another, camaraderie, working toward similar goals, and healthy friendships. In athletics, we all expect these components in a team—shouldn't schools promote similar ideals and the healthy outcomes that students can gain from being members of a team? When students are placed on teams, there is a likelihood of greater student satisfaction and, ultimately, more academic success.

Benefits to Students

The National Forum to Accelerate Middle-Grades Reform (2004), in their policy statement, describes the benefits to students when their classes are arranged into teams:

An extensive body of research suggests that small schools and small learning communities have the following significant advantages: increased student performance, along with a reduction in the achievement gap and dropout rate; a more positive school climate, including safer schools, more active student engagement, fewer disciplinary infractions, and less truancy; a more personalized learning environment in which students have the opportunity to form meaningful relationships with both adults and peers. (1) (cited in Arhar 2013, 617)

Curriculum and instruction are enhanced by the effective use of interdisciplinary teams. Thematic teaching helps students make connections across subject areas, thus avoiding the fragmentation that is often experienced in a departmentalized structure. Learning can be integrated throughout the school day, with each teacher providing specific content and skills to help students explore significant themes. In addition, collaboration with students increases motivation and enthusiasm for learning.

When teams have some control over the class schedule, students have the opportunity to explore ideas for longer periods of time. Flexibility in teaming allows time for

> The best thing about school is that in some ways I like the teams. I know my teachers and like being with other grades. The teachers get close to you.
>
> —**MEG**,
> EIGHTH GRADER

the in-depth research, analysis, and project development that is difficult to engage in when using a traditional approach.

Teachers also develop a better understanding of student needs. They are able to discuss individual student concerns at team meetings, analyze problems, and develop solutions to better meet the needs of each child. In departmentalized middle level schools, collaborating with colleagues about student needs is difficult because of time restrictions and isolation of both teachers and students.

Benefits to Teachers

While the benefits of teaming are clear for students in terms of both cognitive growth and school climate, teachers also reap rewards from this structure. For many teachers, teaming improves the work climate and lessens the isolation that often exists in self-contained classrooms. Teaming reduces the fragmentation of learning from one discipline to another and allows teachers to coordinate assignments, testing schedules, classroom expectations, and classroom procedures. Through common planning time and team meetings, teachers can better serve the needs of students and deal proactively with problems (Mertens et al. 2013; Kasak and Uskali 2012; Schurr and Forte 2009).

Research indicates that teachers involved in teaming perceive that they participate more, have more opportunities for decision making, experience more cooperation than teachers in traditional departmentalized settings, have better time management, more consistent discipline strategies, and "improved coordination of curriculum" (Schurr and Forte 2009, 51). Teachers also believe that they are more supportive of students and more receptive to their needs and ideas. In contrast to teachers in traditional settings, teachers involved in teaming see their students as more motivated and involved. Arhar (2013) summarized, "Interdisciplinary teaming provides schools, teachers, and students with the ongoing and responsive relationships they need to meet the three-part goal of middle grades education: developmental responsiveness, academic excellence, and social equity" (629).

Kasak and Uskali (2012) offer the following characteristics of effective teams:
- They have a culture of discourse at their center.
- They have a clearly defined purpose that guides their work and specific measurable goals that they achieve.
- They are able to define and commit to norms that guide how the team operates.
- They are disciplined in maintaining their focus.

> In contrast to teachers in traditional settings, teachers involved in teaming see their students as more motivated and involved.

- They communicate effectively within the team and with those outside the team. (121)

Successful teams are generally made up of a heterogeneous group of students with a strong team identity. In addition, the most successful teams have a balance in terms of teachers' expertise, age, gender, and race (K. Brown 2001). K. Brown noted that the best chance for successful teaming lies in the leadership of the team, with a formal team leader having specific responsibilities. Effective leadership involves being a liaison between administration and the team, communicating effectively with team members and administration, and keeping team goals in mind by being "task-oriented" (George and Alexander 1993, 293).

Another essential aspect of teaming is common planning time (CPT), defined by Kellough and Kellough (2008) as: "A regularly scheduled time during the school day when teachers who teach the same students meet for joint planning, parent conferences, materials preparation, and student evaluation" (394). Duffield (2013) noticed that AMLE's previous version of *This We Believe* (2003) identified curriculum integration to be a higher priority as a purpose of CPT than the latest version of 2010, suggesting that perhaps a shift in priorities has occurred due to testing mandates and teacher accountability. In this era of high-stakes testing, much of the common planning time (if there is any), unfortunately, is spent analyzing data rather than making curricular and instructional decisions to benefit the students. Teachers in Duffield's study did state, however, that their greatest wish for altering CPT was to have more time to work on interdisciplinary curriculum.

Researchers found that teachers who were fortunate enough to have CPT were more satisfied with their jobs than those without it (Anfara, Jr. et al. 2013). Mertens and Flowers (2003) discovered that schools with CPT "had higher levels of student achievement" (19 cited in Anfara, Jr. et al.). Although administrators may discourage CPT on the basis of saving money, the positive effects far outweigh the costs or change in the schedule to create. For several years, researchers with the American Educational Research Association in the Middle Level Education Research Special Interest Group studied common planning time across the United States. Caskey et al. (2013) released a summary of these studies, revealing that:

- Teachers report very little training about CPT, with very low amounts of pre-service preparation for and little to no professional development about it.
- Perceived benefits of CPT include working individually with students and high expectations for student achievement.

"

The quality of the relationship between teachers and students is the single most important aspect of middle level education.
—**VAN HOOSE**
(1991, 7)

In our advisory, the topics we discussed were peer pressure, safety, how to stay away from drugs, and how to bring our careers together.
—**MICHAEL**,
EIGHTH GRADER

Only 39 percent (of middle school parents surveyed) felt that "There is an adult in this school who knows my child well and can offer advice and assistance."
—**JOHNSTON AND WILLIAMSON**
(1998, 47; cited in Anfara, Jr. 2001, xvi)

- Schools recognized as Schools to Watch (STW) schools had higher implementation of CPT than non-STW schools.
- The least frequently reported team practices are coordinating and integrating curricula across subject areas, teaching interdisciplinary units, and integrating student assignments and assessments across subjects. (334–335)

These results indicate that understanding and implementing common planning time are necessary for both preservice and inservice middle level educators. Incorporating the contribution of teachers of special subjects such as music, art, physical education, computer technology, and foreign languages presents another challenge to teaming. Teams do not usually include teachers of these subjects, because grade-level teachers are best able to meet together when all of their students are attending classes with the music, art, or physical education teachers. Not including special-area teachers on the teams fragments student learning and may give the message to students that those classes are less important. Administrators must work to ensure that special-area teachers are a vital part of the overall planning process for students.

Frequently teams exist in name only. Although teachers may share students and at times are able to meet to discuss their concerns about them, middle level educators often remain subject bound, engrossed in their own area of expertise without regard to what the rest of the team is doing. If teaming is simply an organizational structure, the full benefits of this construct will not be obtained. If students are still sent through the day factory style, traveling from class to class on a rigid forty-two-minute schedule, with no integration throughout the school day, faculty may as well revert to the departmentalized model.

◆❙❙ Advisory Programs

Young adolescents are changing in many ways and need the support of adults in their lives to successfully navigate through these changes. The Association for Middle Level Education (AMLE) emphasizes that it is important that "each student must have one adult in the school who assumes special responsibility for supporting that student's academic and personal development" (2010, 23). AMLE identified advisor/advisee programs as an essential element of effective middle school design. In an advisory program, an advisor (usually a teacher) meets with a small group of students on a regular basis for the primary purpose of helping students develop trusting relation-ships with an adult and close social bonds with a small group of classmates. Advisory sessions may be designed for student-to-student and student-to-teacher discussions about personal topics related to young adolescence. These sessions are essentially nonacademic, ungraded, and planned with young adolescents' social and emotional interests and needs in mind. AMLE (2010) authors suggest, "When students and their advisors meet regularly during the school day, an advisory program helps students develop respect for self and others; compassion; a workable set of values; and the skills of cooperation, decision making, and goal setting" (23).

The National Association of Secondary School Principals issued *Breaking Ranks in the Middle: Strategies for Leading Middle Level Reform* in 2006 with the advice for middle level schools to "Implement a comprehensive advisory or other program that ensures that each student has frequent and meaningful opportunities to meet with an adult to plan and assess the student's academic, personal, and social development" (9, cited in Burns, Behre Jenkins, and Kane 2012, 3). Junior high and high schools initi-ated the homeroom period during the early twentieth century as a way of encourag-ing positive student-teacher relationships, yet the homeroom period is ineffective in establishing relationships between teachers and students.

It is primarily teachers who serve as advisors, but to reduce the ratio of advisees to advisors, other professionals in the building—including counselors, administra-tors, librarians, and district specialists—are often assigned a group of advisees as well. Becoming a proficient advisor requires initial training and regular attention to the specifics of how to organize and deliver an effective program to students. Advi-sors must be willing to develop a relationship with students that is different from the relationship they experience as a regular classroom teacher—one characterized by caring, not authoritarianism (Cole 1992). James (1986) suggested that many students view their "advisor as more of a friend or advocate than a teacher" (53). The primary responsibility of the advisor is to provide a caring and nurturing relationship with students. The advisor becomes the advocate for the student's academic, personal, and social development (P. Brown 2013). MacLaury points out to teachers (2002) some advantages of their participation in an advisory program:

Teacher-advisors often develop closer relations with students, which in turn may increase their motivation to guide and listen to their students. The classroom environment may improve measurably as students also develop closer relationships with others they may not typically socialize with and learn from one another, making the teacher's job easier and ultimately more enjoyable. (249)

Despite endorsements from AMLE, the National Forum, and the National Association of Secondary School Principals, middle level teachers are often reluctant to adopt advisory programs because of the concerns that they have for attempting to meet students' social and emotional needs or add another preparation for an additional class (P. Brown 2013; Burns, Behre Jenkins, and Kane 2012). McEwin and Greene (2013) found that the percentage of schools utilizing advisories in national surveys dropped slightly over the past fifteen years. Often when a predetermined curriculum for advisory doesn't work well, teachers revert to providing a mere study hall. Despite teachers' reluctance, Burns, Behre Jenkins, and Kane suggest:

> Engaging young adolescents in conversations about their friendships, their social and emotional changes, and their positive and negative school experiences may seem less important than activities that resemble the more familiar academic curriculum, but this is not so. Advisory lays the groundwork and builds the foundation of relational support and self-understanding needed for students to succeed academically. Using an academic-type curriculum in advisory diverts time from the important directly relational activities. (23)

The time of the day that advisory sessions are offered and the length of the sessions impact their effectiveness; for example, sessions scheduled at the end of the day are not effective. Schools demonstrate a commitment to advisory when it occurs on a regular basis, meaning more than twice a week, and some researchers suggest it should be offered every day and last for at least 30 minutes to provide time for students to engage in meaningful conversations (Burns, Behre Jenkins, and Kane 2012). Felner et al. (1997) revealed that middle schools offering advisories four or five times a week for 30 to 45 minutes each reported better student achievement and less student stress than schools with fewer and shorter advisories.

Students can be grouped with grade-level peers during advisory sessions. Some schools have multi-age advisory sessions in which sixth, seventh, and eighth graders are grouped heterogeneously. The developmental differences among young adolescents at each grade level may lead to the belief that separating students by grade level would best meet the needs of the students. Data collected from middle level students in one study, however, indicated that the majority of students surveyed preferred cross-grade advisory groups (Ziegler and Mulhall 1994). Teachers reported a great deal of comfort when working with students for extended years, citing the advantages of knowing them well and developing strong bonds with each student (P. Brown 2013; Burns, Behre Jenkins, and Kane 2012).

Although some educators believe that improved student test scores are necessary to justify offering advisory, students may never improve academic performance unless

Middle level education is about helping young adolescents balance their social, emotional, and identity-development lives—on a daily basis.

they experience advisories. The reasons, however, for implementing advisory far out-weigh the intentions of raising students' test scores: Middle level education is about helping young adolescents balance their social, emotional, and identity-development lives—on a daily basis.

Jensen (2009) noted what we believe many teachers recognize about some of their students—that they need explicit direction and instruction in understanding and responding to the emotions of "sympathy, patience, shame, cooperation, grati-tude, humility, forgiveness, empathy, optimism, and compassion" (18). The philosophy behind the need for a program, the roles and responsibilities of teachers, the appropri-ate focus of advisory sessions, and the possibilities for a structured curriculum must be discussed in detail among all stakeholders—students, teachers, parents, and adminis-trators—to ensure the successful launch of an advisory program.

Noddings' (2005) comments about educating the whole child reveal a critical phi-losophy of effective schools at all levels and one that can be advanced through advi-sory programs:

We will not find the solution to problems of violence, alienation, ignorance, and unhappiness in increasing our security apparatus, imposing more tests, punishing schools for their failure to produce 100 percent proficiency, or demanding that teachers be knowledgeable in "the subjects they teach." Instead, we must allow teachers and students to interact as whole persons, and we must develop policies that treat the school as a whole community. (13)

There is no doubt that developing a strong advisory program will help young adoles-cents. Many middle schools have, unfortunately, turned their advisory into a time for test prep or have eliminated advisory altogether in order to work on those skills stu-dents need to pass their high stakes test.

One seventh/eighth grade teacher had this to say about advisory in her school:

In my school we have a period called advisory once a week for fifty minutes. I have the same kids in my homeroom before school for fifteen minutes and for dismissal for six minutes at the end of the day. I meet with these students also three times a week for something called "study block." I have found that my students don't really care about anything we do in that block. Because of the emphasis on grading and testing, my students are trained not to care about anything else. They ask me if some activity will count as a grade. If I say "No," they don't want to do it. I think the advisory concept is important but when we make students think that the only important thing for them to do is pass a test, the advisory is not taken seriously. And that's a shame.

◆▮ **Flexible Scheduling**

Time is the key to working effectively with young adolescents. Schedules can open up and provide that time or constrict and limit it. Days filled with numerous 45-minute periods make it almost impossible to build relationships and learning. (Nesin and Brazee 2005, 43)

Perhaps the greatest barrier to any substantial change in middle schools is the common complaint, and ever-present 800-pound gorilla in the room, depicted in the phrase, "We don't have *time* to do that, because our schedule won't permit it."Teachers clearly recognize the types of activities students need to engage in to ensure genuine learning, but they know that a lack of time influenced by traditional school structures such as forty-five minute class periods will always prevent them from implementing middle level reforms that genuinely affect student learning.

Students require time to learn—especially young adolescents who are moving from the concrete to the formal operational stage of cognitive development. The traditional factory schedule of most middle level schools continues to provide students with the mile-wide, inch-deep surface knowledge that rarely represents genuine understanding of the concepts and principles that are taught. Many teachers have noted positive results of alternative scheduling formats, especially in improved student behaviors and attitudes (D. Brown 2001a; Hannaford, Fouraker, and Dickerson 2000; Queen 2000). Other studies noted that teachers implemented more active instructional processes as a result of longer class sessions, such as lessons involving more creative and critical thinking, more time for student reflection, and greater opportunities for student-to-student collaboration (D. Brown 2001b; Reither 1999).

Over eight thousand sixth graders who were tested from five middle schools in a North Carolina school district showed considerable gains as a group in their mathematics test scores after the schools switched from a traditional schedule to extended periods (Mattox, Hancock, and Queen 2005). Middle level educators must begin to focus on maximizing learning opportunities for students. That may mean replacing traditional views of how the school day is structured and making a commitment to designing the school day so that students are engaged in active learning processes (Merenbloom and Kalina 2007).

◆❙❙ Exploratory Curriculum

AMLE (2010) provided the following recommendation:

The middle school is the finding place; for young adolescents, by nature, are adventuresome, curious explorers. Therefore, the general approach for the entire curriculum at this level should be exploratory. Exploration, in fact, is the aspect of a successful middle school curriculum that most directly and fully reflects the nature and needs of the majority of young adolescents, most of whom are ready for an exploratory process. (20)

We believe that young adolescents should explore—in the school setting and in the natural context of learning each day within their classes. This type of exploration requires that teachers listen to young adolescents to discover their interests within the context of integrated curriculum or any traditional curricular delivery system. This emphasis requires that teachers encourage students' questions, seek their interests through lesson planning, alter curricula to match students' questions and concerns, and pursue lessons that improve students' thinking processes as they relate to their futures.

We want students to explore band, choir, art, physical education, photography, drama, and technology. But we also believe that exploration is a philosophy, an attitude, and an approach, with an accompanying way of teaching that emphasizes personal as well as academic discovery.

As AMLE authors suggest:

If youth pass through early adolescence without broad, exploratory experiences their future lives may be needlessly restricted. They deserve opportunities to ascertain their special interests and aptitudes, to engage in activities that will broaden their views of the world and of themselves. They need, for instance, the chance to conduct science experiments, though they may never work in a lab; to be a member of a musical group, though never to become a professional musician; to write in multiple formats, though never to publish professionally; to have a part in a play, though never to become a paid actor; to play on a team, though never to become a career athlete; or to create visual images through drawing and painting, though never to become an artist. (20)

Middle school is not the time to sift and sort, to tell some kids they can have a part in a play but others won't, to tell some kids they can play in the jazz band and others can't, to tell some kids they can explore an international language and others may not. We don't know what the future holds for young adolescents, but middle school is the time for them to begin to experiment with a multitude of options, and providing exploratory opportunities is the avenue they need to examine in-depth their natural curiosities.

◆‖ Looping and Multi-age Teams

Looping is an organizational structure in which teachers move with their students when they pass to the next grade level. In some schools, an entire team of teachers moves with their students from grade to grade. Other schools have multi-aged looping teams. For example, students stay on the curriculum integration Alpha Team in a Vermont middle school for three years. The seventh and eighth graders serve as mentors for the new group of sixth graders who enter each year. Thompson, Gregg, and Caruthers (2005) reported several benefits to looping. Primary is the idea that "since there is no need to start from scratch, learning new names, personalities, and expectations, teachers estimated that a month of learning time was gained at the start of the second year" (140). In addition, because teachers have students for more than one year, stronger relationships are built. Since teachers are already familiar with learning styles, preferences, and interests, time is saved in student assessment, and teachers can more readily meet the needs of their students (Thompson, Gregg, and Caruthers 2005). Lounsbury, Tarbet Carson, and Andrews (2013) described this time saving:

> They [two researchers] found that of the 3200 total minutes spent in the classroom during the first two weeks of school, the teachers reported spending an average of 390 minutes on the development of rules, routines, and relationships. The one exception was teacher A, who needed only 30 minutes to establish rules, routines, and relationships. This was due to the fact that teacher A was beginning her second year with the same students, and they needed only a very limited review of procedures and connections established the previous year.

Daniel (2007) reported in surveys with young adolescents in multi-age classrooms that they felt a close bond with fellow students and believed the experience positively impacted their self-esteem. All students can benefit from the predictable learning environment that transfers from year to year through looping. Multi-age looping teams have as an additional benefit the previous students initiating the incoming class into the structures and routines of the team. Tarbet (2010) discovered when she started a new year with her previous class that her students were much more comfortable and capable of taking more responsibility for the instructional activities and curricular decision making.

Looping or multi-age grouping have the possibility of addressing the social, emotional, and cognitive challenges that young adolescents face each year through the middle grades. The opportunity to know students well for two or three years and to be able to immediately assist them each year without having to take time to build background knowledge about them is an advantage that educators should provide to middle level students.

PARTIALLY IMPLEMENTING THE MIDDLE SCHOOL CONCEPT

Middle level faculty who implement only portions of the Carnegie recommendations are not realizing the full impact that total implementation can have on middle level students. Too often faculty and administrators change the school structure to align with the middle level concept without changing instructional and curricular practices. Many middle level faculty place students on teams; however, the teachers are given little if any common planning time and limited decision-making authority over the schedule or the curriculum. With no opportunities to collaborate on curriculum, no control over instructional issues, and little opportunity to discuss individual learning needs, young adolescents are denied optimal growth opportunities.

A comprehensive look at research on middle level reform (Lipsitz, Jackson, and Austin 1997) includes the report "The Impact of School Reform for the Middle Years" (Felner et al. 1997). The authors presented results from a longitudinal study that analyzed the degree to which each of the Carnegie Council recommendations in *Turning Points* (1989) had been implemented in specific schools and the resultant impact on student achievement and behavior. The authors concluded, "It appears that when schools attempt to implement these practices but do them poorly (e.g., one or two common planning times per week, interdisciplinary instruction without common planning time, large teams), there may be no effect or even negative effects, especially on teacher attitudes and student performance" (548).

Positive results of the Felner et al. study indicated significant academic gains and personal growth when the Carnegie Council recommendations *were* implemented. Students from those schools reflecting high implementation scored consistently higher than state norms in mathematics, language, and reading assessments. Since the

> Too often faculty and administrators change the school structure to align with the middle level concept without changing instructional and curricular practices.

Felner et al. study in 1997, Erb (2005a) has reported that many other studies have been conducted indicating that "implementing more elements [of middle level reforms] for longer periods of time does, with certainty, lead to improved student outcomes in all three major goal areas—academic, behavioral, and attitudinal" (8). Schools are more likely to meet the academic needs of their students when they simultaneously aspire to address the behavioral and attitudinal areas of development.

McEwin and Greene (2013) reported that in comparing two studies: one of 101 highly successful middle level schools—Schools to Watch (STW) schools—and the other of 827 randomly chosen middle schools, the highly successful (STW) schools:

- more frequently used interdisciplinary team organization, 90% vs. 72%
- more frequently provided core teachers with ten common planning periods a week, 40% vs. 28%
- less frequently organized school schedules using uniform daily periods, 45% vs. 72%
- more often utilized flexible block scheduling plan, 30% vs. 14%
- used direct instruction less frequently, 71% vs. 81%
- used cooperative learning more often, 85% vs. 64%
- used inquiry teaching more frequently, 57% vs. 43%
- had a higher percentage of core teachers holding separate middle level teacher certification [no percentages provided], and
- more frequently had advisory programs, 65% vs. 54%. (96)

As McEwin and Greene note, the successful results of these studies bear well for supporting the continuation of designing middle level experiences for students that reflect the true middle level model. They support this by adding, "However the problem does not lie in a lack of knowledge about the appropriate nature of middle level schools. Rather the problem lies in the failure to fully implement these features in ways that benefit young adolescents" (98).

McEwin and Greene (2013) provide more evidence to support the development and design of true middle level schools:

Data from the Highly Successful Middle Schools 2009 survey, along with other research results, confirm that middle grades schools authentically following the middle school concept/philosophy are more likely to be associated with higher scores on achievement tests and other positive student outcomes. There are also research studies that document middle school programs and practices such as teaming and common planning time do improve student achievement in high poverty schools. (79)

◆▐ Concluding Reflections

Use of interdisciplinary teams, common planning time, advisories, exploratory curriculum, flexible scheduling, and looping result in positive changes in school climate. However, changing school structures alone is not enough. Until the integration of curriculum, instruction, and assessment becomes the focus of change and young adolescents' voices are included in these decisions, the development of a true middle level school will remain elusive and educators will not see the maximum benefits for young adolescents.

"Progressive middle level education may be the best chance for an educational worldview that affirms the worth and dignity of every member of a society that operates on trust, dignity, diversity, and democratic principles."

PART 4:

HOW YOUR CLASSROOM CAN BEST MEET THE NEEDS OF STUDENTS

CHAPTER 8

Creating a Safe

Haven for Learning

> *My own middle school years remain vivid in my memory. I was excluded, and manipulated the exclusion of others. I could be mean, yet, in turn, I was deeply hurt by others. If my friends and I did speak to an adult about these problems we heard such clichés as: "There are plenty of other girls who would love to be your friends" or "Can't you just try to be nice to each other" or my all-time favorite, "Sticks and stones may break my bones, but words will never hurt me." Words break your heart and scar you for life.*
>
> —**LANE** (2005, 41)

> "
>
> Teachers wear a lot of different hats: teacher, doctor, social worker. With middle school age [students], you're wearing all of the hats—almost equally. I find myself playing an advising role all day long.
> —**RODNEY**, EIGHTH-GRADE TEACHER
>
> Teachers shouldn't think they are the coolest people on Earth.
> —**SYDNEY**, EIGHTH GRADER

Any student will tell you that teachers cannot feign caring and believing in students. Your students know what you feel about them. Naima, a seventh grader in an urban middle school, reveals this awareness: "Some teachers don't have respect for us. They only come here to get paid. If they don't want to teach they shouldn't be here." Every student you teach will realize your commitment to teaching and be aware of the extent of your interest.

Every professional educator has a philosophy of education that they are able to espouse when queried, but whether their classroom demeanor reflects their philosophical beliefs is what matters to students. Teachers' beliefs about students, learning, and teaching are evident in the way they greet students each day, provide feedback on assignments, communicate with each student, deliver lessons, choose curricula, and develop relationships with students. Some people may wear their hearts on their sleeves, but *every* teacher shows his or her philosophy in every classroom action initiated. Students experience that philosophy every moment of class. Effective teaching requires knowing the answer to the question, "Will my students describe my philosophy the same as I do?"

You may be saying, "I don't need to read this chapter. Of course I care about students, or I wouldn't consider being a professional educator!" You might be surprised by the kind of teacher behaviors and school policies that deflate students' attitudes and confidence. Middle level classrooms aren't always the caring learning havens that you would expect.

◆⏸ Middle Level Schools and Student Stress

Many situations initiated by teachers can cause fear and stress in young adolescents:

1. yelling at one student or an entire class
2. applying punishment inappropriately or inconsistently
3. threatening students
4. setting unrealistic expectations
5. requiring students to open their lockers, get the appropriate books and notebooks, and get to their next class on time—all in less than four minutes
6. pushing students to learn abstract principles that are beyond their cognitive capabilities without appropriate guidance
7. assigning extensive homework that requires at least an hour or more of work each evening for each subject
8. embarrassing or making fun of students in front of their most significant audience—their peers.

We know you're thinking, "I'd never do any of these things," yet through more subtle actions teachers may also unwittingly disrupt the emotional stability students require in order for learning to occur. These include:

> Middle school is a tough time for many, and I feel as if teachers need to recognize that the adolescent stage is rather difficult because we are too old to do some things, while being too young to do others. So please don't lose your temper when we do something wrong. Teachers are our main role models— disregarding our parents/guardians.
> —**KATIE**, EIGHTH GRADER

refusing to lend a pencil, protractor, or paper to students

caring more about completing the textbook than meeting each student's needs

1. treating each student the same regardless of differences in learning abilities or learning styles

4. preventing students from interacting socially during class time

5. assessing student learning in only one way

6. designing lessons that are primarily teacher-directed without hands-on opportunities for student learning

7. refusing to be flexible in curriculum design, instructional processes, or scheduling

8. using quizzes to "catch" students who may not understand material

9. ignoring young adolescents' stages of cognitive, social, and emotional growth.

These negative actions affect more than students' self-esteem.

HOW STRESS AFFECTS STUDENT LEARNING

Young adolescents experience a multitude of new challenges upon entering middle school. Academic expectations are greater, students are called upon to be more independent learners, their organizational strategies must be honed to be prepared for each class, they receive less individualized assistance than they did in elementary school, and middle level teachers provide less feedback on how to improve than elementary educators (D. Brown 2013a). Eccles and Midgley (1989) found that junior high teachers, "Emphasized social comparisons and competition more . . . and were less trusting and more controlling of students compared to the adolescents' elementary teachers" (cited in Roeser and Lau 2002, 110). Additional developmental stressors affect their academic focus as well, as students experience stress associated with new social situations, awkward physical growth, and hyper-emotional reactions, all of which affect their learning. Further, despite their elementary school academic successes, initial middle level grades often manage to drop well below many students' elementary performances.

Anxiety and stress affect the quality of students' cognitive functioning, disrupting their ability to process information efficiently. Caine and Caine (1994) described what many students experience when perceiving a threat as a "narrowing of the perceptual field" (69). When a situation becomes threatening, students are likely to feel a sense of helplessness followed by a loss of effective cognitive processing, described as

> One of the greatest stressors of being in middle school *is* middle school. Each year we progressively have more and more homework, and also want more and more of a social life. Balancing these two can be extremely difficult, especially when someone plays a sport.
> —**SYDNEY**, EIGHTH GRADER

"downshifting" (69). When stress associated with fear creates anxiety, people drift into a downshifted state, have difficulty using higher-order cognitive abilities efficiently, and are unable "to see the interconnectedness . . . among topics" (70). Caine and Caine added that stress-related issues prevent our brains from forming permanent new memories. A number of studies have identified the relationship between socio-emotional states of mind and cognition (Elias et al. 1997; Perry 1996; Brendtro, Brokenleg, and Van Bockern 1990). These studies indicate that "under conditions of real or imagined threat or anxiety, there is a loss of focus on the learning process and a reduction in task focus and flexible problem solving" (Elias et al. 1997, 3).

For many students schools are the central, if not the only, place where a safe and trusting environment exists. Karen, an eighth grader in an urban middle school, commented: "Students in our school have pressure in the homes and stuff. They can't concentrate in school because at home they've got to be the adult. When they come [to school], they've got to be the child." Even in high socioeconomic communities, schools can be a safe haven for students who are not getting sufficient emotional support at home. A sixth-grade teacher, Edith, who teaches in a wealthy neighborhood, spoke of the "emotional needs" of her students despite their high socioeconomic standing: "Because parents are so busy with their jobs, the children are neglected. Someone's not there to listen to them. There's an emotional component within these children that we have to be aware of."

◆❙❙ Establishing a Caring Environment

Young adolescents, in moving away from the need for parental approval, need to know that someone other than their peers will provide a support system. This comment from John, an eighth grader in an urban school, emphasizes the importance of the teacher–student relationship:

It's not supposed to just be, "I'm your teacher; I see you in school and that's all." It should be like a friend bond also; so you can talk to that teacher—be open to her. That way, they get to know more about you.

According to Elias et al. (1997), "Caring happens when children sense that the adults in their lives think they are important and when they understand that they will be accepted and respected, regardless of any particular talents they have" (6).

I look back on my middle school experience and remember crying almost everyday in seventh grade. We, as teachers, have to be students' personal cheerleaders—we have to connect with each and every kid.

—**HEATHER**,
SEVENTH-GRADE
TEACHER

Researchers in one study discovered that showing care and respect for students "promoted learning and overpowered the comparative effects of instructional methodologies" (Goodman, Sutton, and Harkevy 1995, 696). Lipsitz (1995) added: "Caring did not substitute for learning; caring established an effective culture for learning" (666). When teachers demonstrate caring attitudes, "trust is established and caring interpersonal relationships are built in classrooms" (Chaskin and Mendley Rauner 1995, 673). Creating a caring environment should be a primary initiative for all teachers.

In an interview study with young adolescents, Bosworth (1995) asked students to describe caring teachers. Students reported that caring teachers:

- walk[ed] around the room talking to everybody to see how they were doing [and] to answer questions
- help[ed] students with school work
- noticed and inquired about changes in behavior
- recognized different learning styles and speeds
- sought to know students as unique human beings
- showed respect for students through actions such as "talking in a quiet voice or talking to you in private or alone"
- [did] a good job of explaining the content area, making sure that all students understand
- encourage[d] students to improve. (691–92)

When teachers show their acceptance of students, and students begin to see and understand that teachers care, school can be mutually satisfying to both students and teachers. You can show students you care by:

- sharing some personal experiences with students and conveying excitement for learning
- modeling one-on-one active listening
- helping students develop personal academic and social outcomes
- participating in daily activities such as lunch, recess, and after-school intramurals
- taking the time to discover what is important to your students outside school—hobbies, interests, family stories, pets
- attending your students' musical, athletic, and theatrical performances.

Some teachers make it a point to spend the first and last few minutes of each class session just talking to students about their personal lives.

GENUINELY KNOWING STUDENTS

Roland Barth (1991), former director of the Harvard Principals' Center, proclaimed, "What needs to be improved about schools is their culture, the quality of interpersonal relationships, and the nature and quality of learning experiences" (45). Teachers are responsible for creating the kinds of interpersonal relationships with students that can improve the quality of learning. Once a personal link with each student is established, you will notice that students begin to focus more effectively on academic issues and learn in more meaningful ways.

Rachel, a middle level teacher of eight years, describes how she learned to connect with her students in creating a caring and trusting environment.

It feels like I have been teaching forever! So when asked for advice about how to connect with students I drew a blank. I had to really think and try to remember my beginning years teaching. Early on, I struggled with connecting to students. I made conscious efforts to try to connect to one student at a time. For my first go-round of it I picked the wrong student. He was constantly weary of my questions and looked at me with apprehension when I asked him if he played any sports.

Then I had a dream! No, it wasn't about how to connect with my students; it was about *Twilight*! The *Twilight* book was all the rage one year, so I decided to finally read it. This was the catalyst into connecting with my students. They saw me reading the book and knew we had something in common to talk about. I now was "hip" to the "Team Edward" perspective and could argue for him! The fact that I had a media connection with my students opened the doors to connecting with them in other ways as well. I now try to read books from the school's summer reading list, just to have that connection starter at the beginning of the year even though I don't teach language arts.

I try to stay hip with all the new media around. I have ears like a bat, so I hear conversations about the new "YouTuber" and check him out. I am also always curious about the books my students are reading. It is a glimpse into their lives and an easy conversation starter.

I try to stay genuine to who I am. Middle school students can pick a phony, and they can also pick people who are trying too hard—they don't like it or respect it. I genuinely enjoy the time I get to spend with my students each day.

I also give students "voice" in my classroom. When I hear them complaining about the assignments all due on one day I listen, then change the due date. When I give out assignments I listen to what the students have to say about it. Some of my best ideas have come from students saying, "You know what would work?" This shows the students that I respect them as human beings, and, in return, they respect me as well.

So my advice to new middle level teachers in order to connect with their students is . . . relax, stay true to yourself, and genuinely like and respect young adolescents.

Remember that a caring relationship begins with the development of trust and mutual respect between students and teachers, as Rachel describes. Your job is to create that trust and to maintain a level of respect for each student throughout the year. Respect for students is demonstrated through your modeling of politeness, courtesy, and honesty. Respect is shared between students and teachers when teachers make it a point to recognize students for their efforts and talents—and not merely their academic abilities.

Dave describes mutual respect in a chapter in *Middle Grades Curriculum: Voices and Visions of the Self-Enhancing School* (D. Brown 2013a):

> When teachers' attitudes toward their students are based on mutual respect, students are treated more like guests rather than as malleable objects to be manipulated. Students know the difference between teachers who respect them and those who merely tolerate them. It's teachers' actions that students notice, as they are always louder than their words. Mutual respect among students and teachers creates a learning community in which every student believes he/she belongs in the class and thus becomes an active member of the learning process. (23)

Trust, an essential component of mutual respect, develops between students and teachers when middle level teachers share some of their personal interests with students. Sharing favorite sports teams, family events, vacations, or pets are some of the conversations that incite student interest in you as a person. Your personal stories bridge the gap between their daily struggles as adolescents and your need to help them succeed. These personal stories also help quench adolescents' thirst for what the adult world is like outside of their own families, and their curiosity about you. Maia, an eighth grader, describes teachers' responsibilities in knowing students:

> If I were to advise a middle school teacher, I would start with a single statement: Know your students. You must be able to feel comfortable around your students, and they should feel comfortable with you as well. You cannot teach a bratty thirteen-year-old the same way that you would teach a five-year-old. If you do not care about your students as individuals, you will never truly meet their needs. In addition to this, you must be courteous and respectful.

In developing a collaborative environment, teachers must invite student cooperation. A traditional view of a teacher's role is as someone who controls students' behaviors. Teachers do not control students! Students merely choose to cooperate with us. We suggest that you develop the kind of meaningful connection with each student that encourages students to want to cooperate with you and others. The beauty of establishing a mutually respectful classroom is that it enables students and teachers to reach a common outcome—a comfortable and meaningful learning community.

Sue Luppino, a middle level language arts teacher, describes her strategies for creating a community with her students:

As an ELA teacher, building community is one of the *most* essential foundations of my class. Given that writing (and the interpretation of readings) is an extension of one's heart and soul, I don't think anyone should be expected to share without first working from a foundation of trust and a sense of belonging. Consequently, we engage in a number of "getting to know you" activities and assignments throughout the entire first semester.

One of the biggest components is that any writing my students are asked to create is also an assignment I do. For example, if my students write a "getting to know me" letter, I write one for them as well. We always make something with text and visuals that can be posted on the walls. These include trading cards, magazine covers featuring ourselves, or some other creation. The walls themselves generally are designed by and have an artifact left by last year's seventh graders—often a source of early discussions, a way to connect with their eighth-grade peers, and a means of tangibly demonstrating that student work is valued.

In addition we all complete learning style profiles. These profiles include information we glean from completing multiple intelligence surveys, "What are we good at?" surveys. (Cottonwood Press has a wonderful one: Three hundred items ranging from #29–"I'm good at chilling out" to #246—"Seeing the good in a bad situation.") These are also shared, discussed, and published in some way.

We also play improvisational theater games, decorate journal covers, and, in general, work very hard at acknowledging both what we share in common and what makes each of us unique. We work to build trust so that all of that juicy risk taking can actually happen. Needless to say, I keep a close eye on groupings, partnerships, etc. As the need arises, we build in other opportunities to keep our community strong and supportive. This foundation then becomes the jumping-off point for tackling issues from multiple perspectives. Without a community wherein all voices are heard and valued . . . we'd be sunk!

Developing a respectful community in a school and classroom also includes establishing ground rules for how students treat each other. Middle school teachers realize that students can be unkind to one another. Teachers have a responsibility to assist students in the challenges they face in responding to daily social pressures. Teachers who fail to appropriately address bullying, rude comments, or other insensitive behaviors cause even greater distress for students. Respect for students includes protecting every student and maintaining an environment of psychological safety. Adolescents want their classrooms to be orderly and respectful; it is unsettling for them to have students belittle or disturb classmates while teachers ignore or pretend they don't notice inappropriate behavior.

COMMUNICATING EFFECTIVELY WITH STUDENTS

By the time students arrive in middle school, they have been listening to teachers in formal learning environments all day long for at least six years. As McCarthy (1999) pointed out, "During adolescence they want and need the chance to share their feelings and ideas . . ." (4–5). Developmentally, young adolescents experience a social awakening. They are certainly concerned with interacting with peers, but they also enjoy conversations with adults.

Teachers must provide opportunities for students to be heard, both formally through collaborative lesson design and informally through private conversations. Students notice teachers who genuinely listen to them in conversations about something other than school. When Ladson-Billings (1994) asked a group of eighth graders what they liked about their teacher, this is how they responded:

> She listens to us!
>
> She respects us!
>
> She lets us express our opinions!
>
> She looks us in the eye when she talks to us!
>
> She smiles at us!
>
> She speaks to us when she sees us in the hall or in the cafeteria! (68)

You may not realize that students notice these behaviors in teachers, but obviously they do—and it matters to them.

Teachers' nonverbal actions are even more noticeable to students than what teachers say. Responding verbally to students without a corresponding and congruent nonverbal action sends a message—but perhaps not the one intended. We explained in Chapter 3 how young adolescents' brain development affects their ability to adequately process verbal and nonverbal messages sent by others. Teachers can send a message of listening through the following actions (as suggested by D. Brown 2005):

- make frequent eye contact
- face the student
- listen actively
- rephrase a student's comments when he or she is finished speaking
- listen completely until the student is finished speaking. (13)

Active listening is a critical component of mutual respect between teachers and students. Effective educators find and make time for listening every day and all day.

Roadblocks to Effective Communication

When our students say something to us, we often lapse into familiar patterns of communicating through the voices of our parents. These traditional responses to student behaviors and concerns are often roadblocks to listening and communicating effectively with students.

> Effective educators find and make time for listening every day and all day.

Englander (1986) described some of these roadblocks:

- Ordering: "Go over and apologize to her for what you said."

- Moralizing: "Life isn't supposed to be fair."

- Interpreting: "It's not that big of a deal."

- Reassuring: "You shouldn't be nervous about that; you always get good grades."

- Questioning: "Why did you act that way?" (64)

These sound like innocent and supportive comments; we've heard them for years from the adults in our lives. The difficulty is, when adolescents hear these comments, the problem is not solved and their feelings and frustrations may linger for hours. As Dave (D. Brown 2005) noted: "These roadblocks, unfortunately, send a clear message to young adolescents: 'This person isn't interested in hearing what I think, believe, or feel'" (14). These traditional responses usually indicate that the adults using them are dominating the conversation and imposing their own values and solutions to others' problems (Englander 1986).

The alternative to using roadblocks is "empathetic listening," or "getting inside students' heads":

You make yourself aware not just of their words, but of their deeper hopes, fears, realities, and difficulties. The way to do this is to listen within the student's frame of reference as child or adolescent rather than from your frame of reference as adult teacher. This is the student's perception of reality. (Charles 2000, 52)

Empathetic listening requires listening without judging or moralizing, and encouraging students to be responsible for their own behavior by having them reflect on and begin to resolve their own problems. Young adolescents are more likely to develop an internal locus of control of their behavior, taking more responsibility for their actions and words, when teachers use empathetic listening.

Young adolescents' verbal outbursts that follow emotional situations can be inappropriate. It is easy to feel hurt and angry when a fourteen-year-old swears at you, but a teacher's reaction in that situation can cause even more problems if not designed to defuse emotions and demonstrate mutual respect. A teacher's response to an emotional outburst is also observed by the entire class as evidence of a teacher's professionalism and care for students. Teachers who react calmly despite their own frustration model ways of responding to aggression and can also defuse a problem more quickly. D. Brown (2005) provided a few defusing responses:

- "Swearing is a common response to being embarrassed; however, it offends me and possibly others as well. Plus, it's not acceptable behavior in a public forum such as school. Can you think of something else to say when you're angry that's not so disrespectful?"
- "I noticed you're late again. Is there anything I can do to help you get here on time? It means a lot to me to have you here when class begins."
- "I see you don't have a pencil again. What can *you* do to resolve this problem? Do you need my help in getting supplies?"
- "How do you think your behavior might affect others?"
- "I see you're quite upset. Do you want to talk about it?" (14)

Each response encourages student self-reflection and ultimately also notifies students of teachers' feelings and intent to help. The most inappropriate response is to use sarcasm or to belittle students in any way when they act emotionally.

Teachers cannot afford to take young adolescents' unpredictable behavior personally. Effective teacher responses would include: Calmly and quietly, yet assertively, ask the student to meet privately, and then inform him or her that the behavior was inappropriate. Or, ask the student to describe why you feel the way you do. Or, perhaps have the student describe other behaviors that would have been more appropriate in that situation. If a teacher can't respond calmly at that point, it's advisable to let the student know that you are upset and then arrange a meeting later when you're calm, and the student may be also, to discuss the incident.

ENCOURAGING POSITIVE STUDENT RELATIONSHIPS

Young adolescents must don a strong suit of armor when they interact with peers. Middle school's social battlefields may best be described as places of survival of the fittest, and many students don't have the social strategies they need to defend themselves. Every middle level teacher has seen the havoc that young adolescents can create socially and emotionally for other students. Although many teachers may believe that it is not their place to settle student-to-student conflicts, wise educators take a more proactive role in ensuring that middle level students are polite to one another.

For most students, middle school presents an entirely new social setting. Young adolescents who enter middle level schools as fifth or sixth graders usually begin to establish relationships with many new students from varying demographic backgrounds. Creating safe havens for learning begins with designing classroom activities at the beginning of the year that allow students to interact with one another for the purpose of feeling comfortable together. Until students begin to share aspects of their lives with others, they will not experience the sense of trust needed to cooperate with one another or with the teacher.

Teachers should begin the school year with activities that encourage student-to-student interaction, such as:

- inviting students to share their life histories
- having students meet in pairs to write newspaper reports describing their partner to the rest of the class
- creating cooperative base groups in each class, in which four students work together and accept responsibility for one another's understanding of material and completion of assignments
- pairing students for safe travel between classes
- helping students learn and practice conflict resolution strategies.

Another primary responsibility for teachers is establishing and enforcing appropriate behavioral expectations. Middle level teachers should prevent students from embarrassing each other or inflicting emotional pain. Teachers and students together can develop a set of appropriate social expectations in each classroom and enforce those expectations when violations occur. Charney (1991) values the actions of teachers in creating a community classroom environment because of her belief that "part of our mission is to create communities with fewer nightmares, where self-control and care for others minimizes the possibilities of violence" (17).

◆▌ **The Dangers of Bullying**

Bullying is characterized as an imbalance of power and control in relationships among students. In normal conflicts, each person usually shares equal power. Bullies change that balance and create fear or distress in their victims, who are generally younger, or physically and/or socially weaker (Rigby 2001). Bullying occurs most often during late childhood and young adolescence, thereby making middle level educators responsible for preventing, monitoring, and providing interventions for both bullies and victims (Milsom and Gallo 2006).

> Social media has a big impact on our lives. Kids can get bullied on social media over every little thing, like hair or clothes. They can get depressed as a result.
>
> —**SARAH**,
> EIGHTH GRADER

> Social media really influences our lives. It's the center of bullying, drama, and attention, but it's how you handle it and carry yourself that matters.
>
> —**GRACIE**,
> EIGHTH GRADER

Pardini (1999) defined bullying as "ongoing, relentless infliction of physical, verbal, or emotional abuse by one or more students. It can take many forms, including teasing, threats, extortion, assault, theft, sexual harassment, and social isolation" (26). *Direct* bullying involves face-to-face confrontation and may include verbal as well as physical acts of aggression. With *indirect* bullying, there is no direct contact. It usually involves verbal or written comments about others, often circulated via the Internet or smartphones. Adolescents' prolific use of electronic devices for socializing increases the likelihood that a majority of future bullying will be cyber/electronic—via emails and texting.

In a survey conducted with more than 12,000 fifth through twelfth graders, about half reported "being exposed to relational aggression and verbal abuse regularly" (A. Beane 2011, 5). The high percentage of bullying among young adolescents is confirmed by middle level principals, of which, in one study, 75 percent reported bullying or harassment as a problem in their schools (A. Beane). Olweus and Limber (2007) found that bullying is two to three times more likely to occur at school as opposed to traveling back and forth to school.

A. Beane (2011) recognizes four types of bullying:

1. Physical: Hitting, slapping, elbowing, shoving, kicking, punching, or restraining. It can also involve taking, stealing, or defacing a person's belongings or property.

2. Verbal: Name-calling, making insulting racist, or rude remarks; repeated teasing, harassment, threats, and intimidation, and whispering behind someone's back.

3. Relational: Subtler than other types of bullying, it involves destroying or manipulating relationships, destroying a person's status within a peer group, hurting others' reputations, humiliating and embarrassing someone, gossiping or spreading malicious rumors or lies, hurtful graffiti, and excluding someone.

4. Cyberbullying: Spreading gossip, rumors, and lies electronically; sending or posting defamatory or embarrassing photos and video recordings; sending insulting or threatening email; sending pornography; impersonating someone online; creating a website to humiliate or embarrass someone. (4)

Males and females can and often do engage in all four types, although males are more likely to use physical, direct bullying and females, verbal and relational. Girls are more likely than boys to bully in groups, and females usually cause psychological distress for their victims (A. Beane 2011).

Relational bullying is used to destroy relationships or prevent others from becoming members of cliques. It can lead to serious disagreements or fights. Lane (2005) noted, "Because girls crave close relationships and inclusion, relational aggression causes great emotional suffering for many girls" (43). Relational bullying may begin at school but can erupt into intense viciousness against another student through cyberbullying—via texting and other social media conversations and accusations sometimes posted anonymously (Chu 2005). Researchers from the Pew Internet and American Life Project noted that from 10 to 33 percent of teens report being bullied online (Lenhart 2010). Among teens surveyed for the study, 26 percent reported being harassed via their cell phones.

Females report cyberbullying almost three times as much as males (Chu). The rumors and innuendo that result from the comments about others on the Internet can be devastating to many young adolescents and negatively influence behaviors in school. Cyberbullying can be a much easier form of harassing others for many students because of the anonymity of it. Students who lack the confidence to speak to others at school or lack the physical strength and size to physically bully others may choose cyberbullying due to its relative safety (A. Beane 2011).

The negative effects of bullying can and often do cause permanent psychological scars for adolescents and have profound negative impacts on their futures. A. Beane (2011) describes the consequences: "Bullying leads to loneliness, low self-esteem, depression and anxiety disorders, post-traumatic stress, eating disorders, and other long-lasting harmful emotional effects in the adult years" (5). A. Beane added some other significant effects:

- Bullied adolescents have a higher risk of abusing alcohol and other drugs as they age.
- The possibility exists that they will engage in self-harm, such as cutting.
- Students identified as bullies by age eight are six times more likely to be convicted of a crime by age 24.
- Many who bully during childhood become bullies as adults. (adapted from 5)

Because most bullying occurs at school, students' responses to being attacked are to avoid school. Those who are bullied at school often have poor attendance, are more likely to drop out, can become discipline problems, and have poorer academic performance (A. Beane 2011).

TEACHERS' RESPONSIBILITIES WITH BULLYING

In an attempt to keep students safe, many states have created anti-bullying programs and policies in hopes of decreasing bullying. What policy makers fail to see is that we live in a culture of bullying and until that culture is changed, decreasing bullying in schools will remain a challenge. Children and adolescents see bullying all around them in the forms of racism, classism, and sexism: They see road rage, the person who gets angry at the waiter because the coffee is too cold, and ultimately school shootings. They see corporations that bully their employees, and a government that sometimes blackmails and bullies other countries to get what it wants. We ask students to stop bullying, and yet we don't examine or reflect on how bullying permeates our actions as a culture and country.

Nevertheless, teachers are responsible for keeping their students safe at school and preventing bullying behaviors from occurring or continuing. Bullying patterns are normally established within the first six weeks of school, and students usually don't bully someone they know well (Kerr 2006). Teachers thus have a specific responsibility to develop a safe community in the classroom so that students know and care for one another.

Approximately one-third of students of all ages report that teachers aren't very helpful in stopping bullying. Students reveal that adults don't intervene enough, fail to provide relief or solutions, and fear that the bullying will worsen if they do tell an adult about it (A. Beane 2011). When teachers fail to address bullying appropriately, students are forced to find coping mechanisms of their own—which can be disastrous for students who often lack age-appropriate social skills.

Teachers in the past tended to let students handle these problems themselves. Teachers' roles in responding to bullying are much clearer now. The average length of a bullying incident is approximately thirty-seven seconds, and if onlookers step in within the first ten seconds, it is likely that nothing more will happen (Kerr 2006).

Nutter (2013) offers the following advice for adults in helping students who have been bullied or cyberbullied:

- Make sure the student knows that being bullied is not his or her fault.
- Let the student know that he or she does not have to face being bullied alone.
- Discuss ways of responding to bullies.
- Teach the student to be assertive.
- Tell the student not to react, but to walk away and get help if pursued.
- Tell the student to report bullying immediately to a trusted adult. (adapted from slide #32)

> When teachers fail to address bullying appropriately, students are forced to find coping mechanisms of their own.

A key finding among bullies who were interviewed is that they knew they could get away with their bullying. This confession reveals that supervision and surveillance are essential. Teachers need to take notice of school spaces where students are isolated and hidden from others as well as specific times during the day when bullying is likely to occur. Effective programs against bullying may begin with anonymous questionnaires to determine the nature and extent of bullying problems. Bullying can be reported via short written forms placed in a school mailbox or a special telephone number (Kerr 2006). Specific advisory sessions devoted to bullying are also helpful.

Lane (2005) suggested that encouraging girls to describe their feelings in journals (through words or pictures) can help them handle their hurt and anger. Lane also advised that teachers get to know those students who are often alone and provide them with social strategies to become more involved with others.

Preventing bullying is a responsibility of every faculty and staff member in schools. Protection begins with developing a familial culture with each class of students, jointly establishing classroom rules, planning lessons in which all students are paired with a variety of classmates to encourage mutual support among students, and developing and maintaining a mutually respectful culture.

◆❙❙ Encouraging Risk-Taking

As an educator you are responsible for ensuring the success of all your students—for encouraging them to develop higher levels of motivation and commitment to their own growth. A part of this challenge is to invite the types of risk-taking behaviors required for genuine cognitive growth to occur. Without taking cognitive risks, students limit their learning potential.

We teach reading and writing at all grade levels, from kindergarten through high school. We challenge students to use their minds to solve problems, create stories, and respond to issues and ideas that they've never before encountered. We encourage our students to think critically and generate hypotheses. Behind all successful students is a belief that they can and will succeed at the academic challenges that teachers present. But what about those students who don't do particularly well at reading during the first few years of formal schooling? What about the students who are slow to develop effective writing strategies? What about students who have been persuaded by their teachers that mathematics is not their strong suit? Many of these

> Unless the perception of threat is reduced, the brain persists in doing its primary job—protecting the individual from harm. During fear, sadness, or anger, neural activity is evident in the lower brain, and the reflective, cognitive brain (prefrontal cortex) does not receive the sensory input of important items, such as the content of the day's lesson.
> —**WILLIS** (2010, 50)

students never develop or use the necessary risk-taking behaviors required for substantial cognitive growth.

One characteristic of "good" thinkers is risk-taking (Glatthorn and Baron 1991). Risk-taking is also a characteristic of effective readers and writers at the elementary school level (May 1998). Taking risks is a joy to many of us, but for students who are seldom recognized for academic success, taking a risk, such as reading out loud to the other students in class, is viewed as a losing prospect. Students who meet with minimal success in school because of academic difficulty, learning disabilities, or behavioral problems ask the same question daily: "Why play a game that I will never win?" To protect themselves, these students refuse to participate out of fear that they will never receive recognition for their efforts, only for their products. Their schoolwork may never meet the unrealistic standards often developed by state legislators, local school boards, or their own teachers. These frustrations create a constant feeling of inadequacy.

No adult would be foolish enough to participate in a losing effort for 180 days a year for thirteen consecutive years, yet we expect struggling students to return to school year after year despite their inability to succeed. Let's face it, if you don't believe that you can succeed at something, why would you continue to try—only to fail over and over again? For example, perhaps you don't play tennis well. Every time you play, you become frustrated by your inability to hit the ball, place it in the "right" place on the other side of the net, or to win a game. Imagine your horror if every day a yellow bus came into your neighborhood and took you to the tennis courts for another day of failure! Yet every day, thousands of students get on the bus and head for school knowing that they won't succeed at many of the tasks they are asked to undertake.

Without the confidence, encouragement, or support to attempt new reading strategies, writing experiences, or to learn new mathematical principles, many students wander aimlessly through school, afraid of looking like a fool. Many children begin to believe that they will never succeed as students even before they reach young adolescence. These students are quite capable of learning, but their learning doesn't involve academics and seldom occurs at school!

Teachers need to reach out to these students. Supporting the needs of students who have struggled academically requires assessing their skill levels in reading and mathematics, choosing curricular materials that match their ability levels, and ensuring they reach some form of academic success on a daily basis. Professional educators are hired to meet the needs of all students, not merely the gifted and talented ones. Meeting cognitive needs is secondary to meeting students' emotional needs for a safe learning environment that encourages them to take risks. In taking risks as learners, students will falter—a necessity for them to learn and grow from mistakes. For this risk-taking and eventual comfort with failing to occur, Imordino-Yang and Faeth (2010) explain, "Students will allow themselves to experience failure only if they can do so within an atmosphere of trust and respect" (81). Teachers are responsible for building this classroom "atmosphere."

For students, academic safety means that:

- no one laughs at them when they attempt to ask or answer a question
- teachers establish realistic academic expectations and outcomes for each student
- students' efforts are recognized as well as the products of those efforts
- teachers eliminate competitive situations that create inequity among students
- teachers develop cooperative grouping strategies that encourage students to collaborate in their learning and share their knowledge and expertise with one another
- teachers play the role of learning facilitator to encourage student independence
- teachers choose alternative instructional strategies to meet each student's learning style
- teachers recognize and appreciate talents other than academic skills.

We understand that providing this type of attention to each student may seem impossible. If you're not sure you are up to meeting the challenge, ask yourself this: "If schooling were not mandatory, how would my behavior as an educator encourage each student to return to my class every day?" You affect many young lives as a teacher. Interacting positively with your students is imperative.

◆❙ Responding to Crises

Schools are more than mere brick and mortar buildings designed for ensuring that youth enter adulthood with enough content knowledge to maneuver through the rest of their lives. School is the place where children and adolescents spend the better part of their lives when they're not at home. The people in schools know this, and in effective schools those professional educators and staff members take pride in knowing that they offer students much more than a set of academic skills.

> The World Health Organization defines health as "a state of complete physical, mental, and social well-being and not merely the absence of a disease or infirmity." Schools should accept a similar framework for responding to the unthinkable by having a comprehensive and coordinated plan that includes prevention, preparedness, response, and recovery.
> **—COWAN AND ROSSEN** (2014, 12)

On many occasions, in many communities throughout the United States, professional educators are called upon to help students navigate through the emotional pain that accompanies personal, local, national, and international tragedies. Educators need to be aware of the social and emotional lives of the children and adolescents that enter their schools. Students were in school during the Kennedy assassination, many students watched the liftoff and explosion of the Challenger space shuttle, and 9/11 created an especially challenging time for all U.S. adults and students. Local incidents are also emotionally draining to students—from classmates' accidental deaths and suicides, to towns destroyed by weather events, to the unbearable school shootings. In addition, students experience personal family hardships that can be just as emotionally charged—from divorce to untimely deaths.

Being a professional educator can be an emotional roller coaster on any day of the week, but when our students are exposed to the tragedies that adults often can't comprehend, teachers don't have the luxury of ignoring students' emotional feelings, fears, or concerns. Teachers know that school will be in session soon after the tragedy, and that's when they must have the knowledge and strategies to address students' needs at these critical times of their lives. We share Gregory's story as an example of the feelings that perhaps many of you experienced on 9/11. His story demonstrates what students expect and what educators often may not realize they need to address.

My 9/11 Experience

I was thirteen years old when the 9/11 terrorist attacks happened. I was an eighth grader living in Massachusetts. It was mid-morning when the planes hit the twin towers. The administrators advised the teachers and staff to withhold all information about the events that were unfolding. The staff was told that they were to not answer any questions that students asked them about the events. The school's cable TV was disconnected in order to prevent any teachers or students from watching the news. We had no idea of what was happening and the little information that we had was inaccurate.

We thought that a small plane had accidentally crashed into a building and that maybe a couple of people had died. I remember talking with my friend, Ryan, about the situation late that morning. I jokingly asked him, "Someone crashed a plane into a building? They'll give a pilot's license to just about anyone these days!"

Eventually, the true gravity of the situation became apparent. We found out that more planes had crashed, and that we were being attacked. We had no reliable information, and rumors began to fly. My friend overheard two math teachers asking each other if they thought that schools would be a possible target. There was a rumor that a local vocational school had been bombed.

When the truth is withheld, rumors are treated as facts. We wanted more than anything to know what was truly going on. The inaccurate information and the rumors that followed resulted in far worse fear, apprehension, and confusion than would have been if we had just been told what was actually happening from the beginning. We were filled with questions that would remain unanswered until we got home from school.

I hope that another situation like 9/11 will never happen again. In a post-9/11 world, schools need to be ready to deal with these situations in an appropriate manner. I hope they use my situation as a "what not to do" learning experience.

—*Gregory*

It's likely that many students across the United States experienced similar circumstances on 9/11. Educators were faced with balancing their own need to know what was occurring while also protecting their students from emotional distress. Perhaps many teachers prioritized protecting their students; but young adolescents are not children, nor are they adults, and predicting how any student would react is only a guess. Teachers were scared to do the "wrong thing"; however, few educators know how to appropriately respond to a crisis.

Gregory's response is an indication that young adolescents' developmental levels create the need for genuine conversations with adults during crises. So, how could his teachers have handled this situation more effectively? At many schools, teachers informed students that a serious national crisis was occurring, but explained to students that they were safe at school. Students were told that teachers wouldn't elaborate on what was happening out of respect for their families' concerns about how to handle such a serious event and that their parents should address their concerns at home. At other schools, teachers turned on TVs and showed what was happening, with an honest conversation occurring simultaneously, to address fears, questions, and concerns. In many schools, students were provided with an opportunity to call home and/or leave school upon parental pick-up. The underlying message is the same in all of these examples: In a crisis, teachers and schools must put students' social and emotional needs ahead of concern for keeping to a typical day's schedule.

It is important for teachers to respect middle level students' growing cognitive abilities as well as their social and emotional development. Keeping information from them demonstrates a lack of trust in their abilities. Young adolescents are capable of processing and discussing events that are happening, and we owe it to them to provide a safe place for such discussions.

Every school needs specific plans for addressing crises. Cowan and Rossen (2014) provide four processes that schools should adopt to aid students:

1. *Prevention* efforts create an environment in which students feel valued and empowered, and support successful learning.
2. *Preparedness* activities take place before a crisis and include plans to respond to any number of potential crises or traumatic events.

> Young adolescents are capable of processing and discussing events that are happening, and we owe it to them to provide a safe place for such discussions.

3. *Response* includes actions in the immediate and short-term aftermath of a crisis to ensure physical safety, prevent property damage, and identify and respond to negative mental health outcomes.

4. *Recovery* refers to the task of rebuilding and returning to normalcy or previous levels of functioning after a crisis. (11)

Faculty meetings should be planned for conversations among teachers, advice from counselors and psychologists, and development of definitive plans for the school during possible crises.

Demaria and Schonfeld (2014) describe how some students might respond: "Children will react differently to crises and potentially traumatic events depending on numerous factors, including their developmental stage, cognitive capacity, and skills at managing high levels of stress and anxiety" (13). These two medical doctors state that students may react to crises by demonstrating

- separation anxiety or school avoidance
- avoidance of previously enjoyed activities
- difficulties with concentration and academic work and subsequent failures
- developmental or social regression (being more clingy, less cooperative, or less tolerant of others). (13)

Many students and adults won't demonstrate highly emotional responses, but instead internalize their feelings. Students who hold in their feelings have not "recovered" from their own fears or anxieties from a crisis (Demaria and Schonfeld 2014). Demaria and Schonfeld report that most children recover from crises without long-term lasting effects, adding that assistance from the school community can greatly improve the recovery process. For teachers, that support involves

- letting children and adolescents cry and share their concerns during class
- sharing your own feelings as an adult about how you're handling the event
- providing planned time to listen to students' concerns and stories about how they have been affected by the tragedy
- talking openly and honestly about what occurred—within the cognitive understanding levels of your students
- identifying students who may need additional counseling and arranging it
- encouraging students to write or draw pictures about their feelings
- letting students know that you are available just to listen. (Demaria and Schonfeld 2014)

We would add that many students need hugs following a crisis. They may not tell you, but may instead walk up and unexpectedly hug you. Reciprocating is just what you'd do for your own children, so we suggest not hesitating when your "school children" require this kind of reassurance.

Teachers generally understand that they are not counselors, and therefore they aren't educated or prepared to respond to the emotional pain that their students may experience. However, it's certainly unlikely that the schools in any district will find enough counselors to handle the emotional and mental health challenges of so many students. In a crisis, students will naturally gravitate to teachers they are most familiar and comfortable with, preferring to speak to them during a stressful situation rather than a complete stranger (visiting counselor or psychologist) that they would be meeting for the first time.

Teachers' roles in providing the support students need have always been impossible to predict or define. Just as much of life is unpredictable, so too are students' responses to everyday events, particularly when they are tragic. In those moments of greatest need, we hope you'll immediately respond in ways that reflect what your students genuinely need and your own philosophy of care for young adolescents.

◆❚ **Eliminating Competitive Learning Environments**

One of the most disturbing aspects of the traditional school experience is pitting children against one another. Young adolescents clearly understand how diverse their academic abilities are. Teachers who create competitive learning situations accentuate the weaknesses and strengths of students. Public comparison is embarrassing for less able students. As a result, they refuse to take the risks necessary for learning to occur. If being "the best" is what success means—and that is the idea in many schools—most students will fail. Kohn (1986) stated that a competitive learning environment "distracts you from a task at a given moment, makes you less interested in that task over the long run, and this results in poorer performance" (60–61). Contrary to what you may have been led to believe, competitive environments do not result in increased learning.

Students in collaborative classrooms work together to solve problems, plan presentations, design projects, develop questions, and resolve personal differences. Kohn (1986) explained that "a cooperative classroom is not simply one where students sit together or talk with each other or even share materials. It means that successful

> We hate to be compared, so just don't do it.
> **—ALLY,**
> EIGHTH GRADER

> Never announce grades in front of a class.
> **—MAIA,**
> EIGHTH GRADER

completion of a task depends on each student and therefore each has an incentive to want the other(s) to succeed" (6).

Collaboration among students doesn't automatically occur just because teachers ask students to work together. The teacher's role is to plan instructional activities that encourage student cooperation and to help students develop the social strategies needed to work together successfully.

◆❙❙ Concluding Reflections

Educators must question traditional practices that foster hostile learning environments. Students, like plants, grow well when they are cultivated with care. The more comfortable and secure your students feel when they are with you each day, the more growth they will experience.

D. Brown (2013a) describes the difference between traditional "teaching" and the responsiveness from teachers that young adolescents need:

Educators' guidance for overall developmental growth successes looks entirely different than comparing students, setting exceptionally high academic standards, merely issuing poor grades as a warning to improve, or using traditional teacher-driven instructional and curricular design that often ignores the needs and interests of young adolescents. These traditional and often discouraging strategies have no positive impact on students' efforts, motivation, or cognitive growth. (21)

Jared Diamond (2012) is an anthropologist who has spent most of his life in New Guinea. He commented on the differences between their children and those in the United States:

Other Westerners and I are struck by the emotional security, self-confidence, curiosity, and autonomy of members of small-scale societies, not only as adults but already as children. We see that people in small-scale societies spend far more time talking to each other than we do, and they spend no time at all on passive entertainment supplied by outsiders, such as television, videogames, and books. We are struck by the precocious development of social skills in their children. These are qualities that most of us admire, and would like to see in our own children, but we discourage development of these qualities by ranking and grading our children and constantly telling them what to do. The adolescent identity crises that plague American teenagers aren't an issue for hunter-gatherer children. (34)

U.S. adults are certainly not going to abandon their electronic devices, nor are adolescents. This message, though, from someone outside the education profession reveals that we must begin to understand the significance of young adolescents telling us they are ready to make more decisions, ready to be more independent, and ready for us to "back off" so that they can exercise their newfound cognitive power, sense of responsibility, and physical stature. What better place to do that than at school! As eighth-grader Chris notes, "We are underestimated, and are capable of things people wouldn't usually expect."

TIME FOR REFLECTION

- *Based on your reading to this point, add to the list of effective teacher characteristics that you developed at the beginning of this chapter.*
- *Review your list with a classmate or fellow teacher who has also written one, and compare the similarities and differences.*
- *How do you think the role of teachers has changed since you were a middle level student? How have teacher roles remained the same?*
- *Discuss with your classmates or fellow teachers your views on the importance of using class time to develop a learning community.*

CHAPTER 9

The Power of Student-Designed Curriculum: Exceeding Standards

> *What if, instead of filling students with content, young adolescents developed their critical and creative thinking processes; became seasoned researchers; improved their problem-solving skills; became skilled at asking questions rather than waiting for their teachers to ask them questions; and developed advanced presentation abilities through frequent class debates? Curriculum integration classes are designed to promote cognitive growth for students—not feed them content to be regurgitated on demand.*
>
> —**D. BROWN** (2011, 194)

> Middle school is dubbed as the place to really "find yourself": "What college do I see myself attending five years from now?" and "What will my place in the world be?" are both questions I frequently find myself asking.
> —**KATIE L.**, EIGHTH GRADER

> Don't make the kids fit the curriculum; make the curriculum fit the kids.
> —**ANDREW**, EIGHTH GRADER

A developmentally appropriate middle school curriculum should be the central focus of any middle school. Yet, the curriculum in most middle schools looks like that of most high schools and surprisingly like that of schools fifty years ago despite dramatic changes in our lives. If a school has implemented changes in school structure, the school day, and modes of instruction but has not changed the curriculum, it cannot meet the needs of young adolescents. As Sue Swaim, former executive director of the Association for Middle Level Education, said in 1993, "While a continually increasing number of schools have moved to implement interdisciplinary teams, teacher advisor programs, broad exploratory experiences, skill development programs, and other recommended characteristics, the basic questions of what we teach and how we teach remain for the most part, unanswered and little challenged" (xii). Her statement is as valid now as it was in 1993.

Middle level students want to be intellectually challenged, and their teachers are responsible for creating the conditions for that to occur. Nothing can be as critical to helping them reach new levels of cognitive growth than their involvement in determining the content to which they are exposed for 180 days a year. Yet instead of seeing curricular reform at the middle level, another set of curricular guidelines is foisted upon schools by an assemblage of education wannabees—businesspersons, politicians, and alleged education "reformers"—the latest version known as the Common Core State Standards (CCSS).

TIME FOR REFLECTION

- *What are the most important things students should know and be able to do as a result of being in school for thirteen years?*
- *What thinking processes (e.g., problem solving, critical thinking, research skills) have benefitted you the most as an adult?*
- *What do you wish you would have learned in middle or high school to better prepare you for the daily challenges you face with roommates, the university, your building principal, students' parents, the cable company, your mortgage company, or marriage?*
- *How have all of the standardized tests you've taken during your lifetime impacted your ability to succeed as an adult?*

> Middle level schools have not lived up to their billing as developmentally responsive schools for young adolescents; they have failed to address the fundamental element of the school—its curriculum.
> —**BRAZEE** (1995, 16)

◆▮ What Is Curriculum?

Before we look at what the curriculum of the middle school should be, let's clarify terms. Curriculum *is not*:

- a collection of textbooks or guides
- a fixed course of study
- what the teacher prefers to teach
- a program of study that must be completed before the end of the school year
- a set of content standards (district, state, or some organization's common core) that teachers must cover
- prepackaged scripted lessons or test booklets from the testing companies
- what we teach.

Curriculum *is*:

- the total experience of students at school
- a plan that involves students in learning
- a construct that enables students to access, process, interpret, and make connections to information
- the organizing focus of a school
- curiosities in the lives of *these* students, in *this* class
- what students learn, both planned and unplanned.

Curriculum permeates the school life of adolescents—they are immersed in it. It is their life from the moment they walk into the building until they leave at the end of the day. It includes everything: social times, club times, athletics, lunch, after-school programs, drama, music, social media they access during the day—every planned and unplanned event.

◆▍ Beliefs About Middle Level Curriculum

Tradition is a powerful word in describing what students should learn while in schools. Because education in the United States is so prolific—occurring in every community— many nonprofessionals (businesspersons, politicians, "reformers," testing companies, and millionaires) have been the "arm-chair quarterbacks," influencing what students are to learn at each grade level for decades. Naturally, those influencing what is taught have no research to support their claims or their agendas in steering educators toward another laundry list of facts to teach. Professional educators have seldom been assertive in wrestling control of the curricular decision process, and are frequently mere pawns in a game of delivering content to students.

With the use of one time-tested, but seldom implemented tradition—student-directed curricular decision-making—young adolescents in some communities have engaged in opportunities to reach maximum intellectual growth that no laundry list could ever lead to. By seizing control of curricular decisions, students and teachers engaged in *curriculum integration* break the mold that brings into question the value and validity of any current or future lists of traditional finite, standardized content.

EARLY THINKING

We continue to have, in Kliebard's (1986) words, "the struggle for the American curriculum." How should the curriculum be designed?

1. To meet the needs of business?
2. So that students can compete with others around the world?
3. To help students pass a once-a-year test?
4. To increase the market share of testing corporations?
5. To meet the individual needs of students?
6. Around the disciplines of knowledge?
7. Around a set of mandated content standards?
8. Around the problems and concerns that arise out of students' questions?
9. Around the kind of democracy we value?

Progressive educators in the early part of the twentieth century advocated for a child-centered curriculum that not only met the needs of students but also focused its content on issues in society. These early visionaries wanted a problem-based/project-based curriculum relevant to the lives of the students. The call for such a curriculum resulted in a landmark study during the 1930s, the *Eight Year Study* (1942), based on the idea that

> the conventional high school curriculum was far removed from the real concerns of youth. . . . Young people wanted to get ready to earn a living, to understand themselves, to learn how to get on with others, to become responsible members of the adult community, to find meaning in living. The curriculum seldom touched upon such genuine problems of living. (Chapter 1)

In this study, participating high schools throughout the country offered an experimental curriculum collaboratively designed by teachers and students. The curriculum was experience-based without regard to specific discipline subjects and centered on problems of concern to the students. These students, in other words, did not take the traditional high school subjects—four years of English, two years of social studies, two years of science, or other traditional course work. These high schools were supported by a number of colleges and universities who were willing to forgo the traditional requirements for college admission.

Through this curriculum, students were provided with the opportunity to live and experience democracy and to learn social responsibility at a time when, according to the report, five out of six high school students were *not* attending higher education institutions. The educators wanted the experience of high school to be as powerful as possible for all students, not just for the one of six who planned to attend college.

An analysis of the results of this study indicated that those students who were part of this project did as well or better on standardized tests as students who had attended traditional high schools. Those who went to college earned a slightly higher grade point average and received more academic honors. More importantly, those students involved in the program tended to be more curious and resourceful and have more drive and a clearer vision of where their education would take them, and they continued to be more concerned about world affairs than those students from traditional high schools.

Finally, here was a curriculum that engaged students in thinking about their world, a curriculum based on significant social issues and concerns. These students did not have to take traditional high school subjects, yet in college they performed as well or better than those who were exposed to traditional curricula (except in the foreign languages). Achievement aside, the students involved in the study had many affective and social gains not seen in students from traditional schools.

So what happened? If this approach was so powerful, why wasn't it introduced in high schools throughout the country? In short, World War II interrupted the process. As the country became immersed in the war effort, the results of this significant study became less and less noticed.

The style of curriculum developed in these schools became known as the "core" curriculum (not similar to, or to be confused with, the latest use of the word "core" as in "Common Core State Standards"). Lounsbury and Vars (1978), early middle school visionaries, defined core as "a form of curriculum organization, usually operating within an extended block of time in the daily schedule, in which learning experiences are focused directly on problems of *significance to students*" (our emphasis) (cited in Anfara, Jr. 2006, 48). This core curriculum became an example of democracy at its best. The curriculum was planned collaboratively between teachers and students with a focus on their social concerns. Through this core curriculum all students experienced a general education relevant to their lives.

The idea of a core curriculum based on social issues that used a problem-based approach to learning began to lose favor after the Russian satellite, Sputnik, was launched in 1957. The result of the Russians beating the Americans into space was a return to strict content disciplines in schools with a focus on science and mathematics.

While the concept of the core curriculum was hidden after Sputnik, it was not forgotten. When Donald Eichhorn first engaged in middle level reform in Upper St. Clair, Pennsylvania, not only did he revamp the organization and structure of the junior high school, he also challenged common assumptions about what should be taught and how best to teach it. He believed that the focus on curricular change would ultimately define what middle level education was all about.

In 1969 Conrad Toepfer, another early advocate of middle level education, commented, "It is not difficult to find junior high school administrators who conclude that all that needs to be done to achieve the unfulfilled objectives of the junior high school is to replace it with a middle school organization, add water, and stir. The only predictable result of such a nostrum would seem to be a continued lack of definitive curricular programs for early adolescents!" (135).

Early philosophical discussions emphasized the need to design programs that focused on personal growth and would help students develop the responsibility and skills to interact with their world (David 1998; Dickinson 1993). These discussions were only moderately successful in impacting the curriculum of the middle school. In most middle schools, the curriculum remains essentially like that of the high school.

CURRENT DISCUSSIONS

Present discussions about a core curriculum have nothing in common with the original concept. The latest attempt to influence curricular decisions, designed by political appointees to the National Governor's Association Center for Best Practices and the Council of Chief State School Officers, is one in which *core curriculum* refers to a collection of subject matter in specific disciplines that all students are required to learn to prepare to pass a single test once a year. The vast majority of states have adopted the Common Core State Standards (CCSS), despite being established primarily by non-educators and having no research base to support their design (Gamson, Lu, and Eckert 2103). According to the CCSS website,

> The Common Core State Standards Initiative is a state-led effort that established a single set of clear educational standards for kindergarten through 12th grade in English language arts and mathematics that states voluntarily adopt. The standards are designed to ensure that students graduating from high school are prepared to enter credit-bearing entry courses in two- or four-year college programs or enter the workforce. (2014)

This latest attempt to influence curricular decisions is far from the original meaning of *core curriculum*, and it is rooted in financial interest and in padding the pockets of the standardized testing industry rather than in doing what is appropriate for students (J. Beane 2013). Student voices are also absent from these proposed curricula.

Conversations on appropriate middle level curriculum continue. Authors representing the Association for Middle Level Education (AMLE), in its position paper *This We Believe: Keys to Education Young Adolescents* (2010), wrote, "An effective middle grades curriculum is distinguished by learning experiences that address societal expectations while appealing to young adolescents and offering them opportunities to pose and answer questions that are important to them" (17). The middle school curriculum must touch on those issues that concern young adolescents and help them construct meaning about themselves, their world, and their future. To best meet the needs of young adolescents, AMLE advocates a middle school curriculum that is "challenging, exploratory, integrative, and relevant, from both the student's and the teacher's perspective" (17).

Challenging

"Marshaling their sustained interests and efforts, challenging curriculum actively engages young adolescents" (AMLE 2010, 18). A challenging curriculum provides students with the opportunity to deeply explore significant issues in their lives as they attempt to understand themselves and the world around them. They are empowered to use their knowledge and skills in significant ways and assume control over their own learning.

In the following poem, Richard Bordeaux reflects on his middle school years while studying to be a teacher.

> *A challenging curriculum provides students with the opportunity to deeply explore significant issues in their lives as they attempt to understand themselves and the world around them.*

Absurd

A million miles from nowhere

Sitting alone in my chair

Listening to them whine

A straight line

Is the best way to lose your mind

Doing paper after paper

Where is the laughter

or the learning

It's disturbing

Rote, Rote, Rote

Whipped at our backs

Age old attacks,

It's a fact.

Change to them

is a four letter word

It's so damn absurd.

—RICHARD BORDEAUX (1992)

Exploratory

"The middle school is the finding place; for young adolescents, by nature, are adventuresome, curious explorers" (AMLE 2010, 20). Young adolescents are intensely curious about themselves and the world around them. Their expanding thinking capabilities open their minds to endless possibilities. Middle school should be a time when they can explore these possibilities. A curriculum rich in opportunities can help early adolescents discover things about themselves. Some of these explorations occur in non-academic classes such as art, photography, world languages, music. But exploration should also be part of academic classes. "Exploration is an attitude and approach, not a classification of content" (AMLE 2010, 20).

Integrative

"Curriculum is integrative when it helps students make sense of their lives and the world around them, and when students are empowered to share in making significant, meaningful decisions about their learning" (AMLE 2010, 21). An integrative curriculum is connected to students' lives outside school and goes beyond specified defined content. Skills needed to solve problems are incorporated into the learning process. Effective curriculum design also integrates issues of diversity and democracy; the multiple perspectives of all students are valued, validated, and explored.

Relevant

"Curriculum is relevant when it allows students to pursue answers to questions they have about themselves, the content, and the world" (AMLE 2010, 22). A relevant curriculum is responsive to the questions and concerns that students have about their lives and their world, and it offers students the opportunity to make connections to what they are learning. Such a curriculum engages students as they bridge what is happening in school to the outside world.

◆▮ Basic Approaches to Curriculum Organization

How can a middle level school provide a curriculum that is challenging, exploratory, integrative, and relevant? To help us answer these questions, as well as the difficult question of what the curriculum should be for middle level students, we will first explore and analyze two ways that curriculum can be organized: (1) a subject-centered, discipline-based approach, or (2) curriculum integration.

SUBJECT-CENTERED, DISCIPLINE-BASED APPROACH

For almost a century in United States' public schools, content has been organized and delivered to students around separate disciplines. This tradition of separating subjects is so prevalent that most adults can't imagine learning content in any other way. This subject-centered philosophy has influenced the structure of universities' colleges and departments, the publishing of textbooks, and the design of standardized tests. Despite more than twenty-five years of cognitive science evidence that the brain does not organize learning in subject-centered patterns, considering alternative delivery structures is almost non-existent. Encouraging educators to "think" differently about curricular organization is an overwhelming, if not impossible, paradigm shift for most that causes many middle level and high schools to maintain this archaic system.

Standard Fare—Subject-Oriented Curriculum

Most middle level schools organize their curriculum around discrete subjects. The teachers are specialists in a specific curriculum area, and their responsibility is to teach students the knowledge and skills that their subject area requires.

Subject-specific middle level teaching is often implemented by forming a team of teachers, each responsible for a specific discipline. Usually the team consists of a math, science, social studies, and language arts teacher. Two-person teams are used in some schools, with one teacher responsible for social studies and language arts while the other handles science and mathematics.

In the purest sense of this approach, the teachers, although a team, are concerned about meeting content standards, covering the subject material in their textbooks, and helping students receive acceptable scores on standardized tests. Teachers do not integrate knowledge across subject areas. The single-discipline approach to the curriculum tends to be textbook or content standards driven, and teacher led.

Look at the results. Eighth graders arrive at school. In science class, they learn about the structure of the atom. In social studies, they study Brazil and the Amazon Valley. In language arts they analyze plot and character development in the novel *The*

Westing Game (Raskin 1978). Next, half of the students go to mathematics, where they work on interest rates and percentages. The other half goes to algebra to learn how to solve complex equations. Is a curriculum thus designed challenging, exploratory, integrative, and relevant?

If the answer is "no" (and it is), why do teachers continue to teach that way? Most teachers have been trained as subject area specialists. They are confident about their knowledge and their ability to teach in their area of expertise. Some believe that an "educated" student is one who has learned a limited body of knowledge sufficient in each subject area to eventually progress to the next grade level.

Planning using the subject approach takes less time than attempting to integrate subject matter with other teachers on the team. Any type of team teaching requires collaboration, which necessitates common planning times.

Increasingly, teachers and administrators may feel pressured to maintain a subject approach based on state and local curricular standards and the recent Common Core State Standards (CCSS), as well as required standardized tests. The argument goes that if we don't teach specific items, students will score low on the achievement tests, which will reflect badly on the school. Many teachers feel pressure to follow predetermined curricula particularly in language arts and mathematics to raise students' test scores and to ensure favorable performance evaluations. Furthermore, some educators argue that the structure of the high school mandates that single subjects be taught, each focusing on specific content knowledge.

Concerns about high school and college requirements, state and local content standards (such as the CCSS), and achievement tests also encourage parents to support the subject approach. Parents wonder, "Will my child do well on the SAT or the ACT? Will he or she have the knowledge needed for high school?" Breaking middle level curricular traditions is difficult for some parents to understand.

In his groundbreaking book, *A Middle School Curriculum: From Rhetoric to Reality*, James Beane (1993) questioned the traditional ways of thinking about curriculum and challenged the separate subject approach:

Life and learning consist of a continuous flow of experiences around situations that require problem-solving in both large and small ways. When we encounter life situations or problems we do not ask, "which part is science, which is mathematics, which is history, and so on?" Rather, we use whatever information or skills the situation itself calls for and we integrate these in problem-solving. Certainly such information and skills may often be found within subject areas, but in real life the problem itself is at the center and the information and skills are defined around the problem. In other words, the subject approach is alien to life itself. Put simply, it is "bad" learning theory. (45)

When a curriculum is implemented with few links between subject areas, students have difficulty making connections between what they are learning in school and the significant issues that impact their lives. Who can justify memorizing discrete content area facts when every man, woman, and child has access to any information needed, facts they can access in seconds, 24/7, from the latest electronic device connected to the internet?

John Dewey described the problems with the traditional curricular delivery system in a speech made almost one hundred years ago:

> It imposes adult standards, subject matter, and methods upon those who are only growing slowly toward maturity. The gap is so great that the required subject matter [and] the methods of learning and of behaving are foreign to the existing capacity of the young. But the gulf between the mature or adult products and the experiences and abilities of the young is so wide that the very situation forbids much active participation by pupils in the development of what is taught. (cited in Parkey and Hass 2000, 34)

In addition, textbooks rarely explore concepts or offer connections, often propagate the status quo, and typically present information from a White, male, Eurocentric point of view. Textbooks are also designed by the same companies that have a contract with state departments of education to design, sell, administer, and score the tests that taxpayers purchase for every child in the state at almost every grade level (D. Brown 2012). In this limited context of learning merely for tests, how can what students learn have deep meaning or relevance? James Beane (2013) notes the fallacy of a set of standards, particularly the Common Core State Standards (CCSS):

> These standards (CCSS) are insufficient to define the values and skills that ought to be the center of the curriculum in our nation's schools and learned by all students. To qualify for that position requires values and skills that speak to fundamental principles in our society and essential goals for our schools, applicable across time and place, across occupations and economic circumstances, across social settings and situations. For values and skills to be significant, we must turn to the idea of democracy and the nearly forgotten tradition of the democratic core. (13)

The relevance students crave, the challenges they demand, and the connections they require are difficult to find in traditional curricula.

We are not saying that the acquisition of content is developmentally inappropriate for middle level students. We are saying that we must look at the content and ask how it contributes to helping students explore the significant issues in their lives. What knowledge is important? What knowledge is valued? Whose knowledge is it? The

> "
> In this limited context of learning merely for tests, how can what students learn have deep meaning or relevance?

fragmented, disjointed approach of a subject-centered curriculum makes it difficult to find continuity in learning. D. Brown (2006) noted, "It's no surprise to me that a small proportion of students choose to leave high school before graduating. Staying in school through thirteen years requires considerable patience, in part because of the way students are so often 'inactively engaged' cognitively with the material" (779). Although you may use instructional techniques that make your subject enjoyable, you still must ask whether a curriculum thus conceived is the most appropriate.

When we look at the developing social, physical, emotional, and cognitive needs of the young adolescent, we begin to understand what young adolescents need: a curriculum that engages them intellectually, provides opportunities for wide exploration, encourages interactions with the broader social world, helps them see connections between content knowledge and life, teaches them democratic ideals, and provides active, hands-on experiences. All this activity must occur within a context of learning the skills needed to function in society, now and in the future. In many ways, the single-subject approach fails to meet the developmental needs of the young adolescent.

Multidisciplinary Approach—Still Subject Specific

In a multidisciplinary curriculum, teachers choose themes that can be correlated across two or more subject areas. The teams then determine what each subject and each teacher can contribute to the theme. The simplest form of multidisciplinary planning is called "parallel teaching." In this approach, two or more teachers analyze their curricula for the year to see whether there are common topics to cover and then plan to teach these topics simultaneously. For example, when the history teacher covers the Revolutionary War, students read *Johnny Tremain* (Forbes 1944) in language arts class. As students study World War II in history class, they read *The Diary of a Young Girl* (Frank 1967) in language arts. While students explore the geology of Massachusetts in science class, they study the history of the state in social studies. Although teachers are focusing on a similar topic, no overall goals and objectives are common in the two classes.

A more complex form of multidisciplinary teaching involves the entire team in planning. A common theme or topic is chosen after considering state or local content standards, textbooks, or teacher interests. Once a topic is chosen, teachers engage in discussions about what their specific subject area can offer to the study of that topic. They develop overall guiding questions, identify objectives, plan activities, and devise a final assessment project. As you'll notice in Figure 9.1, once a theme is chosen each teacher develops the activities and skills relevant to the content in their subject area. There is little actual integration of subject areas.

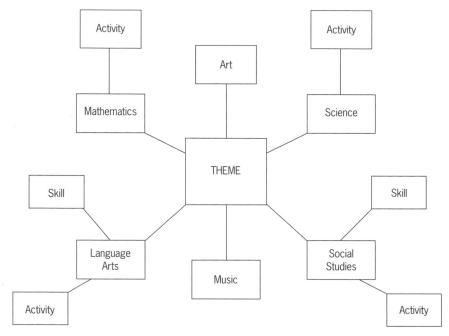

Figure 9.1 Thematic Planning—Multidisciplinary Approach

For example, a team of teachers has chosen to do a unit on the Olympics. The social studies teacher focuses on the history of the Olympic games from ancient Greece through the modern games and discusses how the Olympics have fared during wartimes. Students study world geography. They watch video clips of the parade of nations and investigate why Greece is always first in the parade and why the United States delegation never lowers its flag to the leaders of the host country. Students research countries that have been banned from the Olympics.

The science teacher talks about human anatomy, health and fitness, conditioning, and nutrition. Students analyze video clips of Olympic competitions. They investigate banned drugs and debate the use of drugs to enhance performance and whether rights are being violated with mandatory drug testing (a valid connection to a civics lesson for the social studies teacher). An innovative science teacher might have students research poles used in pole vaults, aluminum versus wooden bats in baseball, why people are running faster now, why changes in tennis rackets have changed the game, the physics of the curve ball, and so on.

In art class, students construct flags for a parade of nations. In music, they learn the national anthems from different countries. In mathematics, they analyze distance, time, rate, height, weight, speed, percentages, runs batted in, earned run averages, and whatever other statistics they can think of. In language arts they read biographies, autobiographies, and novels about former and current Olympians as well as Greek mythology. They reenact the first Olympiad. And, of course, the culminating experience is a mini-Olympics in physical education class.

This type of multidisciplinary teaching is common in middle level schools. The teachers choose the topics with minimal student input. Despite the connections made between the subject areas, topics remain subject bound. The day is still divided into social studies, mathematics, science, language arts, and reading. Sometimes longer blocks of time are devoted to certain activities, but subject areas remain intact.

Multidisciplinary units meet the needs of the young adolescent in a way that discrete subject teaching is unable to do. Students are able to see connections between subject areas. They learn not only content but also how to apply content learned in one area to another.

Affective benefits are just as important. The units can be fun. A sense of team spirit permeates the school day. All the teachers know what's going on in every class. They can talk with the students about their projects for other teachers.

One drawback to such planning is the tendency to make artificial and contrived connections between subject areas. Sometimes it is difficult to see how a specific subject area fits into a theme. For example, how do you relate mathematics to a study of the rain forest—do you graph all the different kinds of frogs? Thematic units lose their power unless clear, meaningful connections are made between subject areas and the topics.

Even more problematic is the tendency to focus on teacher-developed, popular, fun themes rather than significant, relevant ones. The unit on the Olympics was fun, but did it provide significant knowledge? Was it, in fact, challenging, exploratory, integrative, and relevant? Was it truly meaningful for young adolescents? Did it help students understand themselves and the world around them? Did it challenge them to explore their world? Was it the best way to spend student time?

Interdisciplinary Approach

In an attempt to better meet the needs of middle level students, some teams choose themes not based on the textbook or teacher interests but on what they think would be meaningful to the students. Since many students have a heightened awareness of their natural surroundings at this time, a team may choose the *environment* as a theme. Questions to be answered might include: What are some of the causes of pollution? What effect does air pollution have on the human body? What can we do to minimize pollution's ill effects? As teacher teams look at the questions, each teacher decides where he or she can best facilitate learning and develops activities accordingly. Although teachers may still ask what their subject area can contribute to the study of the theme, more attempts are made to integrate knowledge in meaningful ways. Teaching in this model becomes more interdisciplinary; some of the boundaries between subject areas begin to dissolve. The social studies teacher might talk about the historical implications of scientific research in the rain forest. Together, the science and social studies teachers can plan long blocks of time in which students engage in scientific and historical inquiry. On other days, the science and mathematics teachers might have extended blocks of time in which to analyze data generated by students' questions.

Interdisciplinary teaching differs from multidisciplinary teaching in two significant ways. First, to develop themes, teachers consider what they think the interests of the students are. Second, the boundaries between subjects begin to blur as teachers combine subject areas in order to explore principles.

Nevertheless, themes and activities are still chosen primarily by the teacher. Teachers haven't asked students what is significant in their lives. Although the interdisciplinary model provides more opportunities for middle level students to engage in challenging, meaningful learning, can we go even further and organize the curriculum around the questions and concerns of young adolescents and not around content standards, textbooks, mandates, or the interests of separate subject teachers? Can we design a curriculum that not only focuses on significant knowledge and teaches the skills to use that knowledge but also infuses classrooms with the important issues of democracy and diversity?

TIME FOR REFLECTION

In Chapter 1 you were asked what you thought was the most important thing a middle level student could do or learn at school.

- *How did you respond then?*
- *Is your answer the same now?*
- *What experiences have influenced your response?*

◆❙❙ What Students Want

Here's what a group of middle level students said when they were asked what the most important thing to learn in school was.

I think the most important thing to learn is how to live in the real world. . . . We need to learn stuff about life and looking ahead.

—*Eighth grader*

I don't think about what job I'm going to get in the future. I think more about what morals I've learned. I think I should first develop a group of morals that I think are right and then I can deal with what job I do later or what I want to learn.

—*Grace, seventh grader*

I don't think that when we grow up anybody will come up on the street and say, "Excuse me, do you know who Constantine was?" We're learning about Constantine and his son and his son's son and his son's cousin. They didn't do anything in history but we learned about it.

—*Jason, seventh grader*

A CALL FOR A DEMOCRATICALLY DEVELOPED CURRICULUM

We ostensibly live in a democratic society, and there are no reasonable grounds that suggest why the democratic way of life should not be extended to early adolescents or into their schools. The democracy I mean, though, is not simply a matter of individuals selecting alternatives from a menu of limited choices nor the pseudo-democratic "engineering of consent" around predetermined possibilities. In short, it is not simply whatever someone wants to do or whatever someone can get them to do. Rather, I mean that the curriculum ought to be democratically conceived through collaborative planning with involvement of early adolescents. (J. Beane 1993, 19)

The future of a democratic society rests in the ability of each generation to live according to democratic principles and work to propagate and expand those principles for future generations. What are those principles of democracy that we value? In his book *A Reason to Teach: Creating Classrooms of Dignity and Hope*, James Beane (2005) explained,

Democracy is an idea about how people might live together. At the core are two related principles: (1) that people have a fundamental right to human dignity and (2) that people have a responsibility to care about the common good and the dignity and welfare of others. (8–9)

Recent upheavals in governments in the Middle East have created a stage for global citizens to examine the definition of *democracy*—to actually experience democratic ideals in genuine ways. The "Arab Spring" is a testament to a desire to capture the essence of U.S. democracy. As new countries seek their own path to the freedoms afforded U.S. citizens, how can middle level schools provide a forum for students to actually comprehend the democratic system? How about living it—each day within the four walls of their classrooms? *Living* democracy means that middle level students engage in significant decision making each day at school.

◆▊ Curriculum Integration Model: A Different Way of Thinking About the Curriculum

A basic principle of a democracy is that those who will be affected by a decision should share in making that decision. (Lounsbury and Vars 2003, 11)

If we are to have a curriculum that makes sense for the young adolescent, it must be one that is infused with democratic principles. That curriculum must respond to young adolescent concerns about the world, to those issues that they feel are important. A curriculum based on the curriculum integration model does just that— focuses on the lives of young adolescents. In such a model, the curriculum is developed collaboratively by teachers and students, and arises from the questions and concerns of the students rather than the demands of subject areas or standardized achievement tests.

Teachers who adopt this model don't simply turn to the textbook or the latest set of state content standards to determine what to teach. Instead, they ask questions about sources of knowledge and how that knowledge can and should be used within the context of young adolescent lives. Subject area knowledge becomes vital as it helps students answer their questions or solve their problems. The key, however, is that the organizing factor does not focus on subject areas but rather on student questions and concerns. According to J. Beane (1997):

Curriculum integration is a curriculum design that is concerned with enhancing the possibilities for personal and social integration through the organization of curriculum around significant problems and issues, collaboratively identified by educators and young people, without regard for subject-area boundaries. (x–xi)

Young adolescents are intensely curious about their world and their ultimate place in it. They are developing their own values and learning what it means to have ethical relationships in an often confusing social climate. Given these developmental issues, it makes sense to devise a curriculum that puts them and their concerns at the center.

In *A Middle School Curriculum: From Rhetoric to Reality* (1993), J. Beane drew upon the work of the progressive movement in the early part of the twentieth century and advocated a curriculum that focused on young adolescents' lives to design themes for study. J. Beane presented eight guidelines for the middle school curriculum:

1. "The middle school curriculum should focus on general eduction" (17). Middle school is not the time to sift, sort, and select—to put some students in honors classes while others stay in remedial classes, to expose some to significant issues while providing memory games for other students.

2. "The central purpose of the middle school curriculum should be helping early adolescents explore self and social meanings at this time in their lives" (18). The concerns about state content standards are secondary to meeting the needs of young adolescents.

3. "The middle school curriculum should respect the dignity of early adolescents" (18). Young adolescents are not merely hormones with feet, nor are they empty-headed teens with no interests or concerns. Middle level students are dynamic young people who have deep concerns about life and the survival of the world. The curriculum should be designed to take advantage of these concerns and the energy with which students tackle them.

4. "The middle school curriculum should be firmly grounded in democracy" (19). The school environment seldom offers students the opportunity to practice democracy. More often than not, our schools are run as an autocracy in which one person possesses unlimited power over others. As Amanda, an eighth grader, put it, "I think students should have more rule over the school. A lot of teachers will say, 'This isn't a democracy' and they're putting us in a dictator's world in this school, and I don't like it at all." Another eighth grader commented, "In middle school I feel like a robot. You go where you're assigned to go

and do what you're told." If we want students to be firmly grounded in the tenets upon which this country was founded, the curriculum must be democratically constructed through student–teacher collaboration. "Bringing democracy to life in the classroom requires that students have a genuine say in the curriculum and that their say counts for something" (J. Beane 1997, 50).

5. "The middle school curriculum should honor diversity" (19). Multiple viewpoints should be at the core of our curriculum, offering students diverse ways of analyzing and exploring problems and multiple ways of expressing viewpoints. Different ways of approaching knowledge should not only be valued but also validated.

6. "The middle school curriculum should be of great personal and social significance" (20). Although fun units can motivate students, teach skills, and expose students to new content, they frequently lack the significance needed for genuine learning. Students need to study significant topics and themes that help them construct meaning from their lives. One eighth grader noted, "I think you should be able to pick what you're interested in to study. We don't get choices for most stuff."

7. "The middle school curriculum should be lifelike and lively" (20). Seventh-grader Tim said, "Class is so long and boring. Instead of doing fun things, you just read out of a book." The curriculum should embrace wonder, curiosity, exploration, problem solving, challenges, and action.

8. "The middle school curriculum should enhance knowledge and skills for all young people" (21). Knowledge is most powerful when it is used in a quest for meaning. Skills become the tools to access, process, and use that knowledge.

◆❙ Curriculum Integration in the Middle Level Classroom

A curriculum that embraces a separate-subject approach makes it impossible to achieve J. Beane's guidelines. Through curriculum integration, however, all students can access knowledge that has meaning and relevance to them. In this approach, students have a genuine voice in what they are going to learn and how they want to learn it. Themes are chosen by teachers and students through a collaborative effort. These themes emerge from students' personal and social concerns. After themes are chosen, teachers do not look at their particular discipline to determine what to study; instead, students and teachers together determine what activities can be used to explore concepts, solve problems, or answer questions without regard to subject areas. Skills are embedded in the learning process as they become necessary prerequisites for engaging in activities or solving problems. But, and perhaps most important, as a result of collaboration students are exposed to the enduring concepts of democracy, including human dignity and cultural diversity (J. Beane 1993). While you might agree with the philosophy of curriculum integration, it may be difficult to see how you can implement it in a classroom or team setting.

J. Beane (1998) described the most successful way of implementing curriculum integration.

Step One: The initial step involves student reflection. Because students are rarely asked to help develop their curriculum, they will be able to do so more easily if they are first given the opportunity to individually reflect and to answer questions about who they are: "I like horses." "I like going to Hawaii." "I am a swimmer, and I like to play baseball." "In my spare time I play street hockey and football."

Students can then be asked to choose the things they like best about themselves and what they would like to change. They can think about what they would like to be like. These ideas can be kept private or shared in small or large groups.

Step Two: After students have had time to reflect, the second step is to ask students two questions. The first is, "What questions and concerns do you have about yourself?" After individually answering that question, students share their responses in small groups, searching for common questions and combining similar ideas into a group list. Each group presents its list to the class. The key to success is to validate the questions and concerns of all students. Everything gets put on the list during this initial session.

One group of eighth graders listed the following questions about themselves:

1. How does my body repair itself when it's sick?
2. Why do I have certain emotions?
3. How does my mind make decisions?
4. How does the body choose what genes to transfer when I am born?
5. Who am I?
6. Why do we have dreams?

7. Why am I here?

8. Why do we see things differently from others?

9. How do our senses interact?

10. What happens when you die?

11. Why don't we remember our dreams?

12. How old will I end up being?

13. Who will I marry?

14. How many kids will I have?

15. Will they make a medicine that will make me live forever?

16. Will I be wealthy?

17. What will I look like when I am older?

18. Why do people fear change?

19. What would I be like if I was born 400 years ago?

20. How does your brain process light and sound?

21. Why do I have allergies?

22. Why are my feet different sizes?

23. What kind of challenges will I face in life?

24. Will I make a difference in this world?

The second question moves from the personal to a broader category: "What questions and concerns do you have about the world?" Once students have listed, analyzed, and combined the questions they have about themselves, they engage in a similar process with the questions and concerns they have about the world around them—school, family, community, city, nation, world. A class of eighth graders recently developed this list from that question:

1. What will happen when the world is overpopulated and polluted?

2. Why do people discriminate?

3. What if democracy ends in the United States?

4. What happens when we run out of gas and other fossil fuels?

5. What language do deaf people think in?

6. Is social media considered a drug?

7. Why are girls and boys so different?

8. Are jails effective?

9. Would humans ever become extinct?

10. Why do the elderly shrink?

11. What (in the brain) causes a coma, and what happens during one?

12. How does your environment affect your attitude?
13. Will there ever be human life on other planets?
14. With the use of modern technology, why haven't we developed a cure for deadly illnesses?
15. How can we eliminate poverty in the world?
16. Why are pro athletes paid more than people whose jobs help maintain the world?
17. What causes children to be born with disorders?
18. What makes some people smarter than others?
19. Why do some people act violently?
20. What different species haven't been discovered, and will they ever be?
21. Will there be a zombie apocalypse?
22. Will people still be trying to put a stop to global warming?
23. Why do girls create more drama than boys?
24. Will the dinosaurs come back?
25. Will a time machine be created?
26. Will a machine be created that can tell you the day you die?
27. Will humans be able to give birth to animals?
28. How did stereotypes form, and are certain ones true?
29. How did the world start?
30. How are pretzels made?
31. How was the first human made?
32. Was there really a megalodon?
33. How does society affect our perceptions?
34. Is there such a thing as the afterlife?
35. Why do people resist change?
36. Why does the world revolve around power?
37. Where does space end?
38. How do people see God differently?
39. How did Hitler convince a nation to commit mass genocide?
40. How does a mental illness develop?
41. What makes things popular?
42. Why are there social classes?
43. Will there ever be a plague that wipes out the world?
44. What would be the cause of a World War III, if it were to happen?
45. How did languages first form?

46. How do TV and electronics and media influence the public?

47. How can we make gay rights legal everywhere?

48. Do extraterrestrial creatures really exist?

49. How are nuclear weapons made and used?

50. What is the point of mosquitoes' existence?

51. How do black holes work?

52. Why do biases exist?

This process takes time. One student from a curriculum integration class reported when given the opportunity to ask questions on what he wanted to know, "I don't even know what to think right now, because I've never been asked what I want to learn." It's astounding that thirteen-year-olds may have lost an essential part of the nature of learning—asking questions—after being in school for seven years. Preschool children never stop asking questions, yet the structured curricula of traditional schooling somehow manage to destroy the underlying foundation of intellectual growth— *question asking*.

Mark Springer, a teacher who initiated the Soundings curriculum integration program in his school, noted how he almost had to train students to return to their inquisitive nature in his curriculum integration class at the beginning of the year:

> Students play a questioning game in which they begin with a basic question, such as "What did you have for breakfast?" and then try to create as many questions as they can that evolve from this initial question, such as "Why do we eat breakfast?" and "Who decided which foods would be breakfast foods?" (D. Brown 2002a, 55–56)

Most students have never been given a chance to talk about those issues that concern them, and may begin asking questions we think are superficial: "Why do locker rooms smell?" or "Why are coins round?" In fact, these questions are not superficial at all, but reflect the curiosity that is part of the young adolescent's life. These questions may later lead to a wonderful unit on the mysteries of the world.

As students see that their questions are validated and respected they will begin to list ideas that are of deeper concern to them: "Why do people have to judge you by the way you look rather than by what is inside?" "Why do we have gangs, and what can we do about all that hatred?" When given a chance to have a voice, young adolescents demonstrate their ability to think deeply about their world.

Step Three: The third step is for students to analyze both lists, looking for connections between their personal and social concerns to develop some common themes. Students see that their questions about taking classes they don't want to, teachers yelling, the government hiding things, gangs, crime, and the death penalty might all be related to the theme of power. They might look at their questions about technology, aliens, relationships, what job they'll have, high school, and cloning and then come up with a common theme related to the future.

Step Four: The fourth step is choosing an initial theme. Groups present their common themes, which are posted, and students try to reach a consensus about what they want to study first. Sometimes this process involves identifying what themes were mentioned the most, and other times it might involve looking for correlations among themes and combining them. A decision might be reached by having groups choose their top three and bottom three themes and then have students vote. Whatever the strategy, a theme is chosen collaboratively, and the remaining topics are reserved for later study.

Step Five: Once a theme has been chosen, the next step is for students to go back to their original lists of questions and identify those that relate to the theme. They generate new questions, concerns, and problems related to the theme. They brainstorm the knowledge and skills needed to understand the theme well. Students suggest activities that will help them explore the concepts. They determine which resources are needed to research their topics—from interviewing experts from the field to taking field trips to visit local scientists. If they choose the topic of the future, the students might have high school students come talk to the class. They might interview computer programmers, learn how to write résumés and fill out applications, or learn how to develop a family budget. Students also identify ways to demonstrate their knowledge to varying audiences, from parents to fellow classmates.

TEACHERS' ROLES

The teacher facilitates the planning process, helping students explore their concerns and questions. Once a theme is chosen, teachers collaborate with students to develop activities with which to explore the themes. Each teacher on the team analyzes the activities and determines which ones they can best facilitate. Teachers expand and add to student ideas for activities, identify and collect resources, develop lessons related to the activities, create timelines, and integrate the skills students need to answer their questions. Notice in Figure 9.2 that the planning process focuses on the identification

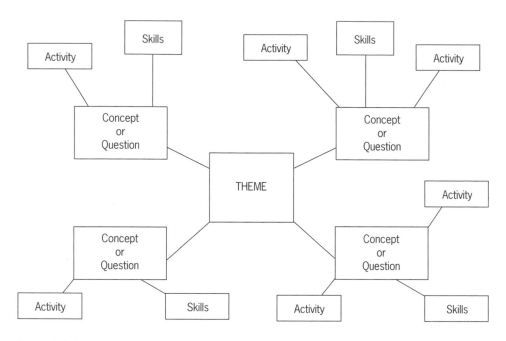

Figure 9.2 Curriculum Integration Model

of significant concepts needed to explore the theme, rather than identifying how each content area contributes to the theme.

Springer (2006) describes student responsibilities in the Soundings curriculum integration classroom:

1. maintaining a daily log book or journal of learning activities
2. maintaining a reading journal with a target of 25 entries
3. completing at least one research project and paper
4. planning and conducting a student-led conference with parents and teachers
5. maintaining a portfolio or file of all work, in addition to the district writing portfolio
6. completing all biweekly assessment documents and the associated sharing procedures
7. demonstrating the ability to use computer technologies including word processing Internet research, presentation programs, and email
8. demonstrating the ability to give effective presentations to various types of audiences

9. demonstrating familiarity with essential skills and concepts established by the district standards, in particular as they apply to the specific themes we decide to pursue in Soundings. (161)

All of these activities are occurring during the school year, and each student has to attend to completing his/her personal learning objectives as well as adding to their small group responsibilities. Curriculum integration teachers are constantly meeting individually with students.

As you can see, developing an integrated curriculum is radically different from developing multidisciplinary units. Curriculum integration begins with and is driven by the questions and concerns generated by students. Activities are chosen because they help students explore the concepts and content needed to answer the questions and concerns. Skills are taught because they are needed to solve problems inherent in the theme. Teachers do not adhere to specific subject areas but use subject area knowledge as needed. Content becomes vital and essential as students attempt to explore the significant issues they have raised.

A curriculum integration model is developmentally responsive, allows for cognitive challenge, emotional self-exploration, social interaction, and physical movement; and, it meets the diverse instructional needs of students and responds to issues of multiple intelligences, ethnic diversity, and students of differing abilities (differentiation). Although students are working collaboratively most days, there is time for students to work individually as they establish their own learning goals each week and evaluate their progress toward those goals at the end of the week (Springer 2006).

In addition, a curriculum that focuses on the real concerns of the young adolescent is highly motivating and leads to significant learning. Collaborating with students demonstrates the values and morals inherent in our society. If we are to teach students the concepts of a democratic citizenship, we must model these concepts in our classrooms. Collaboration between teachers and students gives ownership and power to all involved and respects the knowledge that everyone brings to the learning situation.

If we are to teach students the concepts of a democratic citizenship, we must model these concepts in our classrooms.

MEETING STATE CONTENT STANDARDS AND MEASURING GROWTH

Many teachers fear that by permitting students to choose the topics they'll study during the year state content standards may be ignored, thereby causing students to do poorly on state mandated tests. In the integrated programs that we've studied, students are provided a list of state and local content standards that must be met, and integrate them into their weekly learning activities. Springer's (2006) list of student responsibilities above, for instance, reveals that they must respond to twenty-five texts in their reading journal and complete a research paper. Both of these are state standards for language arts, and students meet those standards as well as others in science and social studies through teacher planned lessons, independent study, or group projects.

In some classrooms, students are provided with a list of the state standards and often determine as a group how they will address the required topics. Addressing content standards is not a unilateral decision by teachers.

In the curriculum integration programs that we have studied, grades are not given; instead, students engage in self-assessment processes. Teachers who initiate curriculum integration programs often obtain permission from administrators to use alternative assessments rather than issuing grades, with an understanding that an ungraded class leads to greater student responsibility for learning. Students, with teacher guidance, collaboratively choose several assignments each grading period that are assessed, and they determine how they will be judged as having met the criteria for successful learning. Students review state standards and design rubrics for each accompanying assignment as a guide to successful completion of those academic tasks.

The emphasis in a curriculum integration class is on each student growing in each area—genuine *mastery learning* versus *evaluation*—in which students are given a grade and often little other feedback that furthers growth. *Evaluation* provides a label and compares students with one another, such as with traditional grades. *Assessment* is a process for determining where the student's skills are at that moment, and it provides feedback on what he or she must do to improve understanding or academic tasks.

One curriculum integration student revealed that her writing improved considerably more than it would have in a traditional classroom: "There's a perspective that things can always be improved [in CI]. We received several chances to improve our papers, so we always think that we can do better" (D. Brown 2011, 202). Students reveal having a much clearer picture of their strengths and weaknesses as learners by engaging in self-evaluative processes in curriculum integration classes rather than being *evaluated* with grades in traditional classes (D. Brown).

Both students and teachers benefit from the curriculum integration model, as these comments reveal:

Having a say is important. It prepares you for later in life when you have to speak out about future issues.
—Molly, seventh grade

Planning with students is the most challenging and most exciting thing I do.
—Sixth-grade teacher

I would probably quit education if I couldn't do this kind of work.
—Seventh-grade teacher

There's nothing more important in the world than empowering students.
—Sixth-grade teacher

I can't imagine doing it any other way.
—Seventh- and eighth-grade teacher

Ultimately, middle level educators are going to have to ask what curriculum model is appropriate for young adolescents. If curriculum integration is the most effective way to educate the young adolescent, why don't we do it that way? If curriculum integration is such a "perfect" and powerful model, why isn't it more widely used?

Poet and preservice teacher Richard Bordeaux (1994) reflects on his middle school curriculum.

Grasping for Air

Four papers

Three worksheets

Too little time

I should have planned ahead

As time passed by

Tick

Tick

Tick

Where are my papers

and my pens

I better begin

Fore the day ends

Too much work

Too little time

Why

isn't quality

more important than quantity?

I know, because it's easier to change lead to gold than a curriculum that's old.
—Richard Bordeaux

RATIONALE FOR IMPLEMENTING CURRICULUM INTEGRATION

The reasons that curriculum integration is *not* more widely used are many and varied. Teacher training, curriculum mandates, pressures from parents, dependence on textbooks, and a society that widely validates the traditional model lead most middle level schools to stay with what has always been done.

Curriculum integration requires a shift in the way that teachers perceive their role in the classroom. The content areas that they have put so much effort into mastering become secondary, and at times insignificant, to their students' search for meaning. Suddenly teachers cannot rely on their advanced content knowledge to guide student learning—and that can be daunting to some educators. Planning is a challenge, as the learning process is dynamic and develops out of daily interaction with students. The uncertainty about what the day will hold can be unsettling when teachers no longer dictate the learning process.

Testing requirements and curriculum mandates, particularly the recent adoption of the Common Core standards, are also important variables. When a state education department requires the teaching of ancient history in the seventh grade, many social studies teachers feel they will have a difficult time implementing curriculum integration. Vars (2001) asked, "Can curriculum integration survive in an era of high-stakes testing?" (1). It is becoming more difficult to find schools and teachers who implement curriculum integration. The narrowing of curriculum accelerated following NCLB and has the potential to worsen with the introduction of the CCSS (J. Beane 2004; D. Brown 2012). When students and teachers live in fear of high-stakes tests, and teachers' evaluations are determined by their students' test scores, democracy cannot flourish in classrooms and highly motivated learning is at risk.

Take a closer look and ask how it is that some group—whether educators, researchers, policy makers, businesspersons, testing companies, or so-called "reformers"—can actually determine which content is essential for absolutely every adolescent to learn. Imagine that ten of your friends join you in a social gathering, and you all begin discussing which books you read in your high school literature classes. Among your ten friends, only three read *The Grapes of Wrath*. Seven of you read *Romeo and Juliet*, but not the others. Eight of you read *To Kill a Mockingbird*, and five friends read *The House on Mango Street*. Some of you took calculus, others statistics; some anatomy and physiology, others advanced physics; three took Latin, but four took Spanish; three took art every year of high school, and three never had an art course but were in the band all four years. You get the picture—all of your friends are successful high school and college graduates, gainfully employed, and obviously academically talented. Yet the discrepancies among your academic backgrounds are gaping.

Who's educated . . . and who isn't? Who determines which academic path is the "purest"? Our response is that the entire conversation is moot, but at the same time it reveals a reality that learning is about much more than content; it's about thinking processes—creative and critical thinking, problem-solving skills, interpersonal strategies, research capabilities, and understanding one's need for lifelong learning. So what content knowledge must be specifically delivered to every adolescent in the United States to ensure quality adult lives? The challenge that many professional educators face in imagining the success of curriculum integration is that somehow students will "miss" learning essential content that will determine their future academic success. Comprehending curriculum integration requires the indisputable fact that curricula are infinite. There is no end to future novels that will be written and become the next essential "read" for adolescents. How many new scientific discoveries are revealed each month? What new technologies will find their way into our lives and completely alter the way we access information or the ability to change medicine and subsequently the way we handle our health needs?

Our own children have access to every bit of information that can be loaded onto the Internet within seconds—constantly; yet, some educators, policy makers, and testing company CEOs cling to content standards and isolated facts as if letting go will destroy their philosophy of what it means to be educated. Now we have a responsibility to prepare youth for using information, for exchanging ideas, and for solving problems. Perhaps medical neurologist Dr. Judy Willis (2010) can help us understand this principle with her advice:

The most rewarding jobs of this century will be those that cannot be done by computers. The students best prepared for these opportunities need conceptual thinking skills to solve problems that have not yet been recognized. For 21st century success, students will need a skill set far beyond the current subject matter evaluated on standardized tests. The qualifications for success in the world that today's students will enter will demand the abilities to think critically, communicate clearly, use continually changing technology, be culturally aware and adaptive, and possess the judgment and open-mindedness to make complex decisions based on accurate analysis of information. (62–63)

It's a victory for teachers to make the paradigm shift from believing in the value of traditional separate content area teaching to acknowledging that curriculum integration is a superior learning approach. The next step, however, is akin to landing on the moon: rounding up your colleagues at your grade level and marching into the principal's office with a plan to initiate pure curriculum integration in your classroom. Don't be the last to don your space suit!

LEARNING MORE, GROWING COGNITIVELY, AND BECOMING BETTER THINKERS: RESEARCH IN SUPPORT OF CURRICULUM INTEGRATION

If we abandon the principle of teaching with separate content and search for another avenue of genuine learning, how can educators be assured that parents will agree? Alfie Kohn (1998) reported that when he asked groups of parents what goals they envisioned for their children as a result of schooling, parents' lists included "happy, balanced, independent, fulfilled, productive, self-reliant, responsible, thoughtful, inquisitive, and confident" (101). When Dave Brown (2006) asked groups of middle level teachers for several years what their list of outcomes should be for students, his respondents replied, "Critical thinking skills, problem-solving strategies and effective decision-making skills, creative thinking processes, effective oral and written communication skills, knowledge of when and how to use research to solve problems, effective interpersonal skills, and willingness, strategies, and ability to continue learning" (778).

It's apparent to us that teachers and parents are closer to agreeing on the essential outcomes for education than many may imagine. A survey of 2,000 Americans revealed, "Many parents assign a lower priority to schools having high test scores or preparing students to take state tests. It's a blunt fact that many parents are less obsessed with test scores than are those who design education policies" (Zeehandelaar and Winkler 2013, 7). In the *Phi Delta Kappan* 2013 Gallup Poll most of those surveyed believe that more testing in public schools damaged schools and made no discernable difference in public school performance.

Teachers often have to sell and defend their use of curriculum integration. Despite these concerns, curriculum integration is alive and well, used by progressive educators throughout the country who believe in bringing democracy into the classroom and giving students a voice in their own education. Students who experience curriculum integration report that they believe the following skills and abilities developed more than if they had been in a traditional class:

- critical- and creative-thinking skills
- problem-solving abilities
- interpersonal skills
- decision-making skills
- research skills
- communication processes. (D. Brown 2011)

Students from two separate classes noted that they were better prepared for adulthood as a result of their curriculum integration experiences. All the curriculum integration students interviewed in one study reported that their reading and writing skills advanced more than they would have in a traditional class.

Vars (1997) noted that students participating in curriculum integration, "Almost without exception . . . do as well as and often better than students in a conventional departmentalized program" (181). Young adolescents are moving cognitively from concrete operational thought into formal operations, and for this to occur they need many opportunities to ask questions, engage in conversations, debates, and research opportunities. Curriculum integration students do this each day. Brown and Canniff (2007) reported that students who participate in curriculum integration receive the following benefits that promote cognitive growth:

- extended learning time needed for cognitive processing
- a risk-free environment that encourages examination of their questions about themselves and life
- the flexibility needed to study topics with the amount of depth required for meaningful learning
- content studied in the context of the connections students make to it and the naturally cognitive way in which students interconnect concepts and principles. (23)

Rice and Dolgin (2005) reiterated the value of student conversations: "The highest levels of reasoning are attained when individuals are given the chance to discuss, argue, and debate with people whose views are different from their own" (137).

Ninth-grade cumulative grade point averages for students from two separate years of cohorts from the eighth-grade Soundings curriculum integration program were from a quarter to a half percentage point higher than their classmates from traditional eighth-grade classes. Vars (2001) reveals more significant outcomes of participation in curriculum integration, "such as love of learning, concern for other people, criti-cal thinking, self-confidence, commitment to democratic group process, and a whole host of other so-called 'intangibles'" (9).

Flying Solo with Curriculum Integration

Curriculum integration requires a philosophy of education that puts students, not subject areas, at the center. If a teacher finds himself or herself on a team with others who do not share this philosophy, it will be challenging to implement the curriculum integration model at a team level.

You can, in fact, do much in your own classroom to propagate the values of democracy and diversity by implementing modified curriculum integration. You can still center your classroom curriculum around students' questions and con-cerns. You can then connect your subject area teaching to broader understandings relevant to your students' lives.

If, for example, your seventh graders are required to study ancient civiliza-tions, develop themes related to their questions and concerns, and ask them how they can integrate a study of ancient Egypt into those themes. For example, themes of *prejudice* or *power* can govern an investigation into the class structure of ancient Egypt. A *technology* theme can guide the analysis of pyramid construction and mummification techniques. Disease and medical conditions in Egypt can be explored under the theme of *wellness*.

To help students perform well on the state tests, teachers in one middle school were told to spend more time on math and reading classes—which, of course, meant less time for social studies and science (Volger 2003). One team of teachers decided to change the way they used the state content standards. These teach-ers showed the students the standards and had them create units using those standards. When achievement tests scores came back, they were higher than in previous years. One teacher commented, "Our team's decision to work with stu-dents to create an integrated curriculum using state standards was more than just a response to a request. It was a course of action designed to bridge the gap between the need for student-centered curricula and the demands and expecta-tions of a high-stakes testing environment" (Volger 2003, 10).

Can you use this model in your own classroom while still being true to cur-riculum standards? Absolutely. Read the story of one social studies teacher who did just that.

Real Learning in My Classroom? Yes!

By J. Scott Clark (1996)

Teaching: Loftiest of professions or daily drudgery? Tradition of Socrates or foolish frustration? Most of us had hoped that we would teach students who would be thirsting for the gems of knowledge we have to offer them; yet, how often has it felt more like we are casting pearls before swine?

In September 1996, I entered my twenty-eighth year as a middle school social studies teacher. I cared deeply about my students and worked well with my interdisciplinary team, but I was prepared for another year of wondering how much my students would really learn, how much they would become engaged in what I had to offer them. I even signed up for one more of those "educational" courses. (You know, the kind where you listen to the drivel from another "expert" professor who you think could never survive an hour with thirty energetic adolescents.)

Little did I realize the "door" she would open for me. Her message was simple and concise: "It's the curriculum, stupid!" She thought the curriculum was the problem? Was she crazy?

Perhaps, but Professor Trudy Knowles introduced me to a group of reformers led by James Beane who have come to realize that student apathy and uninvolvement cannot be remedied by how we teach, what books we use, or the introduction of new technology in the classroom. No, the solution to our problem lies in the simple but radical notion of curriculum change. They do not simply mean selecting another choice from the menu or even teaching it in conjunction with one's teammates. Instead, they suggest that the menu be more relevant to the real world, to the concerns of both adults and adolescents. They suggest that the menu choices be partially determined by student input (What, democracy in the classroom?). They suggest that the classroom experience will be embraced by students when it offers them an opportunity to grapple with the serious, real, and overwhelming issues of our day. Teachers must allow their students to seek, inquire, question, probe, and discover what even the teachers may not know. Then and only then will we witness the student involvement and learning of our dreams.

Aha! Pie in the sky, I thought. I would need the cooperation and support of my teaching team, department head, principal, students, and their parents. What materials could I use? How could grades be determined in this process where inquiry would be its own end instead of tests and quizzes? Were my students "good" enough for this? My optimism and frustration led me to try.

My "recipe" for success? It is really quite simple. Permission to experiment was readily granted, especially since any success could be shared by supervisors, no new technology was required, and the purchase of a new textbook could be delayed even longer. When I approached my students with the notion that we would, together, actually seek answers to the important issues of their world, enthusiasm was overwhelming. In fact, the decision was made not to stop at answers but to actually attempt to implement solutions. They desperately wanted to make a difference, to improve the world they live in.

Students, individually and privately, listed all of the pressing problems they could think of. Taking only one "area" at a time, they listed all the problems of world, country, region, school, family, and self. Already they felt that an adult was truly interested in them and their opinions. These private lists were huge, even the lists of students who usually refused to participate in anything I asked them to do. We then consolidated their individual lists into a gigantic whole-class list. We covered one area at a time and filled up all of our blackboard space. At this point, I was little more than a recording secretary who helped students clarify ideas and refine terminology. No attempt was made to edit or criticize ideas. Everyone felt validated when her/his problems were accepted.

(continues)

(continued)

The next step was critical to our success or failure, to the acceptance of our program by all those "outsiders" like principals and parents. Which one of these problems (well over a hundred in each class group) would they select to study? If their choices proved frivolous, no one would take them seriously. If I exercised control and led them toward the problems I wanted them to study, the students would not take me seriously. Was I in over my head? No! At the end of three days, each class narrowed its list to the seven or eight most serious problems. They did it while I acted only as facilitator. We had to design ways to reach consensus rather than alienating class members. Simple voting that could result in winners and losers was not acceptable.

We began by my reading aloud, slowly and carefully, the entire class list while each student quietly wrote down the problems that were his or her personal top ten to fifteen. I wrote all of these on the board, immediately narrowing our whole-class lists to approximately twenty-five. Students removed problems that seemed less pressing and elevated ones that were more crucial by annotating their personal top ten, marking the three that they considered of paramount importance and crossing out the three that they were most willing to concede. Students suggested such strategies as combining and enlarging to further narrow the lists. After much discussion that floored me with their depth, complexity, and passion, students reached agreement on their final lists.

Their class lists were composed of such problems as crime and violence, war, prejudice, disease, rights and freedom, environment, immigration, starvation, employment, poverty and welfare, taxes, drugs, and education. Not a single frivolous problem had even made it to their semifinal lists. Students really are involved with and tuned into their world. All I needed was to have faith in them.

What next? We had to begin our actual inquiry, our problem solving. After a brief bit of research and some collaboration with my colleagues, I designed a chart that outlined a step-by-step method for solving any problem. It includes:

- careful elaboration of the problem itself
- discovery of the causes
- proposal and analysis of the solutions
- decision as to which solutions to use
- formulation of a plan of action
- implementation of the plan
- a reporting procedure as to what and how it was accomplished.

A simple, hypothetical problem (stolen family car) provided the basis for a practice exercise in using the problem-solving chart. This practice exercise gave both the students and me a chance to try out our new roles within a classroom. Small cooperative learning groups, often preceded by initial attempts by each individual student, seemed an ideal way to structure the class.

Since *prejudice* was on each class list and there were ample materials at hand, the selection was easy. Textbooks, short stories, newspaper and magazine articles, library materials, computer-generated information, and community resources were all possible materials for students to use as they pursued solutions. I discovered that it was of paramount importance for me to act as a facilitator so that the students could pursue their own inquiries and solutions. I asked only open-ended questions that no one even expected me to answer, for they were coming to realize that only their answers matter.

But what about grades? Oh yes, administrators feel the need for them, parents insist on them, and even students want feedback about how they are doing. I utilized four methods to determine students' growth: informal teacher observations; daily journal entries in which students recorded their accomplishments, reflections, and feelings; notebooks that students utilized to record their problem-solving process; and the actual solutions that students devised, contained in written reports documenting what they accomplished (a type of portfolio). This system may not be as mathematically precise as we are used to, but it offers a deeper and more realistic reflection of what a student has really achieved. Classes ended on a reflective note as every student spent the last five minutes quietly writing in his or her journal to sum up what had been learned that day. As the time of departure approached, I was surrounded by a sea of hands beckoning me to stamp their daily entries with a "smiley face," my way of acknowledging and thanking them for their participation.

I am no longer in the memorization business. I am not the game show host who has the answers written out on little cards. I do not have to struggle to motivate bored students. This is real life simply transplanted into a classroom. Real people are seeking real answers to real concerns. As long as it remains their search, the students are the source of their own motivation.

My students are actively engaged in class; they are exploring complex subjects utilizing primary source materials; and they have finally entered into the realms of intellectual problem solving. They feel vibrant and alive because they are not just studying for grades but are actually changing their world. They feel empowered because their opinions and judgments are being actively solicited on a daily basis. They are beginning to understand that problems of this magnitude require cooperation if we are ever going to solve them.

Their journal entries and parents' comments reflect the involvement and interest that has been stimulated. They are preparing themselves for the challenge of the twenty-first century, and I am privileged to witness their progress.

◆▌ Concluding Reflections

As we look at the realities of young adolescence, we are convinced that curriculum integration most clearly meets the needs of the middle level learner. It directly responds to their concerns about the world as they struggle to find meaning. It addresses cognitive, emotional, social, and physical developmental issues. It responds to issues of ethnic diversity, multiple intelligences, and differing abilities. It focuses on high-level conceptual thinking in addition to the development of necessary skills. And it infuses the classroom with democratic ideals.

Chapter 10 introduces several teachers who have implemented curriculum integration in their classrooms. Their stories demonstrate that the curriculum integration model is practical, possible, and productive. All you have to do is take the first step.

Curriculum Integration:

What It Looks Like

in Real Life

> *I believe that, as teachers, we must be responsible for preparing young people for the types of critical thinking and decision making that have little to do with one's work and more to do with one's personal and civic lives. I prefer that schools prepare children to be social leaders, not blind followers; free critical thinkers, not easily brainwashed dolts; creative thinkers, not rote assembly line workers; and actively engaged members of a political community, not apathetic, apolitical zombies. I believe that schools can create empathetic and responsible critical thinkers who are also productive adults—in short, the kinds of people who meet the needs of all of society, not just those of employers.*
>
> —**D. BROWN** (2006, 779)

We have had the honor of working with many middle level teachers whose practice reflects a student-centered philosophy and honors the developmental capabilities of young adolescents. Their teaching is based on their belief, backed by research, that using curriculum integration in a democratic environment is the most powerful way to engage young adolescents. These teachers become facilitators of learning, involve students in decision making, and use student-determined assessment practices that lead to meaningful learning and growth. Here are some of their stories.

◆❙❙ What Teachers Say About Using Integrated Curriculum

In Chapter 9, Scott Clark described how his thinking about his role as a teacher changed as a result of involving students in the planning and implementation of the curriculum in his classroom. In later conversations, he mentioned that curriculum integration particularly helped those students who were disconnected from their schooling experiences. When he first informed students that he wanted to know the questions they had about themselves and the world, heads popped up off desks and students became involved in their learning—some for the first time.

Two weeks into studying their first theme of prejudice, one group of students told Mr. Clark that the problem of prejudice wouldn't be solved unless the elementary students were taught about the problem. So, they developed a lesson plan, contacted the elementary principals, arranged transportation, and taught their lesson on prejudice to kindergartners and first graders. After that experience, they wrote an article describing their project.

These students had not engaged in thoughtful learning until they were given a voice in what they were going to learn and how they would learn it. Mr. Clark demonstrated what can happen when one person on a team decides that he or she wants to change the learning environment in the classroom by negotiating curriculum with students.

You will meet six other teachers who have embraced the idea of democratic classrooms and curriculum integration. They are ordinary public school teachers, made extraordinary by the belief that students have a right to have a voice in their education, to be at the center of making decisions about what they learn, how they learn, and how they determine that they have learned.

◆❙❙ A Middle Level Curriculum Integration Experience: The Alpha Team

The Alpha team at Shelburne Community School in Shelburne, Vermont is a multi-age (sixth- through eighth-grade classroom) student-directed team that has been implementing best practices in middle level education for over thirty-five years.

The Alpha team did not begin because a principal, superintendent, or school board demanded that a group of teachers implement this kind of learning with students. It began because one teacher had a vision of how students learn. She believed in the fundamental idea of a democratic classroom, that students learn more and better when invested in their own work, that students have a right to have a voice in their own education.

A TEACHER'S PERSPECTIVE: MEGHAN O'DONNELL ON HONORING STUDENT VOICE WHILE BUILDING CURRICULUM, ADDRESSING STANDARDS, DESIGNING INSTRUCTION, AND ASSESSING STUDENT GROWTH

Meghan O'Donnell, a National Board–certified teacher, has been a middle level educator for twenty years and a member of the Alpha team for fifteen.

I have had the good fortune of being a middle level educator in Vermont for almost twenty years. For the past fifteen years, I've been a member of the Alpha team in Shelburne, Vermont. Alpha has kept one component at its core regardless of grade groups and size: *student voice*. Honoring student voice is the heart of the Alpha program. It is at the center of all aspects of our program and is the reason for our continued success. This is no small feat in a time when educators are constantly required to conform and restructure their schools and practice based on legislation that emphasizes improved test score results and increased teacher licensing qualifications.

To explore ideas and problems collaboratively with students; to see them assume responsibility for their work, for their peers, for their communities large and small; and to witness their ownership of their learning are all testaments for why curriculum integration works and is an essential practice for middle level education. While the idea appears simple, providing students with this much responsibility for their learning is not easy. I hope organizing my thoughts around the triangle of curriculum development (curriculum, instruction, and assessment) may help shed some light on why I feel this practice works and is so vital to student success.

Developing Curriculum Based on Students' Interests

Our team is made up of three teachers who teach approximately 65 sixth-, seventh-, and eighth-grade students in multi-age groupings for a three-year cycle. In this setting, we intentionally develop curriculum collaboratively with students. At the beginning of each year, we invite our students to create questions about themselves and their world. We model for students what makes a good question so that students spend time considering deep, meaningful questions that are not simply answered with a yes or a no. Each night, students are responsible for developing one set of ten questions: ten about themselves the first night and ten about their world the next night.

Following this homework, students are organized into multi-age, mixed-gender groups to share their questions and identify eight to ten common questions. Following the small-group work, the class meets as a team, and each group presents their common questions. Students begin to see threads of commonality between their "self" and "world" questions.

The students sort the questions around big common ideas, and, together, we create our themes for the year. Students work in small groups to create interesting titles and discuss how they would demonstrate their learning for each theme in some kind of culminating event. Working backward, we and the students plan and organize activities, gather resources, fine-tune the questions, and, finally, coordinate each theme with the year's calendar, taking into account duration, time of year, and resource availability. This entire process consumes the first three or four weeks of the school year.

By inviting students to think about questions they have about themselves and their world, we create an environment that instantly engages kids. We create a dynamic of collaboration and mutual respect among students and with teachers. The Alpha process eliminates the us/them dichotomy that can easily develop between teachers and students in traditional classrooms. As a result, as teachers, we rarely have to respond to "Why do we have to do this?" This student decision making certainly helps with student participation and classroom management. I'm not saying we have perfect angels in our classrooms; we have our share of behavior and motivation challenges. But they are on a smaller scale and occur less often because of the nature and organization of student decision making on our team.

By inviting students to think about questions they have about themselves and their world, we create an environment that instantly engages kids.

Successfully Addressing Standards Within a Student-Designed Curriculum

The challenge we have as teachers each year is answering two questions:

1. How do we reconcile content standards and performance expectations with the students' chosen questions about self and world?

2. How do we do curriculum integration and still hold our students accountable for learning content-specific standards and prepare them for success on standardized tests?

To address the standards, we outline the broad content standards we are accountable for teaching in our three-year cycle. There is a balance in each year of science and social studies standards. Literacy content standards are woven throughout all the student-chosen themes.

Asking students questions about self and world first in our process honors their thoughts, ideas, questions, and concerns and makes the subject matter instantly relevant. By intentionally introducing the standards later in the process, students see that there is an inherent connection between what they want to know and what they are expected to learn. It is validating for them and for us. Students' questions are fresh and current, inviting new perspectives to standards that reflect current issues, concerns, and events.

What I find equally compelling is the universality and depth of student questions. Modeling this process with students from inner-city Philadelphia to rural Vermont shows that students' questions mirror large social issues and concerns regardless of background, ethnicity, and socioeconomic status. Students have a lot on their minds: poverty, health care, natural resources, the environment, war/conflict, religions, technology, earth, the universe, economics, life cycles. Clearly, there is rich content here that has meaning for all members of the learning community.

As educators, we feel an obligation and responsibility to teach what the state mandates and standardized tests evaluate. We have been addressing this balance on Alpha for years, and our students achieve well on tests. Our students' results on standardized tests are comparable to or better than their peers from more traditional settings. Most important, our students are well prepared for high school and beyond. They are active thinkers who ask meaningful questions about their learning.

Providing Meaningful and Differentiated Instruction
Within Student-Designed Curriculum

Curriculum integration inherently creates a differentiated learning classroom. Inviting students to design and implement curriculum they helped create addresses various student learning styles from the start. We have the flexibility to organize students in many different groupings, and we work to vary these groupings often—another aspect of a differentiated classroom. Our roles as teacher are also varied.

A common misconception often associated with student-centered classrooms is that "teacher-as-facilitator" means we don't ever deliver curriculum. Because we move from theme to theme, our roles as teachers change accordingly. At times we act as facilitator, coach, or manager. But we also act as leaders and can deliver an aspect of curriculum in a more traditional manner when we believe that is needed. This theme variation affects students' roles as well. At times, they are expected to be more independent; at other times, more collaborative with their peers; and often, a participant in the classroom with the teacher.

Assessing in a Meaningful Way

Three times a year our students put together a portfolio that is organized around Alpha's five vital results:

- communication
- functioning independently
- reasoning and problem solving
- personal development
- civic and social responsibility

For the first trimester, students collect their work from all aspects of their learning [on the team, in Unified Arts (music, physical education, art), and outside school] and then sort that work as evidence of how they have met these vital results. For example, a piece of writing might be evidence of communication, functioning independently, or personal development. Students decide which category their pieces fit into. They receive guidance from their peers and teachers on how to best categorize their work.

During conferences in November, students present their portfolio to their parents. Students identify areas of success and challenge from the trimester's work, and together with their teacher and their parents set goals for the next trimester based on evident challenges. The process for the March portfolio conference is the same, except that students match their "vital results" with the goals set from the November conference. Students complete a portfolio for the end of the year that goes home with them over the summer.

It would take an entire book to explain the benefits and empowerment that the portfolio process brings to students. Student self-assessment is an invaluable part of our program, in tandem with our curriculum development. The portfolio provides a safe, organized, and manageable vehicle for new sixth graders and advanced eighth graders to speak openly and honestly about their work. Early in the year they see failures or challenges as opportunities for new learning. They see for themselves, with hard evidence from their trimester's work, where they were successful and can identify what they did specifically to create that success. This self-assessment has far more impact on who they are as learners than a letter grade or a percentage score. Our reporting process includes student and teacher narratives on students' successes and challenges in each vital result area. This, with local and standard assessment results, provides the assessment profile for each student. Alpha students speak differently about how they learn. The differences in their learning from their previous experiences are noticeable, and they are the greatest advocates for themselves and this process because they speak genuinely, articulately, and openly about learning.

A TEACHER'S PERSPECTIVE: CYNTHIA MYERS SHARES STUDENTS' AND PARENTS' COMMENTS ON INTEGRATED CURRICULUM

Cynthia Myers was with the Alpha team for over a dozen years. She shares her thoughts on why Alpha has been so successful, focusing particularly on the importance of the relationships that can be built when teachers and students work together and honor one another.

The Alpha program fosters best practice for optimum learning for all. The curriculum is student centered, is connected to real-world experiences, is a testing ground for new ideas and technologies, and models and helps students build skills needed for a democratic society while maintaining high academic standards.

Students Describe the Benefits of Integrated Curriculum

One former Alpha student wrote in his college application:

> As Robert Fulgham said, "All I Ever Needed to Know I Learned in Kindergarten." But I must have been a late bloomer because everything I know I learned in Alpha. The relationship between teachers and students is unique. The students refer to themselves as family, and there is a strong sense of community. In Alpha, I learned to evaluate my work and myself and then set personal and academic goals. I also learned to lead groups of students, big and small. Alpha stressed the importance of community, responsibility, and leadership. The Alpha experience taught me principles I use every day in high school. My abilities to self-assess, lead others, and set priorities, while maintaining balance, have been instrumental to my success.

The teaching of young adolescents brings great joy and rewards. They have taught me to be a leader, a mentor, a friend, and sometimes an expert. I have also learned that each child is fragile and filled with self-doubt and wants to be valued and respected. I have found that when I have a personal relationship with a student, it leads to them wanting to do well and feeling comfortable to take risks. One seventh-grade girl commented,

I remember in sixth grade how nervous and small I felt. I was placed in your theme group, "Evolution." I also remember how kind and encouraging you were and how great it felt to come into that classroom every day. I have many more memories like this, and in all of them you remained caring and helpful. When I think of school I think of your warm smile and great attitude. You understand that different people work at different paces and incorporate it into the way we learn. You also understand we have lots of stuff going on outside of school and you help us manage our time.

An eighth grader who was on an Individualized Educational Plan described her experiences on the team camping trip. "When we got to the campsite, it was like we were a family laughing and working hard to get a job done. We did everything that a family would do. We slept and ate together. It is something I can't fully explain, it's just there in my heart and in my eyes."

Parents' Reactions to Integrated Curriculum

Building strong relationships with parents is key to supporting student success. We encourage parent involvement and have designed many vehicles to encourage open communication. This helps foster understanding and build trust. We know that many Alpha parents feel pressure from other parents who wonder how Alpha students are prepared for high school and grading. Parents can be and are some of our strongest advocates. The support carries on with some even after their child leaves the school. They also give us feedback to help us make the program better.

Here are some comments by parents of Alpha students:

"High school teachers can pick out the Alpha students because they are organized and ask good questions to help with their learning. They approach learning differently."

"My son knows how to look at his work and find both his strengths and areas he needs to improve."

"They don't work for a grade so their learning goes beyond normal expectations."

Holly Pasackow's three children were on the Alpha team for a total of nine years. She shares her reflections:

I have had the good fortune to have my third child "graduate" from the eighth grade at Shelburne Community School. Over the past sixteen years my children have been sprinkled throughout the educational system. I have spent a lot of time, energy, joy, and heartbreak in the halls of our schools. Nine of those years have been spent with a child on Alpha. Amazing. Awesome. Incredible.

(continues)

(continued)

On Alpha, my family has seen three teachers come and go, one to reassignment to a lower grade, one to retirement, and the third to another district. We have worked with numerous paraprofessionals and student interns, all who have added to the history of Alpha. We have been there with many dedicated families who believed in their children, and in our children, and in Alpha. We have been one of the fortunate families who have been a part of something bigger than middle school and bigger than public school. These incredible teachers, students, and families believe in community, and they have been willing to be the village that collectively raised all the children on Alpha. Imagine taking on the responsibility of raising sixty adolescents, year after year.

Alpha is big, much bigger than just a middle level team at Shelburne Community School. Alpha is bigger than its dedicated professionals and paraprofessionals, past and present. Alpha is about the students, their families, and their community, from yesterday, today, and into tomorrow. I am proud and privileged to have been a part of Alpha over the years, and so pleased and relieved to know my fourth child will have the opportunity to be a part of something so big.

Meeting Students' Developmental Needs with Integrated Curriculum: The Power of Caring Relationships

Working with ten- to fourteen-year-olds has taught me that small acts of personal interaction are so important. We who choose to work with middle school students have a chance to make a difference when children are struggling with who they are as a learner and a person trying to build a life without regret. I cherish the special relationship with students. It is teacher–student, yes, but also something very close to friendship. Their trust is inspiring. A former Alpha student writes,

---

During sixth period, you sat down with me and Morgan to talk about the book we were reading, *Monster*. I know I had work to do, and I'm sure you did too, but you took the time to just talk. We assumed the boy was innocent, and you showed us some parts in the book that made us question that. This is exactly what you gave to me: the ability to question and be bold. I thank you for your never-failing ability to be my friend, not just my teacher.

> The profession of teaching is complex and challenging. We have a huge responsibility as the cognitive and emotional link to the hearts and minds of emerging adolescents.

The profession of teaching is complex and challenging. We have a huge responsibility as the cognitive and emotional link to the hearts and minds of emerging adolescents.

Our greatest rewards are intrinsic: watching the spark of light in her eyes when a student discovers the world of ideas and learning. There is great joy that cannot be measured but must be seen or felt. The payoff is that by nourishing young minds and spirits we, as teachers, reap the rewards of doing something that is meaningful and fulfilling. An eighth grader sums up his feelings about Alpha this way:

> I don't think I would be the same if I hadn't been on Alpha. I came here a young kid, and I am leaving a capable young adult who feels he was offered all the opportunities in the world, because of what Alpha gave to him.

An eighth-grade female shared these feelings:

> Throughout all of the three years I've been on Alpha, I have never wanted to leave. I liked where and who I was. All good things must come to an end. It is time for me to go. I will always have a place for Alpha in my heart and it will keep growing. Even though I may not physically be in Alpha, I can carry my leadership, communication, and skills wherever I go.

Nothing is more special than spending three years in a young person's life watching him or her grow from a shy sixth grader into a responsible adolescent ready to take on life's challenges.

◆❚❙ An Eighth-Grade Curriculum Integration Experience: Soundings

Mark Springer initiated and taught in curriculum integration programs in southeast Pennsylvania for approximately thirty years.

In 1998, Mark implemented a fully student-designed curriculum with eighth graders called *Soundings*. Mark describes the reason for choosing the name:

> The word soundings connotes probing and measuring depth, and the Soundings program encourages students to explore the topics they study deeply. The name also refers to the sounds of students who have a voice in their own education and opportunities to share their learning with their community. Finally, just as whales sound for fresh air, students and teachers in this program are revitalized and refreshed as they experience the benefits of the program's self-directed, integrated curriculum. (D. Brown 2002a, 54)

As in the Alpha program in Vermont, in the Soundings program these eighth graders determine the curriculum based on their questions about themselves and the world.

TEACHER PERSPECTIVE: MARK SPRINGER ON CREATING AN INTEGRATED CURRICULUM PROGRAM

Every middle school teacher should know that there are viable alternatives to the conventional curricular formats used in most schools serving young adolescents. What's more, some of these alternatives can better serve our students because they more closely fulfill characteristics that research has shown improve learning.

Curriculum integration (CI) is purposefully designed around the needs of young adolescents, and it uses their questions as the essential organizing principle driving curricular content and pedagogy. As a result, CI empowers students to take charge of their learning, which, in turn, provides students with both the vested interest and a meaningful context for learning. Because they have asked the questions important to them, the students want to discuss possible answers; this enables students to approach required skills and standards as means to that self-determined goal. In addition, this approach establishes and reinforces the validity of the students' questions and concerns, thus giving them confidence in their cognitive abilities and a willingness to push themselves even further.

Having witnessed amazing growth of young adolescents who experienced curriculum integration practices, I believe success stems in part from the atmosphere promoted by CI. By definition, the CI learning community is a truly democratic one and supportive of each individual—a claim that most traditional, teacher-directed classrooms cannot make. Students empowered to determine their curriculum start to see themselves in a different light from those in conventional curricula. These young adolescents see themselves in a working partnership with their mentor-teachers and with each other. They are being invited to share in the decision-making process, rather than being told what to do. Schools often talk about democracy, but they tend to be the least democratic institutions in our nation. Every middle school teacher should know that there are ways to put democratic ideals into practice. Curriculum integration is not easy; neither is democracy. The two go hand in hand, however, and I would argue that the future of democracy in America may well be decided in our public schools over the next few decades.

You can read more about Mark Springer's program in his book Soundings: A Democratic Student-Centered Education, *published by the Association for Middle Level Education in 2006.*

TEACHER PERSPECTIVE: DAVE MERCURIO ON EMBRACING CURRICULUM INTEGRATION AS A VETERAN TEACHER

Dave Mercurio currently team-teaches in the Soundings program with Danielle Bajus, continuing Mark Springer's legacy. Here, he explains his journey from traditional instruction to curriculum integration.

As a college undergraduate studying how to become an educator, I was introduced to some of the best teaching practices that master teachers employed. As I was given my student-teaching assignment, I was ready to employ these best practices with my soon-to-be students. I quickly realized that all those best practices we were introduced to as undergrads were not so easy to utilize in the classroom, as there are books that must be read, a curriculum that must be followed, and limitations as to what can and cannot be accomplished during a forty-five minute period. Unfortunately, the real-world classroom is much different than the one we hear about as undergraduates.

Almost ten years into my teaching career, I was partnered with Mark Springer, the creator of the Soundings program. Mark trained me to rethink my view of education, specifically at the middle level. What role should grades play? How important is a standard curriculum? What role should the students play in their own education? What role should the teacher play? How can we get kids interested in what they are learning in school? What are the most important skills that kids could come away with at the end of a year? What were those best practices that I had heard about as an undergraduate? These were the questions for which I needed answers. Some answers came quickly; others, not so much. However, at the end of my first year teaching in the Soundings program, I came to believe that this model is what is truly best for kids.

The program puts the emphasis on the student, not the teacher. As teachers in Soundings, we truly become facilitators, not givers of knowledge. The students are given choice, true choice, on what they want to learn. Therefore, they are engaged in their own learning. With the elimination of grades, students are able to focus on the quality of their work and don't have to compare themselves to the rest of the class. They are able to genuinely push themselves to produce quality work on a consistent basis. Our students are not required to memorize random facts for a test, and then forget those same facts they "learned" thirty minutes later.

Ultimately, what I believe we all, as educators, want from our students is that they be better managers of time, be productive members of small and large groups, have the ability to speak in front of their peers, be able to advocate for themselves, be self-motivated, be active and engaged in their own learning, be able to make connections across disciplines, and be thinkers. Soundings does all of this, by providing the students with a voice in what they want to learn, a framework for them to be invested in their own education, and the opportunity to motivate themselves to be successful.

What we see from our students, at the end of the year, is major growth in all areas. That growth is different for each student—which it should be. As we know, not all students are the same, which then begs the question, "Why does the traditional setting force students to do all the same assignments and evaluate them on the same scale?" There was a time that I thought that was the way education should be. How wrong I was.

Our students learn that they are the most important part of their own education, not the teacher. They need to take an active role in their learning if they are going to get the most out of it. The Soundings program empowers students and allows them to become risk-takers. The students do not need to be fearful of digging themselves a hole they cannot dig out of because they "failed" an assignment. With the stress/pressure of grades removed, the students focus on what is important, the quality of their work, and being proud of what they produced—not whether the teacher gave them an "A."

This model can work for anyone, anywhere, in any district, at any level. It might not look exactly like Soundings but for those willing to allow the students to have choice in what they learn, to let go of the traditional evaluation system and limiting model of grades, and to become facilitators rather than givers of knowledge, it can and will work—of that, I am certain.

TEACHER PERSPECTIVE: DANIELLE BAJUS ON FINDING NEW ENERGY AS A TEACHER THROUGH CURRICULUM INTEGRATION

Danielle's educational experience before joining the Soundings program was diverse: She student-taught overseas, worked for an experiential education nonprofit organization, and taught elementary school. She now has a permanent position co-teaching with Dave Mercurio in the Soundings program that Mark Springer established.

The experience I gained in the traditional setting was invaluable. Over time, however, I grew frustrated with the realization of the increasing focus on "teaching to the test." Ultimately, with students being categorized by data points, the fire I once had inside for the philosophy of good teaching and learning practices began to fade. I was disheartened. Yes, I took a statistics class in college, and data, when used in a meaningful way, can be helpful—but this was overkill. Deep down, I knew it was time to make a change.

I found out about an opening as a long-term substitute in the Soundings program. I chose to leave my position teaching fifth grade to join this one of a kind program. Most people, including my new teaching partner and principal, repeatedly questioned my sanity in giving up the security of a teaching contract in a fantastic school district for a temporary position as a long-term substitute for one year. To me, learning how to co-teach in a democratic classroom setting with curriculum integration, even if only for a year, was too good of an opportunity to pass up—so I took it.

This transition reignited my passion for teaching and learning, and also restored my faith in the public school system. Dave and I spend three periods per day with the same forty students. We become a close-knit learning community, which provides each Soundings group with a "home base," a "school family" of sorts, and a safe place to be—or better yet, become—themselves during an often-difficult stage of development.

Students develop an individual and collective love of the process of learning through "real-life" experiences, and as a result they are more than prepared for ninth grade—they are ready to take on the real world. All of the components of the program help them develop a stronger sense of self.

As an educator, the workload, energy, and time spent are extraordinary, but so are the results. Due to the fact that we spend a large part of each day with our Soundings crew, we get to know each and every one of our students well. Therefore, we are able to meet their individual learning needs. Both students and teachers become highly invested in the learning process, and the time and energy feels well spent. It is a different kind of exhaustion that I feel after each day, not the overwhelmed, stressed out, disempowered feeling I often had in years past. Integrating the curriculum and allowing middle school students to take more ownership over their learning benefits both teachers and students. Young adolescents need time and many "real-life" opportunities to practice skills in order to master them, and Soundings' integrated curriculum creates the space and time for them to do so.

◆‖ A Small-Scale Curriculum Integration Experience: Gert Nesin's Class

Gert Nesin embraced the curriculum integration model in 1992 while teaching in a small, rural, traditional school in Maine. Throughout her years as a middle school teacher, she and her teaching partner have created democratic classrooms that include collaboratively planning curriculum with students. She has also taught at the University of Maine where she used that model in creating curriculum with her college students.

TEACHER PERSPECTIVE: GERT NESIN ON STARTING IN "OUR OWN LITTLE CORNER"

When I started teaching, I made all the decisions about teaching and learning without significant input from students. It was how I was taught through school and college, and I never knew there was or should be any alternative. My students and I were mostly successful because of the caring relationships we developed. I chose to start including students in the process of learning when I took a class, based on John Dewey's Experience and Education (1938), that opened my eyes to the idea that students could learn better and more when content started with their experiences, interests, and concerns. I tried it that school year with one group of students, and it really worked! It was reinforced the following summer when I watched James Beane and Barb Brodhagen plan curriculum with students in Maine. At that point, I began to connect with a network of educators who believe in the value and dignity of all students in the learning process and in society. Since then, I have never considered returning to teacher-centered education.

Standards never disappear in my college or middle school classrooms. At the beginning of our time together, I make sure students understand that there is required content, which we spend time looking at and defining. As we plan learning, we carefully include knowledge and process standards on which we will focus. Those standards become the substance that helps them answer their questions rather than be an end in themselves.

College students and young adolescents respond similarly to collaboratively achieving common learning goals. At first they are hesitant to believe that they truly do have significant input into the content and direction of their own education. They look for manipulation, unstated expectations, and hoops. When students finally figure out that no hidden agenda exists, they relax and get down to the business and fun of learning together. Some students, usually the individuals who have been successful in more traditional classrooms, hold on to their skepticism further into the school year.

After a year of integrative curriculum, most of my students have changed in significant ways. Probably more important than any other outcome I've observed is that students think they matter, both personally and as part of a learning community. Their ideas, concerns, and talents are valued and they are supported in their challenges. Every student becomes part of the community, with all of his or her abilities and disabilities.

I have also seen many other important changes. The students become expert in how they learn. They become skilled at the process of making decisions that work for individuals while also considering and meeting the needs of diverse group members. They learn content in depth, and they learn how to apply it in important ways. They figure out how they can make a difference in their classrooms, schools, communities, and the world. They become effective researchers—finding, evaluating, understanding, and synthesizing a variety of primary and secondary resources and reaching logical conclusions. They find confidence in who they are and their abilities and contributions. Given significant choice and input, they take responsibility for their learning and behavior. These changes are especially pronounced for students who usually flounder in school, academically and/or behaviorally.

Students overwhelmingly approve of integrative curriculum. Some of my seventh-grade students anonymously responded to the question, "What are the benefits of being in this class?" in the following ways:

> "I learned to think about what I am going to do when I get older and choices I have."
>
> "We learned to be more independent."
>
> "I've become more responsible, and I've learned how to get involved in activities and stay committed to them."
>
> "I've gained more knowledge about different topics in my class than I probably would in any other. Our program is more 'advanced' than other classes."
>
> "I think I do my homework more, and school is more interesting."

As a teacher, I find benefits that improve my teaching and me as a person. Teaching becomes a process of solving problems with students rather than dispensing knowledge to them. We're all in it together, and I mostly get to enjoy them and their learning rather than finding a way to force them to do what I perceive as best for them. I

Working with students to develop meaningful relationships and learning experiences gives me hope that we can create a better world, starting with our little corner.

am absolved of the sole responsibility of being the one who creates interesting and engaging learning activities, since the students share that responsibility. I help students build relationships with one another, me, other adults, and the larger community. For me, I have felt most privileged to watch students who think little of themselves and their abilities realize that they are competent and valuable. Working with students to develop meaningful relationships and learning experiences gives me hope that we can create a better world, starting with our little corner.

The Alpha teams, the students in the *Soundings* program, and Gert Nesin's two-person team are different classrooms with different structures, yet the philosophy underlying all of them is the same. They are all based on the belief that the most effective and powerful learning occurs in a democratic classroom in which all involved are given a voice. These classrooms are designed around the philosophy and belief that students have a right to a voice in their learning and that teachers have an obligation to honor that right by listening to what students have to say.

In these classrooms, significant learning is occurring and students are performing well on high-stakes tests. But more importantly, these students are attaining meaningful learning, using thinking processes daily, and living by democratic values that will carry them through life. In interviews, several former *Soundings* students from three separate years noted that by participating in curriculum integration, they made significant growth in their creative and critical thinking, decision-making, and problem-solving abilities (D. Brown 2011; Brown and Morgan 2003). They also believed that their oral communication skills and ability to work well with others developed better in *Soundings* than they would have in a traditional classroom.

Some teachers may be concerned that students won't ask sophisticated enough questions to warrant studying them, but every class we've surveyed has developed complex and often abstract themes to study—from stem cell research to questions on the nature of violence. Traditional middle level classes don't generally have an opportunity to delve deeply into such time-sensitive, meaningful, and theoretical principles.

Many teachers might be reluctant to consider using curriculum integration without a definitive response on its impact on students' test scores—particularly if their own evaluations are dependent on students performing well on tests. Evaluations of educators that currently teach in these programs will also be partially based on students' test scores. Their principals tracked their students' test scores throughout twelve years of NCLB, with no demands to cease their curriculum integration classes. Parents saw their children's test scores, and would have had every opportunity to warn other parents of the disastrous effects of CI classes on their students' test scores—yet none of these events has occurred, and these programs are flourishing.

Test data indicate that these students, who have a wide range of academic abilities, have done as well as, and often better than, students from traditional classrooms in both their high school grade point averages and on standardized tests (D. Brown 2011; Springer 2006, 2013; Vars 1997). Springer (2013) noted the immeasurable growth items, which should have a greater impact on their lives than their middle school test scores:

> These include self-motivation and enhanced self-confidence, improved attitudes toward learning in general and toward specific skills such as reading and writing, increased retention of information, and improved abilities to analyze and apply information. Also noted by researchers, teachers, and the students themselves are improved social abilities, such as cooperation skills and heightened tolerance for differences, and the ability to make responsible decisions. (211)

If you're nervous about students' test scores, it's imperative to understand, as we mentioned in Chapter 9, that these teachers purposely interweave state content standards into the topics students choose, and if student-chosen curricula don't match content standards, teachers use direct instruction to reach those principles (Springer 2006). Introductions of any new set of standards for the 21st century can be similarly managed. Curriculum integration teachers are apt to say that fear of CI students' test scores is "much ado about nothing," especially considering the thinking processes and social skills that students gain as a result of participating in curriculum integration.

Two Soundings students who were in their junior year of high school provided their thoughts on transitioning to high school:

> I remember thinking how ridiculous that people would think that Soundings wouldn't prepare you for high school. I think Soundings prepared me better for high school than regular classes would have. I was bored in regular classes in ninth grade—I mean, did someone think the information we're learning this way [teacher directed] was supposed to stick?

> I may have been better prepared because of writing and research skills. Soundings also helped me to be self-motivated—something you need in high school. (Brown and Morgan 2003, 27)

Two students from the 2013–14 Soundings class had this to say:

Honestly, I don't know where I would be without the Soundings program. This style of learning has helped me in so many ways. I have improved the overall quality of my writing. Also, I have enhanced my public speaking skills drastically. I believe that teachers should understand that it's not all about giving worksheets, and testing them to see what they know. You can't just grade students with a percent or letter. I believe teachers around the globe should incorporate some of the things we do in Soundings.

—*Eddie, eighth grader*

Another thing I feel is important is failure. Most teachers disparage failure, but it's always important to learn from your mistakes. Soundings is a place where we find things out for ourselves or dig for our own answers. It's impossible to make everything flawless, but that's the best part: Impasses and blunders are crucial to education, and are just like real life.

—*Katie*

◆❚❚ Concluding Reflections

Middle level educators can play a large role in helping students know themselves as learners and as people. Teachers can make all the excuses they can think of for not implementing these kinds of student-directed learning experiences. The truth is, *you* can make your classroom more democratic, and *you* can give students a voice in how the classroom is structured. You just need to use your courage and your willingness to take risks as a professional educator and begin.

CHAPTER 11

This Is Learning:

Making Instruction

Meaningful

What every middle school teacher should know about middle school students is that there are only a handful of kids who come to school actually ready and willing to listen. So the more interactive and light-hearted the lessons are, the more kids likely will listen.

—**MARY**, EIGHTH GRADE

When one approach doesn't work, you don't give up! You've got to go back into that bag and keep pulling out different approaches until the children learn.

—**MARIA**, FIFTH-GRADE TEACHER

Eighth-grader Julia's remarks reflect the need for responsive teaching in middle level schools:

All middle school teachers should be open to feedback and questions. Teachers should be able to explain things in different ways. Just because half the class gets it doesn't mean the other half does. Also, you have to be interested in your own material. Lastly, try to make your class interesting and engaging.

Another student, Glenn, offered, "I would tell teachers to focus their class on the students and less on just giving knowledge. If the class is interesting to the students, they will take in more information. Having this interest will lead to a more focused and productive environment."

Whether you design curriculum and activities collaboratively with students, develop instruction as part of a team, or teach a separate content area, the lessons you plan and the learning experiences you choose will have an impact on whether meaningful learning will occur.

In their position paper, *This We Believe* (2010), the Association for Middle Level Education (AMLE) states "Successful middle grades schools are characterized by the active engagement of students and teachers. It could not be otherwise, for everything that is known about the nature of young adolescents and the principles of learning points to the reality that the most successful learning strategies are ones that involve each student personally" (p. 16). AMLE authors suggest, "Teaching approaches should capitalize on the skills, abilities, and prior knowledge of young adolescents; use multiple intelligences; involve students' individual learning styles; and recognize the need for regular physical movement."

Instructional practices in middle level schools should focus on what we know about the learning needs of young adolescents and their varied cognitive developmental processes, along with what we know about how learning occurs. Although high expectations are set for all students, Jackson and Davis (2000) stated that "uniformly high expectations should not lead to uniformity in instructional practices: teachers need a broad range of approaches to enable students in a heterogeneous classroom to excel" (175). Student success should be a guiding principle for how teachers choose to design instruction.

TIME FOR REFLECTION

- *What is learning?*
- *How does learning occur?*
- *How is learning out of school different from learning in school?*
- *What specific characteristics of young adolescents might affect their ability to learn? How?*

◆❚ How Learning Occurs

Research on cognition and how the young adolescent brain develops impact our understanding about how learning occurs and the teacher's role in the learning process in a middle level classroom (Sousa 2011; 2010; Walsh 2004). In addition, understanding how we construct knowledge and the role that socialization plays in that construction helps teachers make better curricular and instructional decisions in the context of young adolescent development.

TAKING ADVANTAGE OF NEUROSCIENCE TO PROMOTE LEARNING

When we design our instruction based on neuroscience, it is more likely that meaningful learning will occur. Learning is not only a cognitive process but also involves physical, emotional, and social factors (Sousa 2011; Willis 2010; Jensen 1998; Caine and Caine 1994).

Sousa (2011) offers the following questionnaire for educators to assess their use of brain-compatible strategies (adapted from 12):

1. To what degree do you adapt the curriculum to recognize and coincide with the windows of opportunity of cognitive growth that students have at their ages?

Because of the hypergrowth of dendrites in the brain during young adolescence, more connections can be made between concepts and principles being studied. Young adolescents need cognitively active learning experiences in which they are intellectually engaged and challenged by the content they are receiving.

2. To what degree do you provoke strong, positive emotions in students during the learning process?

Adolescents' cognitive processing is often more regulated by the amygdala or the emotional center of the brain than the prefrontal cortex or reasoning center. When students are stressed, there are negative impacts on their learning; but the opposite emotion is joy, and teachers can display that emotion in school by demonstrating their enthusiasm and excitement about learning, by using humor, and smiling often. J. Willis (2010) reported that students who experienced happy faces during simple recall assessments performed better than those who viewed grumpy faces. Hardiman (2010) summarized, "Reducing stress and establishing a positive emotional climate in the classroom is arguably the most essential component of teaching" (236).

3. To what degree do you help students adjust their self-concept to be more successful in learning situations?

Brinthaupt (2013) described the self-perception challenges that young adolescents experience. Greater academic expectations, more competition and comparisons among students, and socialization challenges create low self-esteem for many middle level students. Teachers can positively affect students' perceptions of academic ability by helping them establish personal learning goals, recognizing students' academic efforts rather than merely products, providing constructive feedback on completed assignments, and assigning work that matches students' cognitive developmental levels. *Realistic*, not just *high* expectations ensure that students receive academic tasks that they are capable of understanding yet still lead to growth.

4. To what degree do you provide an enriched and varied learning environment?

Sousa (2011) suggests that enriched learning occurs when teachers use novelty in lessons by using movement, multisensory instructional activities, and music in classrooms when appropriate (38). Designing constructivist classrooms also provides a rich environment. We discuss constructivist classrooms in-depth below.

5. To what degree do you search for opportunities to integrate curriculum concepts between and among subject areas, and ensure that these concepts are relevant to students' lives?

We described curriculum integration (CI) in Chapter 9 as a way to design curriculum that provides relevance to students' lives. Springer (2013) offers the following advantages of CI for student learning:

Tackling significant social concerns raised by the students offers opportunities to apply content knowledge in significant ways, thus creating contexts and helping students construct meaning patterns they will retain. In addition, as Beane tells us, this same process enables students "to engage with the world in meaningful ways, heighten their sense of responsibility and encourage their growing sense of autonomy." (J. Beane 2007, 9) (Springer 2013, 209)

Even in classrooms that are not designed for pure curriculum integration, teachers can help students make the connections between and among content areas in ways that create much clearer understanding.

6. To what degree do you offer frequent opportunities during class for students to talk about what they are learning?

Research reveals that when students have opportunities to discuss the principles being studied they are more likely to remember the information and use it later when necessary (Roake and Varlas 2013). Surveys of adolescent learners reveal that many do not feel challenged while in school, with two-thirds of over 40,000 students surveyed noting that they enjoyed discussions in which there weren't clear answers (Sousa 2011). Eighty-two percent of that same surveyed group reported a desire to be creative while in school. Students who engage in discussions improve critical thinking processes as they listen and respond to comments made by classmates. Tim, an eighth grader, reveals how discussions affect his learning:

I think that every middle school teacher should be aware of the power of discussion. This is very helpful to students because they can hear what other students have to say and get ideas from them. They should know that kids learn more effectively in an open classroom meeting . . . you have the opportunity to explore and discuss.

Listening well is a key component to effective discussions. Modeling listening, paraphrasing, and "bounce" remarks help students learn to improve their conversation skills. When students bounce ideas from each other's comments, they demonstrate their listening and critical thinking skills. Effective teachers also spend less time talking during genuine discussions and more time listening so that students understand that it's their words that count—not the teacher's. Palmer (2014) suggests that by assigning roles to some students, there's a greater likelihood that all students will participate.

Researchers caution educators that brain research isn't always interpreted appropriately to become effective pedagogy. The neuroscience information available, however, is often applied to learning situations and confirmed as appropriate strategies for engaging learners and improving their academic successes. Using Sousa's questionnaire for engaging learners can help teachers develop appropriate pedagogical strategies for improving young adolescents' cognitive growth.

CONSTRUCTIVISM: A THEORY ABOUT LEARNING

We constantly construct knowledge and meaning throughout our lives as we are confronted with problems, new ideas, and new knowledge. A toddler learning how to stack blocks, a first grader learning the connection between letters and words, a fourth grader exploring maps, and a seventh grader examining the meaning of *prejudice* are all constructing knowledge about their world. It is evident from looking at the principles of neuroscience that in order to construct meaning, students must have opportunities to manipulate ideas and materials. Teachers can't make students construct knowledge—students do this naturally and without external prodding. Teachers can, however, establish an environment that promotes active learning by providing authentic hands-on and minds-on learning experiences within a social context. Michael, a seventh grader, told us, "You've got to learn by doing it. You can't learn about it by taking notes." An eighth grader concurred: "I think kids would learn a lot better if you do something hands-on."

Several significant differences exist between learning in a traditional classroom and learning in a classroom that models constructivist philosophy. A traditional classroom might be characterized by a focus on discrete, often unrelated skills. Teachers are viewed as dispensers of information and follow fixed curricula, guided by textbooks and curriculum guides. The emphasis in a constructivist classroom is on general principles and concepts. Teachers support learning by providing materials and ideas for students to manipulate, and facilitating personal and group reflections as students interact with the material. Teachers carefully introduce and embed needed skills as students engage in the process of exploration. Brooks and Brooks (1993) summarized the principle of constructivism this way: "We look not for what students can repeat, but for what they can generate, demonstrate, and exhibit" (16).

In designing constructivist classrooms, the important consideration is that students are not told what they should find, but are given the opportunity to make sense out of the information themselves. For example, students experiment with pendulums to determine what factors affect their rate of speed. They may analyze lists of words to determine spelling patterns, explore music to develop an understanding of a cultural era, and look for patterns in the survey data they collect. In addition to setting up the conditions for student exploration, teachers point students in the right direction, providing frequent feedback to ensure accurate understanding.

AMLE (2010) suggests that teachers go further:

Developmentally responsive middle grades educators take the concept of hands-on activities further by promoting what might be termed "hands-joined" activities, ones that teachers and students work together in developing. Such activities foster student ownership and lead to levels of understanding unlikely to be achieved when students are simply completing teacher-made assignments. (16)

When students are provided with opportunities to build their own understandings by interacting with the environment, their knowledge about topics is enhanced in a meaningful way. In addition, providing young adolescents with opportunities to construct their own knowledge enhances their movement from the concrete to formal operational thought processes (Santrock 2013).

FOSTERING GENUINE INTELLECTUAL GROWTH

Teachers should design lessons that offer more time for students to engage in problem solving, critical thinking, and creative thinking. Constructing new knowledge may mean asking questions of one another and tinkering with new ideas and manipulatives.

Traditional instructional practices often involve asking questions following an assigned reading. Many times only a few students respond, so just how many students are learning? What would happen if teachers let students ask the questions? Although students may not initially have the skills to ask the kinds of questions that reveal the central issues, with teacher guidance they eventually will. Wilhelm (2006) advised, "Students must be the ones asking the majority of the questions and doing the bulk of classroom talk" (10).

Until students are responsible for asking the questions they have about curriculum, teachers will never really know what students are curious about or what they misunderstand. Educators may present exciting lessons, but without genuinely knowing what questions students have, they waste instructional time and students' time.

One example of perceived student growth is the new vocabulary words in every content area. Teachers introduce a new set of words for a science unit, the next social studies chapter, or a novel for language arts. A common problem is that students never actually "own"—that is, understand—the words once the unit or chapter is completed. They hear them, may memorize a definition, even use the word correctly in a sentence, but they have no long-term memory of the word and are unlikely ever to use it. Beers (2003) described one teacher's realization that she was teaching too many words each week:

I never really expected that they'd [students] learn them to actually *use* them. It never bothered me that there were so many [words] because I always must have known deep down that they were only learning them for a test. (182)

Teachers must teach fewer new words with each lesson and provide many concrete experiences if they expect students to understand new concepts and principles associated with those new words. They must allow students to use these words in an authentic context. English language learners (ELLs) are particularly challenged by these incessant vocabulary lists, as teachers don't provide the context necessary for ELLs to comprehend new words.

Encouraging students to explain their thinking and erroneous beliefs about abstract principles also promotes cognitive growth. Asking students to keep journals in which they describe the confusion they experience in understanding new concepts and principles begins the process of deepening their metacognitive awareness—that is, their analysis of their own thinking. Students should also be asked to describe their level of attention to learning and their attitudes toward learning. These activities lead to real brain growth as opposed to temporarily raising test scores—in other words, learning that matters.

> Only in U.S. classrooms are individuals asked to find every answer, solve every problem, complete every task, and pass every test by relying solely on their own efforts and abilities.
> —**KLINE** (1995, 23)

◆❙❙ Collaborative Learning

Advice from neuroscientists, constructivist theory, and the needs of the young adolescent all point to the positive role that socialization can play in the learning process. Young adolescents will talk to each other in the halls, during class, during breaks, at lunch, and in the evenings. They're never more than a class period away from responding to each other's texts, staying in touch through electronic conversations when they aren't face-to-face. It should not be difficult then for teachers to get students talking in the classroom about their learning.

In school, students can learn to work collaboratively with others in developing questions, reaching consensus, solving problems, creating projects, and resolving disagreements. As Wolfe and Brandt (1998) suggested, "learning is enhanced when the environment provides [students] with the opportunity to discuss their thinking out loud, to bounce their ideas off of their peers, and to produce collaborative work" (11).

Never assume that students already know how to work collaboratively. Many students may have had cooperative learning experiences in elementary school, but often these past experiences resulted in failure and frustration. To ensure success at the middle level, ample time in the first few weeks of the school year should be devoted to helping students develop interpersonal strategies needed to progress successfully as a team. Dave Brown (2002a) described how teachers in one curriculum integration classroom encouraged students in their social development at the beginning of the year:

> During the first few weeks of school, students engage in several socialization and trust-building exercises. Cooperative games help build a community spirit. Success is defined by everyone's willingness to cooperate, to communicate clearly, and to be concerned about and react to the safety needs of others. These activities provide students with the social and emotional tools they need to engage in meaningful learning with one another. (55)

Pairing students together for short periods to work on small projects is one strategy for encouraging students to trust each other and develop productive working relationships. After students have engaged in collaborative activities, teachers should facilitate a discussion on the pitfalls and advantages students experience when working with others. Sharing concerns about the process of teamwork early in the year may help students more successfully navigate future team efforts.

Writing workshop (Davis and Hill 2003; Atwell 2002; Ray 2001) offers the opportunity for students to construct their own knowledge about writing while collaborating with others. Writing workshops feature opportunities for students to choose writing topics, hold student-to-student conferences, take part in peer revision and editing sessions, and have one-to-one conferences with the teacher.

Literature circles are another example of a collaborative activity (Daniels 2002). In a literature circle, four to six students read and discuss books that they choose based on their interests. Literature circles present opportunities for students to process information, create meaning from text, and use critical thinking skills.

Research-team investigations and group oral presentations are other examples of collaborative activities that lead to meaningful learning. Groups of students analyze primary or other source materials to generate ideas about an event, culture, or historical period. Information is interpreted from diverse and multiple points of view. Students then collaborate on the best way to present their understandings to the rest of the class.

The real value of social learning occurs when students share their questions about issues, offer alternative points of view, devise creative solutions to problems, and provide feedback to each other on the products of their learning. Young adolescents are also more likely to take the risks associated with learning new concepts and principles when they have opportunities to collaborate.

Many schools have infused technology into collaborative learning activities that were previously handled in face-to-face meetings. If students in a class have electronic access to a teacher's Moodle course, they can post ideas about an assignment and immediately those thoughts are shared with everyone in that class. One student described how his teacher's texting improved class discussions:

Before class, one of my high school teachers would text us a question that you had to answer in class. Sometimes you'd know the answer. Sometimes you wouldn't. So you'd talk to classmates to get their thoughts. There were big separations of groups in my school. These questions would break the separation. Because you don't usually talk to that one guy, but he may know the answer [sic]. By the time you show up for class, everybody has talked about everybody else's reading assignment. So it made us study as a group. It made us more of a community. (EL online 2011, 46)

It is not surprising that, when structured correctly, collaborative learning provides many benefits. Slavin (1991) described some of the advantages of collaborative learning:

- enhanced achievement
- improved self-esteem
- improved relationships among students of different races, genders, and abilities
- greater acceptance of students with special needs.

Collaborative learning is not a cop-out, a way for students to ignore their own academic growth by riding on the coattails of the work completed by more conscientious peers. The intent is for students to grow, which occurs when they have opportunities to speak to one another, sharing experiences, ideas, and solutions in their daily learning.

While we know that collaboration works, teachers must always be aware of the emotional needs and social issues of their students when grouping for instruction. As eighth grader, Bridget, says, "Group projects or work isn't always fun. Even if we can choose groups, keep in mind we don't always have friends in that class, leaving others left out." Teachers may think that it's a positive strategy for students to be grouped to do work. Bridget's reaction reminds us that sometimes it's not as easy as it looks to "find a friend to work with."

> To make teaching and learning work . . . teachers must develop an alternative approach to instructional planning beyond "covering the text" or "creating activities that students will like."
> **—TOMLINSON**
> (1999a, 14)

> The teacher is literally a designer who takes bigger ideas and fashions them into learning experiences so young adolescents can learn.
> **—BILODEAU-CALLAN**
> (quoted in Brazee and Capelluti 1994, 71)

◆❙❙ The Teacher's Role

No educator should ever use the phrase, "I covered that already, so they should know it." *Learning* and *covering* are indeed not the same in the context of what occurs in a classroom. An understanding of the learning process can help teachers make better decisions about what goes on in the classroom. And yet, often, after repeated hours of teacher planning, numerous homework assignments, and all that grading, we dare to ask, "Do you suppose students are really learning?" Effective teachers ask that question after every class, every day, because no one else is around to ensure that teachers are really doing their jobs—except your students, who are the best at determining "accountability." No other organization or policy maker needs to be consulted on whether you're *accountable*—your students' voices are the most significant measure of teacher effectiveness.

Each student encounters new ideas and information and constructs meaning based on his or her own understanding of the world. The teacher is not passive in this endeavor. Although they may collaborate with students regarding instructional strategies, it is ultimately the teacher who must plan and design the school day.

Effective instructional practice involves more than designing lessons to fit the curriculum guides, implementing teaching strategies, and following the scripted lesson plan. Teachers who limit themselves to these traditional activities ignore the latest research on cognition and discount the ability of young adolescents to search for their own understanding.

WHAT DOES GENUINE LEARNING LOOK LIKE?

Teachers often say that students learn best through:

1. experiencing something hands-on
2. collaborating (having conversations) with classmates
3. experimenting with objects and principles
4. taking risks
5. making mistakes and correcting them
6. developing personal theories through experimenting
7. solving problems individually and in groups
8. developing their own questions about content
9. role-playing
10. engaging in case studies. (D. Brown 2003)

These processes are components of authentic learning—the kind of learning that is often more likely to occur for students outside school instead of inside. Bringing these activities inside the classroom is how teachers make learning a significant activity.

In talking to students it becomes apparent that they also want something other than traditional forms of direct teacher-controlled lessons. A seventh grader told us:

Spend more time and try to do creative things, like hands-on. Have kids have their own opinion on something, not just say, "This is the way it is." There are always two ways to learn something. Maybe one way is always easier, but you are always going to come up with your own way of learning something so I think they should give kids more of an opinion. They shouldn't just be so out of the book.

Knowles (2006) asked a group of students diagnosed with attention deficit hyperactivity disorder what would help them learn. She summarized their preferences:

They were the most engaged in lessons that were active, hands-on, and gave them some choices and control over their learning. They talked about making learning relevant, meaningful, and fun. They talked about having direct connections with those things they were learning. They talked about constructing their own understandings about knowledge and about truly understanding something, not just spitting back facts. They talked about what they will truly value and use in their lives. In addition, they saw a great need for flexibility on the part of the teacher. (79)

Teachers who engage in effective instructional practices use everything they know about their content area, learning, young adolescent development, and instruction in order to make the best choices. But most important, effective teachers know their students—how they think, their academic backgrounds, previous successes and frustrations as learners, personal interests, and learning profiles.

WHAT DO YOU KNOW ABOUT EACH OF YOUR STUDENTS?

Before the school psychologist started the evaluation with me she asked me a couple of questions about myself, how I feel going through school, what my experiences had been. With a few things I told her she said, "A lot of these are typical of symptoms or signs of someone with ADD. This is really surprising that no one's really noticed this before." And I said, "Well, no one's ever asked me anything."
—*Christina* (cited in Knowles, vii)

Teachers must identify how their students learn, discover their cognitive strengths and weaknesses, and determine how they can help their students grow. In addition, teachers need to know their students' lives in all their complexities. To know these details, teachers must become expert kid-watchers. Kid-watching begins with an attitude of willingness and a belief that only through knowing students well can we create learning environments for all.

Teachers should have a method for keeping notes on every student. At the beginning of the year, students can write a letter to the teacher explaining what they know about how they learn. Some teachers ask students to tell them four pieces of information they should know about them as learners and four other details they should know about them as a person. Learning about your students' interests, learning preferences, needs, and personal lives begins on the first day of school and continues throughout the school year.

Some teachers carry a clipboard containing notecards or use sticky notes; as they observe or hear something they note it on the card or sticky note for that student. Some teachers keep notes on address labels that can be peeled and placed in the binder or folder. Other teachers reflect on students' behaviors or academic performance for the first few minutes of their prep time or after school, adding notes to the binder. Teachers should discuss students needing assistance at team meetings, gathering information from colleagues about what strategies they use that are effective.

By the end of the first two weeks of school, teachers should have some notes on all students. You may find that you have lots of entries for the students who command your attention, but ask yourself, "Are there students with no entries? Do I have any notes for the quiet student, or the student who completes all the work easily? Are there students who are confusing to me who I need to know more about?" Many experienced teachers will admit to not knowing some students well enough to help them until the last month or two of the school year. We hope this won't happen to you.

One eighth-grade teacher commented that she really learned the power of knowing her kids when it was too late.

I lost a student one October. She died after a freak accident while riding in a truck. I realized after she died that I still didn't know who she was. I didn't know her strengths, her passions, her interests, her family, the way she learned. I became determined after that I would get to know my students deeply starting from the first day I met them.

Wilhelm (1997) described what he does as a language arts teacher: "I study every student who comes into my classroom. To do less would be to not take each student with the seriousness she or he deserves" (28).

As you become acquainted with your students, you will begin to perceive their learning preferences. You will see how students process information, you will notice the kinds of activities they need in order to be challenged, and, wisely, you will assist students in designing learning experiences that capitalize on their strengths and build on their weaknesses.

When teachers analyze those notes, they can begin to make decisions about how to help students succeed, using the information to differentiate instruction, find developmentally appropriate curricula, make appropriate accommodations, or hold conferences with students. The observations, along with frequent conversations with students about what's working and what's not, both inform and drive instructional

designed to help students reach academic success. When teachers know
well, they can help students set daily, weekly, or semester goals for improv-
academic progress.

ents who drop out of school don't merely think about it on one weekend
ninth or tenth grade and then decide on Sunday night to sleep in Monday
ng and never go back. The decision to drop out is a reflective process that begins
g the middle level years based primarily on the relationships they have at school
classmates and particularly with teachers. Cameron (2012) interviewed sev-
high school dropouts, and three of those respondents, Steve, Cole, and Hannah,
revealed the overwhelming need for teachers to notice them and care about them.
That "care" has to be more than analyzing students' test data and speaking to them
about grades or late assignments; care has to be demonstrated by recognizing students' challenges at home, in their lives away from school, as Cameron (2012) explains:

> If young people could leave their out-of-school lives outside the school house door and if school culture
> didn't punish kids whose lives complicate their school experiences, Hannah would have graduated. The
> kind of help Hannah most needed, like Steve and Cole, was someone to *see* her needs, to listen—*really
> listen*—to what was going on in her life and to support her. (18)

Just *one* student saying that you were the reason she chose to complete high school
rather than drop out has a much more powerful impact than half of your students' test
scores rising. Your most significant job during an academic year is to know each of
your students as if they were your own children—that's what it means to be *accountable* as a professional educator.

FACILITATORS IN ACTION

"Teacher as facilitator" is perhaps an overused metaphor that some have even interpreted as a way to ignore instructional responsibilities. Being a facilitator, however,
requires a great deal of effort, energy, and perseverance.

Some teachers use the "KWL" approach as facilitators to help students get a
handle on their topic: What do students *Know, Want* to know, and *Learn*? It doesn't
make sense, however, to start a unit by asking, "What do you know about Nubia?" or
"What do you know about the Hausa people?" If students don't know anything about
a specific topic, it's difficult to generate questions. Teachers often find that student
questions do not really guide the unit development, thereby making the KWL chart
simply an exercise and not an effective learning tool.

"

Know each of your
students as if they
were your own
children—that's
what it means to be
accountable as a
professional educator.

Rachel Knowles, a seventh- and eighth-grade teacher, explains the evolution of her use of the KWL charts and how she developed the use of what she calls "KiNL" charts as a facilitator of learning.

All throughout my university education classes, KWL charts were touted as the key to engaging young adolescent minds. So when I began teaching, I began using these charts. What I found though was not an engaging tool. Instead, I experienced students being put off by the "Know" section and shutting down. Very often they didn't know anything about the topic. The "Want to Know" section was equally frustrating for me. Students frequently said, "I don't want to know anything about this, I just don't care," leaving them to try to think of filler questions to make the required amount of questions. If they didn't know anything about the topic to begin with, this section became even more frustrating.

After this section it was difficult to add their questions into my unit, for the unit had already been planned! I hoped that the students would forget about their questions because I felt like I was letting them down. Two things would happen by the time I got to the "Learned" section: I would either forget about it, or the students would lose their paper.

This led to my evolution of the KiNL charts: What do you *Know* or what can you *infer* about the question I asked? What do you *Need* to know to answer the question? What did you *Learn* that answered the question? I was looking for a way to help define what students needed to look for in reading or in analyzing any document or visual image. This process has helped students focus in on what information they are trying to find as they begin to generate their own specific questions and needs for themselves individually.

The process always begins with the question that I want students to answer through studying this topic. I may ask my seventh-grade students "Is Hinduism monotheistic or polytheistic?" "Was Shi Huangdi a good leader or a bad leader?" "How does geography affect the culture of China?" Students then create three columns.

The first column is the "Ki" column. In this column students answer "What do I already *know* or can *infer* about this topic or this question?" When I first began these charts the "I" was not part of it. I quickly realized that inferring is an important step in answering questions. For instance, if we know that monotheism is one god and polytheism is more than one god, then we can infer that Hinduism is a religion. If we know we're studying China, we can infer that Shi Huangdi is a leader from China. If we know that there are many mountains in China, we can infer that these mountains impact the culture there. I may have to do a brief lesson on inferences at the beginning of the year, but they quickly pick up the idea. I always preface this step by saying that I expect this column to be short. If it were long then I'd be wasting my time teaching them.

The next column is the "What do I *Need* to find out in order to answer this question?" Students pose their own questions of things they need to know in order to answer the bigger question. They might ask: "Where is Hinduism practiced?" "Do Hindus have many gods?" "When did Shi Huangdi live?" "What were some of his policies?" "What are some landforms in China?" "What are some of the celebrations or traditions that the Chinese people practice?"

The last column is the "Learned" column. This column is to be completed while reading or researching. The only information that goes in the learned column is information that answers a question from the *Need* column.

(continues)

(continued)

Throughout the years my KiNL charts have evolved in order to help students access text. I sometimes utilize questions from the end of the chapter in the book and, using those questions, I do the KiNL chart as a reading strategy. I find that students sometimes get bogged down with all the information that is out there. The KiNL charts help eliminate extra information and focus on the essential questions that lead to understanding the content and the text.

When you collaborate with students on activities, they may suggest a wide variety of ways to approach the acquisition of knowledge. Many students want to do some kind of project to obtain and demonstrate knowledge. As Brodhagen (1998) explained, "Projects . . . provide students opportunities to use multiple resources including technology, popular culture, common 'experts' (people in their personal community who know much about a topic), multicultural resources, and personal experiences" (51).

For example, students might want to interview experts. You could conduct a mini-lesson on how to generate questions or conduct an interview and then help them set up the interviews. Students might want to conduct a school survey. You will help them develop survey questions and analyze, interpret, and report data.

Authentic instruction requires attention to each student's needs and flexibility in teacher response. It is necessary for teachers to hold frequent conferences with individuals or groups to set goals, establish timelines, and monitor progress toward a final product. Students can focus on their learning during these conferences by responding to teacher questions such as:

- What do you hope to learn as a result of studying this topic?
- What are some ways you could demonstrate your learning?
- Who would you like to share your new knowledge with once you have researched the topic?
- How would you assess your final product?

During conferences, students can explain their work, talk about their explorations, and seek new avenues of research. Conferences with students become paramount in deciding how they will demonstrate their newfound knowledge to others. Students may need extensive instruction, guidance, and feedback as they develop final presentations, pieces of writing, works of art, or scientific demonstrations. Conferences that include parents encourage students to take ownership of their own learning.

As you can see, teachers are highly involved in structuring learning processes. Brodhagen (1998) discussed some of the instructional strategies that teachers use:

Cooperative learning groups can be a powerful instructional strategy when used correctly. Direct teaching can be effective when used appropriately. Presenting information through both visual and auditory methods increases retention of material. The use of advanced organizers, anticipatory sets, or scaffolding helps students understand and remember more when ideas or information are connected to prior learning. (50–51)

Nesin and Lounsbury (1999) observed that although many of these strategies can be viewed as traditional and may be used in any classroom, in curriculum integration classrooms "strategies and activities selected result from student-teacher planning rather than teachers' unilateral decisions" (34).

RECOGNIZING DIVERSE LEARNERS

Tim, a seventh-grade teacher, admitted after a few months of teaching, "I wasn't prepared as a secondary education major for these kids!" It is easy to recognize the physical differences of young adolescents as they enter a classroom; however, perceiving cognitive, social, and emotional differences is challenging. It is naïve to think that students in the same grade level are also at the same levels of intellectual processing. Noticing that students look entirely different from one another should signal to you that they are also just as different in what they bring intellectually into the classroom: their background knowledge, previous academic success, levels of basic skills (reading vocabulary knowledge and comprehension, mathematical computation), and their attitudes and efforts toward learning.

They differ in the way they process and understand knowledge and in the way they construct meaning from knowledge. Sally, an eighth-grade teacher, revealed the diversity she sees in her students: "Each child learns differently. One child might have only a two-minute attention span. Another child might come to school with a host of issues and just be completely exhausted." Students see this diversity also. Jake, a sixth grader, told us, "There is such a wide range of smartness in the school in each class. It's hard because some kids move faster than others, and they [the teachers] have to know the needs of some kids."

Traditional curriculum design and many traditional instructional strategies do not account for the diversity of students' learning needs. The belief that "one size fits all" when it comes to preparing students for life after high school results in every

A good teacher is one who understands your needs—understands what you need as a student. I'm not saying they have to sit down and write, "Jason needs this, Tom needs this, Anne needs this, Marie needs this." But they have to be able to know if I don't understand something.
—JASON,
SIXTH GRADER

student being exposed to the same curricula, reading the same book, receiving the same assignments, acquiring information through the same instructional model, and completing the same tests to demonstrate growth. Using the same methods for all students will only ensure that some are *not* successful.

Legislative initiatives like No Child Left Behind and Race to the Top have exacerbated the one-size-fits-all model. With their focus on high-stakes tests and data-driven instruction, administrators and teachers can easily forget that all students are not alike and that our instruction should be "student-driven," not data-driven.

UNIVERSAL DESIGN FOR LEARNING

Recognizing diversity in learning means that teachers understand that each student has a unique way of accessing, processing, and applying information. Learning preferences and differences may be based on environmental conditions; on genetic, neurological, or other physical challenges; or on a combination of environmental and physical factors. One student's learning preferences may differ from another's based on broad issues such as developmental level, gender, race, ethnicity, socioeconomic class, or native language. Learning differences may be very specific, such as a preference for learning from parts to whole or vice versa, the need for social interaction versus independent study, the preference for analytical methods of learning, the need to write to enhance learning, or the need to engage in physical movement when learning. Personal interests, learning disabilities, and degrees of background knowledge also impact learning preferences (Tomlinson 1999b).

The causes of individual differences are not as important as the responsibility for teachers to ensure that every student has opportunities to succeed at learning—daily. Teachers' attitudes, philosophies, and actions in recognizing differences in students determine the degree of success that students will experience. Meeting the needs of all learners by differentiating instruction begins with accepting the fact that your students are all cognitively different from one another.

In the past, teachers often designed lessons and, as an afterthought, they would think about how to modify the lesson for specific students in their classrooms. That's how architects used to design buildings. They built them and later determined how to modify those buildings to make them more accessible to all people. Just as architects now use a universal design model for buildings in order to make them accessible for all, using principles of Universal Design for Learning allows us to frame our lessons in a way that meets all the needs of students in the classroom. We design instruction up front, with all students in mind. No one is an afterthought. Using this framework removes the barriers from learning and optimizes learning opportunities for all.

> Meeting the needs of all learners by differentiating instruction begins with accepting the fact that your students are all cognitively different from one another.

The Center for Applied Special Technology (CAST) (2014) has been working for more than a quarter of a century to help students with disabilities access the curriculum. Their work has expanded to focus on Universal Design for Learning (UDL), a framework for teachers to think about all of their students when designing curriculum rather than simply when the lesson plan is complete.

The three main principles of UDL call for providing multiple means of representation, multiple means of action and expression, and multiple means of engagement when designing lessons (2014):

Principle 1: Provide multiple means of representation. Students learn in different ways, so it is important for teachers to present and represent information in different ways. In its simplest forms, teachers must make sure that information is presented through various modalities (visual, auditory, tactile, musical). Teachers might think about providing a written transcript for certain students when watching a video or listening to an audio piece. Other students might benefit from highlighted text or the use of a written outline for a lesson. Advanced organizers, concept maps, data-collecting sheets, and graphic organizers for presenting information might be helpful. The key is to represent the material in as many ways as possible to provide multiple entry points for students.

Principle 2: Provide multiple means of action and expression. Students can demonstrate their understanding of knowledge in various ways. While we might offer options, keep in mind that we want all students to be able to respond to the big ideas and essential understandings of the topic. While some students excel in written expression of understandings, others might excel in physical means of expression (dance, movement, drama, role play, use of manipulatives). Some students might tell you what they know while others visually represent their understandings.

Principle 3: Provide multiple means of engagement. Students will not/cannot learn unless they are engaged. As teachers, we must do everything possible to provide multiple ways for students to enter the learning process. The greatest engagement occurs when students are presented with authentic learning experiences that respond to their questions, concerns, or interests (designed collaboratively using a curriculum integration model). When students are given choices for how to complete projects (essay, chart, poster, journal, song, dance, diorama, multimedia presentation) they become more invested.

The more choice and power students have over their own learning, the more engaged and invested they will be. Allow students to identify their own reading materials, choose topics to research, write from their own voice, and create personal goals for learning. Find out what students want to learn and actually teach that. Provide flexible groupings. Use small groups, large groups, pairs or individual work, and interest groups. Keep students engaged by not having them continually do what they already know how to do, such as when teachers assign more math problems even though their students already know how to do them.

When principles of Universal Design are used to frame lessons, all students benefit. Students will not only be able to access information, they will also be able to use that information in meaningful and powerful ways. No standardized model for designing learning experiences can meet the needs of all students in every classroom. Understanding, validating, and responding to student learning differences is a professional responsibility of educators. All students have a right to succeed, and teachers must provide the necessary environment for that to happen. Using principles of Universal Design can make that a reality (CAST 2014).

◆▌▌ Culturally Responsive Teaching

Immigrants have entered American public schools for centuries. Early perspectives on educating culturally and ethnically diverse students drove educators to use traditional teaching methods in attempts to Americanize students. By using traditional instruction and curricula, educators ignore students' rich cultural and ethnic heritage that they bring from home and also ignore diverse learning profiles that accompany students' cultural backgrounds. Many African American students bring unique socioeconomic challenges and personal family perspectives that impact their academic efforts and successes. Teachers are well intentioned, yet some prevent students from reaching academic success by delivering what is often viewed by students as a stifling curriculum that prevents ethnically diverse students from connecting their daily schooling experiences to their lives. D. Brown (2012) described the following schedule for students at an urban middle school as evidence of disempowering many ethnically diverse learners:

8:30–9:00: Test preparation period for reading (M, W, F) and math (T, Th)
9:01–9:54: Corrective reading activities via the scripted reading program
9:55–10:39: Corrective scripted mathematics program
10:40–12:09: Core literacy classes
12:10–12:54: Student lunch (No reading or math teaching at this time!)
12:55–1:39: Special classes (physical education, music, art, foreign language)
1:40–2:10: Additional literacy (reading or English curriculum)
2:11–2:24: Science and social studies (Notice this is only 13 minutes.)
2:25–3:09: More mathematics lessons (194–195)

I think American society has shortchanged itself and minorities by insisting that immigrants, African Americans, and Native Americans deny their cultures and languages to become "real" Americans.
   —**WEINER** (1999, 7)

To address the low achievement of black males, schools must be willing to accept that there are ways of looking at the world, modes of communication, and approaches to teaching and learning that are unique to black males. At the same time, educators must also acknowledge that these unique ways of being are just as complex as those of other students.
   —**EMDIN** (2012, 13)

What component of this schedule would arouse the natural curiosity of young adolescents? All over the United States students have their minds wasted by scripted lessons and drills to improve their basic reading and mathematics scores. This schedule represents the antithesis of culturally responsive teaching and denies students any opportunity to engage in critical or creative thinking, problem solving, or interpersonal communication processes—all needed to improve future learning.

Students don't need to speak perfect English before they have an opportunity to learn in an engaging manner, such as having class discussions on the reasons for poverty, the challenges of the Arab spring, or the latest conversations in Washington on the passage of an immigration bill. Often English language learners (ELLs) and African American students who primarily speak African American English Vernacular (AAEV) are treated as if they have limited cognitive capacities merely because they lack the vocabulary to maneuver through some content. Just as you don't lose your cognitive capacities when you travel to Europe and don't speak the native languages, neither do your ethnically diverse students as they sit in your class waiting for a chance to use their brains for something more than completing basic skill worksheets.

Mikael, a 20-year-old African American male college sophomore, had this to say about the plight of Black male students: "We (Black males) have been brainwashed and socialized to believe that the darker your skin is, the less capable you are" (Sparrow and Sparrow 2012, 46). The previous schedule demonstrates the perfect storm of high-stakes testing, scripted curricula, teacher accountability systems, and low expectations that often define teaching and learning in poorer socioeconomic communities.

For African American students to become successful, motivated learners, they must: (1) be given opportunities to use their intellectual capabilities, (2) be given forums to speak about their lives and their futures, (3) be provided with lessons that connect their daily circumstances with content standards, (4) have opportunities to discuss how their chosen identities can help or hinder their educational opportunities, and (5) be given leadership opportunities within the classroom to begin to demonstrate their academic capabilities. Emdin (2012) reveals the challenges some Black males have experienced: "Many others have performed the role of disinterested black male for so long that it's become almost second nature to underperform in school. Unfortunately, as students have performed these images, educators have failed to acknowledge that they have a responsibility to help students overcome these expectations of disinterest and low achievement" (14).

Teaching ethnically diverse students requires specific actions that positively impact student success. Wlodkowski and Ginsberg (1995) explained the need for mandating cultural responsiveness:

> Few of us . . . would care to admit that the way we teach compromises the learning of certain cultural groups. Yet, to avoid or remain insensitive to the cultural issues and influences within our teaching situations under the guise, for example, of maintaining academic standards or treating everyone alike is no longer acceptable. (8)

Culturally responsive pedagogy requires a positive attitude toward change and a commitment to alter instruction and curriculum for the benefit of diverse students. D. Brown (2002b) noted, "Culturally responsive teaching begins when teachers recognize, demonstrate, and celebrate an equal respect for the backgrounds of all students" (21). Ladson-Billings (1994) further explained, "Culturally responsive teaching is about questioning (and preparing students to question) the structural inequality, the racism, and the injustice that exists in society" (128).

It may be easy, particularly for White teachers, to believe that no injustices exist for our students, or to be unaware that much of American teaching reflects traditional cultural norms about how learning occurs. Those beliefs reveal ignorance about the lives of our ethnically and culturally diverse students and their families. Ethnically diverse young adolescents recognize the differences in how they are treated in American society, by peers, and also by teachers who may ignore how their lives are affected by their ethnicity (Emdin 2012; Hurd 2012; Brown and Leaman 2006). Sheets (2005) stated, "Adolescents notice that their groups' accomplishments may be missing or distorted in the school curriculum" (61).

Cultural responsiveness begins by engaging in frequent conversations with students about their families, backgrounds, language, and preferred learning styles. Teachers who enact cultural responsiveness purposely initiate classroom conversations about their students' lives—conversations about students' heritage, homeland, religion, and language. Teachers initiate discussions that connect content standards with students' knowledge of poverty, injustice, White privilege, language barriers, and governmental actions that deny equality to many of their families.

Cultural responsiveness does *not* imply that "I treat all my students the same—I don't see color." If you believe this, then you may completely ignore your students' differences and the behaviors and learning preferences associated with their ethnic profiles, and you may reduce their chances for academic success.

A primary goal of culturally responsive teaching is to adjust instruction and curriculum so that ethnically diverse students will have equal opportunities for learning (Ruddell 2006). Gay (2010) described many diverse students' needs for more active instructional processes. English language learners have a particular need for direct contact with information through manipulatives and hands-on experiences (D. Brown 2002c). Dong (2014) also describes ELLs' needs: "Research has shown repeatedly that language learners' prior knowledge—which includes their previous learning history, native language, cultural and life experiences, and any understanding they have about the topic at hand—is a key ingredient of their meaningful learning" (30–31).

Gay (2010) contends that African and Hispanic American students also need more contextualized learning experiences. D. Brown (2002c) sees these as opportunities for

- telling stories
- sharing experiences related to new vocabulary and content
- engaging in kinesthetic reenactments of historical events
- designing physical models of new principles
- drawing graphic organizers
- taking field trips associated with key units. (adapted from 65)

An essential component of culturally responsive teaching is educators' ability to respect and respond to their ethnically diverse students' communication styles and native languages. Howard (2001) discovered that "the achievement of students is increased when teachers modify their instruction to make it more congruent with the cultures and communication styles of culturally diverse students" (183). Several nonstandard forms of English are spoken at some of our students' homes: Hawaiian Creole, Appalachian English, and African American English Vernacular (AAEV). Teachers demonstrate their awareness and respect for their students' culture and ethnicity by not correcting them each time they use their language or dialect of origin. Teachers can emphasize the differences between Standard English and the discourse students' families speak at home politely and in the context of class discussions, writing assignments, and private conversations. As D. Brown (2002c) noted in response to some African American students' use of AAEV, "To overly correct or dismiss students' use of AAEV denigrates young adolescents' ethnic and cultural backgrounds while creating negative feelings between students and teachers" (67).

ELL students need many opportunities for public and private conversations during class time. Teachers must permit them to *code-switch* during these conversations, that is, to use both English and their native language to effectively learn English. Frequent conversations with your ELL students will give you an idea of their English skills and the help they need to improve their use of academic English. African American students who speak AAEV also need direct instruction that permits them to compare their spoken language to Standard English, particularly when they write (Wheeler and Swords 2010). Side-by-side comparisons of Standard English and AAEV help students to see the differences that they often don't hear. Teachers should encourage students to discuss circumstances when it may be necessary to use Standard English versus speaking AAEV.

Garcia (1999) suggested that teachers use these instructional strategies to improve ELL students' academic success:

- Increase wait time following your questions and after their responses to promote elaboration and more processing time.
- Simplify your language—don't speak louder; rephrase comments or questions instead.
- Don't force students to speak.
- Pair ELL students with proficient English speakers.
- Adapt instructional materials to make them more comprehensible.
- Support the student's home language and culture. (cited in D. Brown 2002b, 178)

Conversational exchanges among students as well as between students and teachers during lessons better match the learning profiles of ethnically diverse students than traditional fast-paced question/answer sessions. Quick responses to questions during recitations and discussions may prevent many ethnically diverse students from engaging in learning activities. This type of quick exchange also discourages some students from becoming engaged in learning activities.

Becoming a culturally responsive teacher requires developing and believing in a philosophy of differences among students—differences that must be studied and that teachers must respond to through explicit efforts. Making a difference in our ethnically diverse students' lives depends on our willingness to plan curriculum and instruction collaboratively with students and to make instructional and curricular decisions that take into account all the learners in the classroom. The most significant teacher response that matters to ethnically diverse students is listening, inquiring about their lives, and then more listening.

TECHNOLOGY USE IN TODAY'S CLASSROOM

While using technology in education raises a number of issues related to student access to technology and appropriate uses of technology, it is undeniable that students will need to use technology for real purposes in their lives beyond school. As teachers, it is our responsibility to help them to do this safely and efficiently. While technology in education is still an evolving field, researchers are working to provide guidelines and activities for engaging students in learning with technology.

Coiro and Fogleman (2011) provide the following advice on using websites during lessons:

- Identify the purposes of a lesson before assigning it to students.
- Ask the question, "How can informational websites support your learning goals?"
- Determine the value of certain types of websites in providing developmentally appropriate information for your students.
- Assign specific activities for students to do while they're using the website.
- Consider sending students to websites that offer interactive games to reinforce specific curricular guidelines. (34–38)

Kolb (2011) provides a list of activities that students can engage in during school with their cell phones, including "pod casting, oral recordings, and oral quizzes" using *Google Voice* accounts; "mobile *geotagging* where teachers can post media from a mobile phone to a specific place on a map"; using *digital storybooks* in which students can create their own stories "using a mobile phone"; and using "*photo-sharing* sites such as *Flickr* and *Photobucket*" to help students connect concepts to everyday items outside of school (40–42).

The use of technological devices in education settings can create excellent opportunities for *flipping classrooms*. Flipping involves presenting the big picture first—showing the video before reading the book, doing a demonstration before having students read the text or define vocabulary words. Most of these activities are common in many classrooms and especially advantageous for ethnically diverse learners, as we mentioned earlier.

Bergmann and Sams (2014) suggest using *Moodle*, a personalized virtual learning environment, to create the excitement about topics outside of class. It can be used for assignment submissions, a discussion forum, or online quizzes. Or, Moodle might be used to post a video that explains a principle better than an oral presentation would. Bergmann and Sams warn though that some topics posted on Moodle might be too abstract for students to comprehend without teacher assistance. They believe, however, that Moodles developed by teachers with their explanations may be better for students who are able to understand their own teacher's instructional style rather than someone they've never heard of or seen before.

Finally, we offer a cautionary tale and a student's wise advice. Gorski (2013) mentioned the following after his visit to an urban school:

> During a recent visit to a high poverty school, I asked eighth graders how many of them had a working computer and Internet access at home; only a few of the forty students raised their hands. Then I asked how many of them had been assigned homework that required access to computers since the last grading period ended; everybody raised their (sic) hands.

Teachers must take the pulse of their students' access to computers and the Internet before assigning every student to use their computers at home no matter which community they're teaching in. The most obvious issue with "bring your own device" (BYOD) is inequality: Not every student will have a device, and the students who have devices will not all have the same software. BYOD requires careful structuring by the teacher: How will the devices be used? How can students without devices fully participate in lessons and assignments? However, in schools that do not have funding for technology, some teachers are finding ways to allow students to use the powerful digital tools they have in their pockets: their cell phones.

When it comes to technology, students can teach us when we're not sure how to use some devices. One student explains, "I'd rather explain some technology thing to a teacher than sit there and watch them try to figure it out for themselves. Just admit you don't get it. We all know you don't know. Because if you knew, it would be up already [sic]. Just don't be afraid to ask for our help" (*EL online* 2011, 45). Experimenting with technology might be an appropriate time to model what risk-taking looks like for your students. The advice offered herein may be used as guidelines for future technological devices, although we recognize that new inventions may completely alter how educators infuse technology into learning experiences.

◆❙❙ Concluding Reflections

We are fully aware of the position in which teachers are sometimes placed when they don't cover the curriculum or complete the textbook; however, time, textbooks, and curriculum guides do not have to be impediments to implementing active learning activities within your own classroom. A traditional school structure is no excuse for refusing to use best practices based on effective research-based pedagogical principles (Bizar and Daniels 2005; Daniels, Hyde, and Zemelman 2005).

Being a teacher is a complex task. You will not find a recipe that tells you what ingredients to use to be successful. You must first remember the young adolescent population with whom you are working. Young adolescents are vibrant and alive, curious and questioning, passionate and intense. If you can capture and use their vibrancy, curiosity, and passion and see learning through their eyes, you have taken the first step toward facilitating meaningful learning. Couple that with your extensive content and pedagogical knowledge, as well as the flexibility to use what you know in response to student needs, and you will be able to develop an environment in which students are genuinely able to create meaning and make sense of their world.

CHAPTER 12

Assessment That

Promotes Active Learning

I'll never forget the expression on the principal's face when I told him that the district's standardized tests could not help me know what the students in my English classes needed to learn.

—**BARR** (2000, 20)

Decisions about whether or not students are learning should not take place in the legislature, the governor's office, or the department of education. They should take place in the classroom, because that is where learning occurs.

—**DOUGLAS CHRISTENSEN**, cited in Roschewski, Gallagher, and Isernhagen (2001, 611)

◆▌▌ What Is Assessment?

I went to school where we didn't have grades, and we didn't have tests. We never got a report card. I was much more willing to learn.
—**DAN**, SIXTH GRADER

A message posted on the campus where one of us teaches states, "Good luck on exams!" You have undoubtedly heard the same "good luck" from friends and family as you prepared to take tests. We find it humorous that luck would have anything to do with determining what you have learned. How can students spend so much time learning in school only to have the level of their knowledge determined by a test that relies as much on luck as it does on skill or knowledge?

The kind of assessment that takes luck to succeed involves students memorizing facts, and then attempting to recall them for the test. Students who experience assessment this way usually have no knowledge of the questions they will be asked to answer until the day they take the test. This reminds us of owl pellets—those small, cylinder-shaped, gray hair balls that owls regurgitate after they eat because they can't digest the hair and bones of field mice. All of us have taken a test in which we regurgitated pellets that represent the information we couldn't digest! We don't consider that type of assessment an accurate measure of learning. We question the validity of such tests; that is, do these traditional assessment strategies measure what they claim to measure? Do they measure what teachers want students to know?

Most significantly, do the tests, no matter who designs them, actually lead to students growing intellectually—not merely receiving improved test scores from last year—but actually cause them to think better? The premise of effective teaching is based on this simple principle: When teachers design learning opportunities, students should actually grow cognitively as a result of those experiences. This philosophy should be the driving force for all the decisions that educators make in designing the school day. Educators who lose sight of this mission deny students the opportunities they deserve and, in the process, waste students' time.

ASSESSMENT *ISN'T* TESTING, EVALUATION, GRADING, OR ACHIEVEMENT

We need to develop a "big picture" view of assessment and increase our understanding of how to help young adolescents become more involved in assessing their own learning. When we think about determining what students know, we may think of words such as *testing*, *evaluation*, or *grading*. These words do not have the same meaning as *assessment*.

Testing is a method for determining what someone knows. We usually think of teacher-generated tests as multiple-choice, true/false, or essay questions. Tests may not actually measure what teachers want students to know or be able to do as a result of studying a particular topic. Tests often do and can, however, label students—as in "Yep, she's an 'A' student" or "I expected him to be average, and this 'C' confirms it!" These arbitrary labels—grades particularly—don't usually take teachers on an educational journey of understanding their students' needs.

Evaluation is the most dangerous word commonly used in place of assessment. Evaluation is a judgment of a child's performance. Most evaluation of student learning uses external sources instead of being personally generated by students. The typical end products of evaluation are grades. Evaluating students does the following *to them*:

- labels them, as in "proficient," "below grade level," "basic," "gifted," "learning disabled," "an 'A' student," or "just an 'average' Joe"
- compares one student to another
- tracks them in homogenous groups based on ability, such as "ready for Algebra I," "belongs in advanced science," or "remedial reading class"

- designates them as either "college-bound track" or "basic classes for possible trade school."

Evaluation does *nothing* to help students understand their current skill level, abilities in specific content areas, their amount of effort, or their attitudes toward learning. It creates a label that students use to determine their future efforts and attitudes toward learning for the remainder of their middle level years and throughout high school. Students are apt to proclaim during their middle level years, after receiving that first report card in November, "Looks like I'll be in the 'dummy' class for the rest of my years at school," or "I don't like math anyway, so this 'C' confirms that I won't get into Algebra until I get to high school, and I'll never understand it!"

Grading is merely a component of evaluation and is an arbitrary label used to place students along a continuum, from best to worst or to compare students with one another. Grades in any format, such as *A* to *F*, *satisfactory*, or *at grade level*, describe student performances over a period of time on a number of tasks. Although grading has a strong tradition, a number of problems exist with this practice. According to Tombari and Borich (1999): "[Grades] assume equal amounts of learning have occurred for individuals who achieve the same grade, fail to acknowledge continuous progress or development in learning, and may mask an individual student's learning strengths and needs" (39). Marzano (2000) noted, "Grades are so imprecise that they are almost meaningless. This straightforward but depressing fact is usually painfully obvious when one examines the research and practice regarding grades with a critical eye" (1).

Dressel's (1957) portrayal of grades might make you laugh initially, but then sigh, realizing his accurate description of this erroneous, yet hallowed, long-held tradition: "[Grades are] an inadequate report of an inaccurate judgment by a biased and variable judge of the extent to which a student has attained an undefined level of mastery of an unknown proportion of an indefinite amount of material" (cited in Kohn 2006, 32). Dressel's explanation reveals just how arbitrarily grades are assigned, how insufficient they are at measuring anything worth knowing, and how grades are unlikely to improve students' intellectual growth.

Convincing parents and other educators of the insufficiency inherent in grading is a lifetime battle. Grades are not motivating for many students and rarely have little to do with learning. Marzano noted: "A single letter grade or a percentage score is not a good way to report student achievement in any subject area because it simply cannot present the level of detailed feedback necessary for effective learning" (106). The two essential words in this comment are *feedback* and *learning*. When students receive credible feedback about their work, the chances for academic growth are greater than when grades are merely used to summarize a teacher's opinion.

Perhaps the most abused word in the education world is *achievement*. The U.S. Congress and the Federal Department of Education personnel use it in legislation, such as NCLB and in the funding provided by Race to the Top (RTTT), to describe student growth. Educational researchers have adopted the word, too, to evaluate policy and programs. *Achievement* doesn't actually have meaning in the field of cognitive science because *learning ≠ achievement*. Much of the learning that parents and teachers want for adolescents cannot be described by the word *achievement*. Kohn (2006) adds to the ambiguousness of this word and its misuse:

Most researchers, like most reporters who write about education, talk about how this or that policy affects student "achievement" without questioning whether the way that word is defined in the studies makes any sense. What exactly is this entity called achievement that's said to go up or down? It turns out that what's actually being measured—at least in all the homework research I've seen—is one of three things: scores on tests designed by teachers, grades given by teachers, or scores on standardized exams. Each is seriously flawed in its own way. (31)

Achievement has nothing to do with learning in your classroom. Students with high test scores would probably be considered "high achieving," but the most significant question you must ask as their teacher is, "Have they grown any during the year?"

ASSESSMENT IS . . .

Assessment has a more generalized meaning than testing, grading, or evaluation. D. Brown (2002b) noted the following meaning: "The historical origin of the word *assess* is Latin, *assidere*, meaning 'to sit by' (American Heritage Dictionary 2000, 108). Seems a perfect description of the requirement to determine what students really know—sit by them!" (189)

Assessment is a set of strategies for discovering what students know or can do as a result of engaging in learning experiences. It is a comprehensive act that includes consideration of a student's goals for learning, processes of learning, progression toward established goals, and revision of goals when needed. All assessment should have as its primary purpose the improvement of student learning. All instruction should be informed by what we learn about students in formal or informal ways.

All instruction should
be informed by
what we learn about
students in formal or
informal ways.

Effective assessment begins with discovering who students are when they enter your classroom each fall. D. Brown (2002b) suggested teachers be aware of the following information about each student:

- attendance records
- learning preferences and primary modes for accessing information
- comprehensive reading strengths and weaknesses
- writing level and strategies
- study skills
- personal interests not associated with school
- leisure activities
- parents' beliefs about their child's academic progress
- health issues that may affect learning
- personality traits that may affect learning
- English proficiency level
- grade level abilities in major subject areas. (adapted from 187–88)

These activities require systematic kid-watching throughout the year (as described in Chapter 8). Finding the answers to all this information about students takes time—especially if you are responsible for as many as 100 to 150 students a day. However, without understanding your students you miss the opportunity to determine whether genuine growth is occurring each day.

The Role of Metacognition in Student Self-Assessment

Despite the emphases on teachers' responsibilities for knowing their students well, young adolescents have reached the cognitive ability levels to recognize their own learning needs, called *metacognitive* skills or strategies. *Metacognition* is often defined by professors as "thinking about thinking," but this vague definition does nothing to describe young adolescents' newfound intellectual abilities. We view metacognition as encompassing three significant components:

1. Students' *attitudes* toward learning: Are they interested, positive about what they're doing cognitively at the time of the lesson? Do they feel good about their prospects for succeeding on what they're asked to do?

2. Students' *efforts*: Are they focused on the tasks at hand? Will they give it their best shot as they engage in the lesson? Will they persevere even when it gets challenging?

3. Students' *knowledge of strategies*: Do they know what to do when they are stuck? Do they have a set of solutions to challenging tasks? Do they know where to go when they lack a solution?

Middle level students are capable of demonstrating these three components of mindful behavior, but it may take some coaching on teachers' parts before they use them on a consistent basis. We suggest that teachers ask students these questions on a regular basis: "How do you feel about what you did? "Is that your best effort?" "What strategies did you use and what could you do now?" Some students will need help responding to these questions initially. You may need to demonstrate explicitly what positive attitudes look like, how students can attend efficiently during lessons, and what maximum effort means in your classroom.

TIME FOR REFLECTION

- *Make a list of the reasons for assessing students.*
- *Discuss with a classmate or colleague how the reasons you've listed support young adolescents' cognitive growth.*
- *Describe some of the frustrations you've experienced with traditional assessment techniques.*

◆❚❚ Students' Roles in Assessment

Young adolescents are capable of and should be involved in monitoring their own academic and cognitive growth. From setting goals, to developing guidelines for monitoring their progress, to creating the criteria for assessing projects, to conducting conferences with parents to talk about their growth, young adolescents can take increasing responsibility for their own learning.

The first step is for them to be involved in personal goal setting. These goals should relate to what students want to or expect to learn or be able to do, or behaviors they want to acquire over a period of a week, month, semester, or year. To help students initiate their own goal setting, teachers can begin by brainstorming with an entire class what goal setting looks like. Students should work collaboratively, writing goal statements and specific objectives describing how they'd like to improve their academic

(Y)oung adolescents are capable of being active participants in both assessing and judging their accomplishments.
—**AMLE** (2010, 25)

skills and in what areas. As students share their group responses, teachers can identify which ideas represent effective goals and objectives for learning, and then transition into students writing individual goals and objectives with teacher guidance.

When students are involved in their own personal assessment and goal setting they should be asking such questions as:

- What do I want to accomplish next week (or month)?
- Do I possess adequate background knowledge in this subject area?
- What academic behaviors do I demonstrate at this time (appropriate reading strategies, basic mathematical skills, effective study habits)?
- What specific help do I need to be able to succeed on this assignment?
- What can I do to improve my study habits and in-class academic behaviors?
- Is my effort genuine and my attitude positive enough to ensure that I'll learn from this assignment?
- How would I describe my learning profile (style)?
- What accommodations do I need to address my learning needs in this situation?

Not requiring students to develop goals and not knowing the answers to these questions prevent students from being engaged learners, but instead creates an *external locus of control* for students in which they can blame teachers for their academic failures or successes.

A natural extension of student goal setting is frequent monitoring of progress toward reaching their goals. Student-teacher conferences should be conducted frequently to determine student progress in meeting their goals, and to redefine and develop new outcomes and goals. Revisiting and possibly revising these academic goals are imperative to ensuring appropriate academic growth.

When students have helped to develop goals for their learning, they can use those goals to reflect on themselves as learners. As they share their new understandings about themselves with teachers, parents, or peers, they learn to take increasing responsibility for their learning. As Davies (2001) explained:

Involving students in communicating their learning signals a shift in roles and responsibilities. Instead of searching for evidence that students have learned, teachers now help students find evidence of their own learning. (49)

A critical aspect of this type of frequent communication between students and teachers and possibly peers is the constant feedback that students receive about their progress toward meeting their personal learning outcomes, feedback that helps them make adjustments and ensures academic growth. The Soundings curriculum integration program engages students in designing the year's curricula based on their personal questions. An eighth grader in the Soundings curriculum integration experience provided this perspective on his frequent teacher feedback and self-assessment: "The way we were assessed in Soundings gave me constructive advice about how to better my performance in school. I also received feedback from my own reflection on my writing and presentations" (Brown and Morgan 2003, 19).

Davies (2001) noted the opportunities for student growth through communication:

When students communicate with others about their learning, they learn about what they have learned, what they need to learn, and what kind of support may be available to them. Research shows that when students are involved in the assessment process and learn to articulate what they have learned and what they still need to work on, achievement improves. (47)

Students can focus on assessment issues during student–teacher conferences by responding to these questions:

- What are your goals for next week?
- What do you hope to learn as a result of studying this topic?
- How might you show your understanding of this information?
- How does what you already know compare with what you'd like to know?
- With whom would you like to share your new knowledge?
- How would you evaluate your final product?

Helping students develop a course of study, choose strategies for learning information, and select ways of presenting their learning to classmates, parents, and teachers is a journey that is continually evolving. Teachers help students identify process skills and work habits they need to develop, such as analytical and research skills, time-management strategies, persistence, and collaboration with classmates (Educators in Connecticut's Pomperaug Regional School District 15, 1996). In providing options for ways to demonstrate knowledge, teachers allow students to choose how they will demonstrate their learning so that assessment matches the students' abilities while strengthening their weaknesses.

This process involves ongoing teacher guidance and conferencing, student risk-taking and experimentation, and careful design and possible redesign of final projects. Learning occurs as much in the unfolding of the process as it does in the completion of the final product or culminating performance.

Rick Stiggins (2004), internationally recognized for two decades for advising schools and assessment organizations on appropriate assessment strategies, believes that educators must "stop being so adult centered in our thinking about assessment. We must build classroom environments in which students use assessments to understand what success looks like and how to do better the next time" (25). We can only hand responsibility over to students if we believe that they are capable of communicating about their own learning needs and if we provide them with the strategies and time for reflection on their effort and progress.

Few middle level schools have adopted a student-managed assessment philosophy, in part because of a belief that young adolescents are incapable of independent learning and reflection. We know, however, that emerging metacognitive abilities permit young adolescents to evaluate their performance on academic tasks. Young adolescents are able to see their mistakes and correct them without intensive teacher direction, think creatively when given opportunities for reflection, use analytical strategies that they had not been capable of prior to this growth period, and develop advanced questioning strategies that provide teachers with insights into their depth of understanding.

Eighth graders in a class that used the curriculum integration model believed that they improved their critical thinking skills more than they would have in a traditional classroom as a result of "thinking about and critiquing what others said or presented; the many circumstances of evaluating each other; their responsibilities for frequent self-evaluation; and their need to review and consider the constructive criticism received" (Brown and Morgan 2003, 23). Stiggins (2006) insisted that students be involved in their assessment so that they develop an understanding of what academic success looks like and have an opportunity to take responsibility for reaching it.

Wiggins (1993) noted in examining the true meaning of the word *assessment* that, "It is something we do *with* and *for* the student, not something we do *to* the student" (14).

THE PROBLEMS WITH STANDARDIZED TESTS

The pressure placed on teachers and students by the No Child Left Behind (2001) legislation (NCLB) altered the way students were taught, what they were taught, and how teachers determined what they knew. The Race to the Top (RTTT) initiative with its focus on Common Core Standards, data driven instruction, and required teacher evaluation based on students' test scores has made matters worse. Already students must pass high-stakes achievement tests to graduate. The new PARCC assessment (Partnership for Assessment of Readiness for College and Careers) will start being administered in the third grade to determine whether students are advancing according to scripted curriculum guides. Despite these pressures, you as a teacher are the only one who can know whether your students have gained the necessary skills, strategies, and attitudes they need to successfully complete a year of learning. You also know that these high-stakes tests are not a measure of whether learning or intellectual growth have occurred.

Many tests are incapable of assessing students in ways that help teachers improve instruction, but national or state standardized tests may be the *worst* measuring devices for helping teachers and students. Standardized tests have not traditionally been given as pre-test/post-test assessments to determine student gains in knowledge, but instead are administered for a one-time-only view of students' learning of concepts and principles—content that may not even match what you are required to teach. Attempts by some testing companies to begin offering pre-tests and post-tests are rife with the challenges of matching states' and schools' content standards to test items, even if tests are aligned to another set of temporary content standards such as the Common Core State Standards. Educators, unfortunately, will not have an opportunity to verify whether test content matches what they teach—called *content validity*—thereby negating any claims by testing companies that these standardized tests have value for students or teachers. This lack of content validity and of the opportunity for teachers to verify it make the testing mandates untenable as realistic measures of students' academic growth.

Many educators across the nation have similar concerns that the latest standardized tests aligned with the CCSS don't match their current curricula (D. Brown 2013b). It is likely that one of the primary purposes of encouraging states to adopt the CCSS was to force each public school district to purchase the next new textbooks that conveniently match the CCSS (J. Beane 2013). Beane clarifies the "gestalt" of the CCSS movement:

The Common Core State Standards are, like virtual schools and voucher programs, an example of how far we have drifted from an understanding of education as a human, professional endeavor toward a more technical impersonal, corporate model. There is definitely some big money to be made here. And for that reason, it might not be too far-fetched to rename the Common Core State Standards "The Corporate Core." (10)

James Beane's prediction will become reality, as test-publishing companies produce curricular products and practice tests that match the CCSS. The real question becomes, how long will it be before educational professionals and parents across the United States refuse to accept the testing culture that has ruined effective teaching and learning?

Students should know what content is going to be on a test so that they can prepare for success. Logic tells us, therefore, that all teachers should also know explicitly the items that are to be on a test that has high stakes for students and teachers, such as the state tests mandated by NCLB and RTTT. Yet each year teachers have no idea what the content of the tests will be. How can it be considered cheating to prepare students for success? Popham (1999) suggested that educators be provided with an opportunity to "scrutinize the test's items one at a time to see what they are really measuring" (15). Until teachers know what will be tested, many students will suffer the consequences associated with unacceptable scores, and teachers will continue to alter instruction and curricula in ways that discourage meaningful learning (Musser et al. 2013).

Proficiency as used by the NCLB authors does not describe genuine student learning. Proficiency may have nothing to do with students learning the critical principles that they need to know. Your students may be proficient in the skills measured by a mandated standardized test yet lack the necessary information and strategies needed to achieve the learning outcomes you have identified for them. "Proficient in what?" is what you should ask following your students' experiences each year with state or national standardized tests.

The difficulty with most of the external examinations required for students throughout America is that these tests in no manner help students learn better or teachers instruct better. Students are given the tests in the spring, and the results are released the next fall after students that you taught for the year have completed that grade, meaning you'll never teach them again.

The results of these state tests are seldom if ever indications of students' academic growth during the year. Teachers recognize the folly of taking these tests seriously as a way to determine genuine student learning and growth. Popham (1999) noted, "The better the job that teachers do in teaching important knowledge and skills, the less likely it is that there will be items on a standardized achievement test measuring such knowledge and/or skills" (12). Teachers who choose to focus on the subskills of content, such as memorizing vocabulary, may prepare students for tests, but cause them to lose the ability to use active thinking processes.

Teachers are less likely to use creative teaching strategies or spend as much time as is needed to study topics that interest students when they feel pressured and responsible for raising students' scores on external standardized tests. Instead of improving the curriculum and instruction, high-stakes standardized tests tend to narrow the curriculum, increase dropout rates, and decrease graduation rates—especially for ethnically diverse students (Stiggins 2006; Kohn 2000). Stiggins noted that despite legislators' desires to improve student performance by using high-stakes standardized tests, there has been no significant improvement in students' test results since the 1960s. D. Brown (2002b) added, "Shouldn't standardized tests at least help students and teachers, considering all the money and time spent purchasing, administering, and scoring them" (220)?

Most teachers believe that they are responsible for helping students learn content and skills. They are often pressured to change instruction to a skills-based, direct-instruction approach with a belief that it will improve students' chances for test success. Adopting this structured teaching approach ignores what is best for young adolescents and may in fact prevent students from learning what is important to learn.

Teachers who use a structured approach in the hope of achieving high test scores likely will not achieve their goal: Wilhelm (2006) discovered in reporting on an analysis of test score data from the National Assessment of Educational Progress (NAEP) and the Third International Mathematics and Science Study (TIMSS) "that better student test scores are associated with inquiry approaches that emphasize deep understanding" (14). This research runs counter to the belief that structured teaching improves test scores. Instead, we find that implementing active instructional processes, student-designed curriculum, and student self-assessment practices helps your students reach learning gains on meaningful outcomes.

Surviving and Fighting the Testing Insanity

We provide direct evidence that traditional, rote teaching and curricula have detrimental effects on genuine growth for young adolescents. After reading about and comprehending the developmental traits and needs of middle level students, we hope that you'll consider and adopt both a philosophy and strategies that lead to exceptional learning environments. Despite educators' philosophies though, when one's job evaluation and sense of pride is based on students' successful test scores, it is only common sense to find ways to improve student success on these standardized assessments.

We have worked with many teachers who have felt a great deal of stress to ensure test score success, so we understand the high-stakes pressure that affects teachers' instructional behaviors. With these expectations in mind, we advise teachers to continue to dovetail a philosophy of personal care, individualized instruction for each student, and an overall instructional delivery that provides students with a fighting chance of success on standardized assessments.

Effective educators, however, make a habit of prioritizing their students' needs each and every day of the school year. When students need comfort for their emotional distress, good teachers prioritize that over teaching about gerunds; when ELL students need help with basic English, good teachers provide time for casual conversations despite falling behind with daily vocabulary lessons; when a high percentage of students are below grade level, good teachers provide content with which they can succeed, regardless of grade level of that content; and when some students need additional assistance to behave appropriately, good teachers take time away from planned lessons to show them how to act. Some may call these critical decisions by teachers acts of *creative insubordination* when they detract from test preparation activities, but every teacher with a philosophy of care for students eventually recognizes that adhering to content standards to ensure that students' test scores meet unrealistic expectations is a disservice to many of their students.

We encourage creative insubordination because these actions lead to student learning. Teachers' classroom behaviors, however, must also be accompanied by a constant individual and community response to change the culture of testing. Many organizations, both professionally and among parental groups, advocate that testing have a lesser role in determining what occurs at school. We urge educators at all levels to converse with fellow colleagues, students' parents, and local administrators to find common ground and strategies for changing the culture. The future of the education profession as the most influential voice in determining how we teach requires a measured and aggressive response to the testing culture. By doing so, schools can continue to provide hope and a successful future for all students.

ASSESSMENT *FOR* LEARNING

Assessment is not the end product of a unit of study. It should not be focused on the number of facts students have memorized but rather on meaningful learning experiences. Stiggins (2006) described a critical distinction between assessment *of* learning and assessment *for* learning. Assessment *of* learning is the traditional and standardized testing view of assessment that notes how much students have learned as of a

> With the elimination of grades, students are able to focus on the quality of their work and not have to compare themselves to the rest of the class. They are able to genuinely push themselves to produce quality work on a consistent basis.
> —**DAVE MERCURIO**, SOUNDINGS TEACHER

particular point in time (the day of the test). Assessment *for* learning, in contrast, is based on the idea and practice of assessing students so that teachers can help each of them grow cognitively (Stiggins).

Another essential component of assessment is *feedback*, the responses that students receive about their assignments and projects. Students need teacher feedback to determine the next steps in their growth (Brookhart 2008). Effective feedback provides students with information that they are able to understand and to use constructively to change academic behaviors. Feedback should be provided within a reasonable amount of time so that students can recall the assignment among the many that they complete each week. When students use both teacher feedback and self-assessment, there's a greater chance that they'll change behaviors. Butler and Winne (1995) refer to this as *self-regulation*, and it mirrors self-assessment processes in that students determine their next learning outcomes and discuss strategies for reaching those objectives.

Brookhart (2008) notes that feedback can be addressed on three meaningful levels: (1) specific feedback about the learning task or product itself, (2) feedback concerning the strategies used, and (3) feedback on the student's perspective of the work. For students to understand how to improve their effort, feedback must be descriptive rather than evaluative; that is, rather than be a general label such as a grade, feedback must provide suggestions for change or ways to improve the product.

Students need opportunities to hear, see, or reflect on their academic performances and become familiar with the strategies needed to improve their next performance. The emphasis of meaningful assessment is on individual growth, not student-to-student competition. Every student should understand that he or she is responsible for improving *his or her* knowledge, skills, and strategies. There is a better chance of that occurring when students receive appropriate, timely, and frequent feedback (Stiggins 2006).

Assessment should be ongoing and frequent rather than only occurring at the end of a unit. *Formative assessment* is the information that teachers collect about students' skills and abilities every day of the week, including watching students, collecting daily assignments, listening to them contribute to discussions, noticing their interactions with classmates in small groups, or meeting with them to evaluate their monthly goals. Assessment doesn't need to be formal; in fact, the most informative assessment occurs during daily learning activities. *Summative assessments* conducted at the end of a grading period or unit, such as a test, are not frequent enough to provide the meaningful feedback to students or teachers in a timely manner.

One of the reasons that standardized tests dominate the education field is because many promote and believe the misconception that teachers' evaluations are too subjective. However, parents want and need subjective information about their children to discover their strengths and learning needs—and teachers are responsible for providing it. When young adolescents engage in self-assessment processes, they are being subjective about their skills, abilities, and areas of needed growth. Subjectivity is essential in every learning situation in life. Trust your insights as a teacher to provide essential feedback to students to insure their continuous growth through your subjective lens.

◆‖ Connecting Assessment to Curriculum and Instruction

The strategies chosen for determining what students know differ considerably from those of traditional practice when *learning* is the anchor of one's assessment philosophy. Assessment practices must be closely connected to curriculum and instruction. The beliefs that a teacher holds regarding these three components affect the choice of how he or she determines what students know or are able to do as a result of learning. Separate-subject curricular design, teacher-centered instruction, and traditional testing techniques often fail to meet the criterion for connecting curriculum, instruction, and assessment in a meaningful way. When teachers design the curriculum collaboratively with students, students become responsible for helping to design not only how they want to learn information but also how they want to demonstrate their learning. The assessment is in fact part of the instruction and drives the learning experiences.

For instance, students who choose as a small group to study the source of pollution in a local stream are engaged in learning a topic of interest. Students take part in genuine learning as they develop hypotheses, determine how to collect information, analyze samples, and reach conclusions about the stream. Learning occurs through the reflective processes of determining how to design a project that demonstrates their newfound knowledge and then employing their chosen method to present their findings. Students' assessment decisions provide direction to purposeful learning activities.

Some schools have adopted a grading system that uses state content standards as the determinant of grades, called *standards-based grading* (SBG). SBG is a principle that matches students' assignments and the grades they receive on them to the same content standards used on state tests. Instead of receiving traditional grades on assignments, students receive an assessment of *proficient*, *partially proficient*, or *advanced.* Varlas (2013) describes SBG as a better method of providing feedback to students than grades, which often provide little or no feedback. With the *partially proficient* label students can make changes to the assignment and return it later to receive a better "grade." This type of feedback has the potential to encourage self-assessment. Some teachers using SBG have stopped giving grades for nonacademic behaviors; for instance, teachers don't penalize students for late assignments, or lack of neatness.

Although the SBG philosophy is based on the same sound assessment strategies that have been used for years, particularly in providing timely feedback and encouraging self-assessment, the strategies are not used until after students have completed their assignments, a fault that prevents SBG from eclipsing the self-assessment processes that have been used consistently in curriculum integration classes. Another difficulty with SBG is that by using content standards as criteria for receiving grades, more significant outcomes, such as critical and creative thinking, problem solving, and the development of public speaking skills, are ignored. Objectives that are aligned with content standards are a narrow band of cognitive subskills, thereby limiting young adolescents' intellectual growth.

◆❙❙ Authentic Assessment Leads to Meaningful Learning

Assessment of the young adolescents' abilities and growth should be authentic, providing opportunities for students to connect curricula to events occurring in their lives and to people with whom they interact. Authentic assessment emotionally engages students as they use information in real-life contexts that have meaning to them (Schurr 1999). Scientists and historians don't answer multiple-choice questions or define vocabulary words from a textbook. They develop research protocols, conduct research, and then analyze findings. They report those findings through oral presentations, slide shows, and written journal articles. Writers write. Musicians create and perform music. Mathematicians solve problems in life using mathematical concepts. Geographers create maps. These are *authentic* actions. These types of activities demonstrate how young adolescents are able to use many of their developing cognitive skills, such as creative thinking and problem solving, rather than their ability to memorize isolated facts.

Perhaps the greatest advantage of authentic assessment over traditional testing is the chance it provides young adolescents to extend their knowledge through reflection and application of information to real-life contexts. Authentic assessment is a dynamic process that cannot be confined to a forty-two-minute period one day a week.

Of primary importance when using authentic assessment is that young adolescents need to be challenged in a way that encourages them to find solutions to personally developed questions and hypotheses. The value of authentic assessment is that it encourages students to engage in specific processing strategies to reach desired results.

Effectively designed authentic assessments become the uniting force for content and process. These assessments provide the learner with the opportunities to make connections more meaningfully than he or she would with teacher-designed or externally administered tests. Teachers are responsible for helping students identify authentic exercises and activities that match their learning goals, and then monitor students' efforts while they develop their end products.

ASSESSING STUDENT PROGRESS WITH RUBRICS

Rubrics have become a common avenue for communicating clearly to students what is expected of them to successfully complete academic tasks. Many teachers, school districts, and state departments of education use rubrics to evaluate students' performances and to describe expected student academic behaviors. School districts may use common rubrics for the evaluation and feedback of students' writing at all grade levels. Computerized rubric scoring mechanisms have become popular in some schools and states as a way of tracking students' academic performances year to year throughout their basic education.

Although there may be numerous advantages to this constant record keeping, we caution against the use of a standardized rubric that becomes foreign to students—that is, one that denies them the opportunities to engage in designing, evaluating, and altering rubrics to fit their learning needs. The more localized assessment processes are, the greater likelihood that the assessment processes will improve learning.

The most powerful rubrics are those that are designed with student input. When students are involved in determining what a quality product looks like, they become more aware of what they need to do to reach acceptable performance levels. As students help design rubrics, teachers become aware of the level of knowledge that students bring to the class about specific curricula and can determine how to help students grow in that content area.

Rubrics should not be used for the purpose of assigning grades; rather, they should be created in collaboration with students and given to students prior to an assignment so that they have clearly stated performance expectations. After the assignment has been assessed using the rubric, students can identify how to improve their performance in subsequent assignments.

An example of student-generated rubrics leading to self-assessment occurs in Soundings. Students establish their own rubrics for most of the assignments they complete during the year. As a result of student self-assessment, their efforts and products are more about mastering the principles they're learning rather than merely covering them. Danielle Bajus, who teaches in the Soundings program, describes students' roles and the effects on their growth:

Since the program is ungraded, we rely on rubrics to assess students' progress. They have to change what they've often done in the past, which was to put little time or effort into an assignment, turn it in, and receive a high grade due to their innate ability. Students in Soundings have the opportunity to rewrite initial assignments and turn them in again and again to be reassessed until they are satisfied with the quality of their work. In essence, they develop a sense of integrity and accomplishment because they learn the value of hard work when it's not merely a grade they're receiving, but an expectation of a better product each time they try again. Additionally, they receive and learn to use constructive criticism to improve the quality of their work. Isn't this what we want our middle school students to learn? How to make mistakes, learn from them, and try again?

PORTFOLIO ASSESSMENT

The use of portfolios is another meaningful assessment tool for young adolescents. Schurr (1999) described portfolios as a "systematic, integrated, and meaningful collection of a student's day-to-day work showing that student's efforts, progress, or achievement in one or more subjects" (4). Students are the primary decision makers regarding which items to include in the portfolio and are also responsible for evaluating its contents (Schurr 1999). Teachers, parents, and peers might also have a voice in deciding what to place in the portfolio. No mandates should govern portfolio creation; however, here are some examples of items that may be included in portfolios:

- student-established goals
- journal entries
- pertinent questions
- written hypotheses
- book reviews
- creative writing and graphic designs

- peer reviews
- videotaped presentations
- parents' comments on work
- teachers' comments
- self-evaluations
- self-designed rubrics
- evidence of collaboration with other students
- computer-generated projects.

The list and variety of items are endless. What is important is that the items represent the essential strategies and knowledge the student uses to explore significant themes.

It is not the collection of student work that makes portfolios an important form of assessment but rather the students' analyses and reflections on their work. Student-developed rubrics or checklists can offer guidelines for how to construct, design, and decide what may go into a portfolio and help students engage in personal reflection of their progress in achieving personal academic goals.

Growth portfolios (Stiggens, cited in S. Willis 1997) contain items that represent evidence of students' increased proficiency in specific areas of the curriculum. Students have the opportunity to examine their own growth when they are held responsible for collecting and evaluating their schoolwork. Personal attention to their progress can motivate students to improve performance and effort.

◆❘❘ Student-Led Conferences

Teachers are encouraged to have middle level students conduct their own conferences with their parents. Student-led conferences put young adolescents in a position of responsibility for their academic growth (S. Willis 1997). In student-led conferences, students join their parents to discuss their progress throughout an academic term and clarify progress toward personally established outcomes. They share with their parents their strengths and areas of needed growth as they display samples of their work. These conferences are empowering for students, because the audience for their growth is more personally focused on them than in traditional teacher-led conferences.

Kinney, Monroe, and Sessions (2000) reported that as a result of using student-led conferences, "Students became much more responsible for completing assignments, more articulate in explaining work, and more accurate at analyzing themselves as learners" (5). Ultimately, student-led conferences lead to greater learning opportunities.

ORGANIZING STUDENT-LED CONFERENCES

Student-led conferences don't reduce teachers' responsibility for being involved with the parents on conference days. Together, the teacher and the student develop plans for collecting data to be put in the conference portfolio. This portfolio includes the student's selected goals and evidence that the student has met those goals. Teacher evaluations and peer reviews may also be included. Kinney et al. (2000) suggested that student academic work prepared for conferences meet the following criteria:

- show multiple skills and processes
- address national/state/local curriculum standards
- emphasize process as well as quality of product
- use examples of "real work," not work contrived for show. (13)

Students should have an opportunity to practice conducting their conference. Effective review and organization of the portfolio are imperative if it is to be useful for conferences. Danielle, from the Soundings curriculum integration program, describes the effects of student-led conferences on her students and parents:

> One of the biggest components is student-led conferences in which students direct their own meeting with their parents/caregivers. Often, it is a turning point for many of our students, in that they have to *own* their lack of quality work completion, or, for those students who "get it" quickly, it is a celebration and a time to keep setting the bar high with new goals. This experience helps our students develop character, and serves as a catalyst for growth and improvement. Many of our students' parents/caregivers, during student-led conferences, share how impressed they are at how comfortable their thirteen- to fourteen-year-old has become in speaking with adults, including themselves. They have more in-depth discussions at home about matters of importance, such as what is currently going on in the world.

Research in middle schools indicates that parents note considerable honesty and candor from their children during student-led conferences (Marzano 2000). Davies (2001) noted:

> When students communicate their learning using a variety of work samples, they go beyond what grades, numbers, and scores alone can show; they are able to examine the depth, the detail, and the range of their own learning to figure out their strengths and what they need to work on next. This is all part of learning to self-monitor—an essential skill for self-directed, independent, lifelong learners. (48)

Student-led conferences are a perfect fit for matching the cognitive growth processes of young adolescents with learning opportunities and self-direction that are necessary for genuine cognitive development.

◆❚ Concluding Reflections

Grades, competition, and the incessant measuring of students have nothing to do with intellectual growth. Every effort must be made by middle level educators to deemphasize external assessment processes. Educators should never lose sight of the primary outcome of the three processes of curriculum, instruction, and assessment: overall student growth. Effective meaningful assessment occurs for middle level students when they are engaged in analyzing their own growth. Young adolescents have the cognitive capacity to self-assess and improve their learning through personal reflection and student-designed assessments.

◆‖ Epilogue: What This Means for You

Adolescence is one of the most fascinating and complex transitions in the life span: a time of accelerated growth and change second only to infancy; a time of expanding horizons, self-discovery, and emerging independence; a time of metamorphosis from childhood to adulthood. Its beginning is associated with profound biological, physical, behavioral, and social transformations that roughly correspond with the move to middle school or junior high school. The events of this crucially formative phase can shape an individual's entire life course and thus the future of our society. (The Carnegie Council 1996, 7)

In the first chapter of this book we asked you to list the characteristics you felt a middle level teacher needed to have. Have your ideas changed? Middle level students told us the kind of teachers they want: "They should be nice." "They should make learning fun and interesting." "They should care about us."

Listen to middle level students. Listen intently to what they have to say to you. Sit at the lunch table with them. Chat with them in detention and as they wait outside the principal's office. Listen to them as they roam through the halls or respond to other teachers. Volunteer to chaperone a middle school dance. Observe band and choral rehearsals. Attend track and soccer practices. Eavesdrop on the conversations that occur during physical education classes or in the bus lines after school each day. Seek their opinions about curriculum, instruction, and assessment, and then listen to their responses.

Young adolescents are vibrant, alive, curious, energetic, and exciting to be around. They need a school environment that responds to these qualities. Too often their schools are dull, detached, sometimes even cruel places. These students are captives of a system that suppresses their natural needs, capacities, and desires. They need teachers who love the excitement of young adolescence and want to guide teens in their journey through the middle level years. In addition young adolescents need:

- curriculum that is relevant, meaningful, and student designed
- instruction that is challenging and active
- varied assessments designed to promote growth rather than simply measure it
- kind, caring teachers who listen to students
- adults who constantly strive to know them well and whom they can trust
- opportunities to socialize with peers
- a healthy and physically and psychologically safe school environment
- opportunities to question and explore their social, emotional, cognitive, and identity developmental processes.

Paul George (2011), one of the most influential contributors to the middle school movement, continues to advise middle level educators at all levels, and these thoughts add to his passion:

Eleanor Roosevelt once said, "The future belongs to those who believe in the beauty of their dreams." Middle level educators have always been dreamers. So, dream on. The education of millions of young adolescents depends on what you dream, what you deeply believe, and what you say and do in the years ahead. Progressive middle level education may be the best chance for an educational worldview that affirms the worth and dignity of every member of a society that operates on trust, dignity, diversity, and democratic principles. That's worth dreaming of and fighting for. (51)

As young adolescents make that often frightening move from the dependence of childhood to the independence of adulthood, teachers need to support them, to enjoy them, and to provide guidance as they search to make meaning from the many changes occurring in their lives.

◆‖ Supporting Young Adolescents

What do these research findings mean for you? You must speak up! Do not be content with being a teacher in a middle school in name only. As middle level educators, we have a responsibility to be advocates for those programs that improve the quality of education for young adolescents. The data clearly demonstrate that gains in achievement as well as improved student behavior and emotional adjustment are the result of implementation of recommendations for middle level reform. These gains are representative for all, including at-risk students. If we implement reforms that group students to ensure success, provide a common core of knowledge for all, expand opportunities for learning, maximize the use of time and space, and involve students in decision making with respect to their learning, many young adolescents' needs will be addressed.

Not only must we develop a community of learning in middle level schools, we must also garner parental support and community resources. We have discussed at length the pressures that exist against many middle level reform policies, including societal expectations, legislative dictates, parental fears, mandated tests, and concerns about being able to succeed in high school or college. Joining professional organizations, attending conferences, and reading professional journals are all strategies for you to expand your knowledge and keep current on middle level reform. You must share this knowledge with administrators, parents, and other adults so that we can continue to help young adolescents grow in every developmental area.

◆▌ The *True* Middle Level School

A primary objective in writing this book was to describe the characteristics and conditions needed to create a true middle level school. Some will say that creating such a school is not possible or practical. We know it *is* possible, because across the country we find teachers and administrators who are establishing a vision, developing a plan, and implementing the components that we have described in this book. They establish teams, collaborate with students on curriculum and instruction, institute flexible schedules, develop advisory sessions, and, in effect, create successful schools for young adolescents. Chapter 10, with its stories of teachers who embrace curriculum integration, alternative assessment, democratic classrooms, and dynamic learning experiences, should encourage you also to take the risks associated with developing the true middle school concept.

The critical components needed to establish effective middle level schools don't spring from politicians' mandates, national or state content standards, administrators' policies, school board members' proposals, or parents' complaints. They develop when professional educators speak clearly, loudly, and knowingly about what is best for young adolescents—and then act on those pronouncements.

A true middle level school reflects much more than program or structural reforms, however. It is more than just a place of learning. It is a place where students experience the support of caring adults who provide liberal amounts of prodding, encouragement, understanding, and celebration to the experiences that young adolescents encounter. A true middle school is a place where students are genuinely valued—not merely in words but in the very way that they are treated. We've asked many middle school students what advice they would give to someone who wants to be a middle level teacher. Their suggestions are straightforward and from the heart:

> "My advice to people wanting to be middle school teachers is to be strong. The students are going to give you a hard time. You need a lot of patience and you have to make it fun. Being in middle school is really hard."

"My advice to teachers is to listen to the kids' half of the story, get to
know the kids, get to be their friends and not just a teacher—but
don't be too much of a friend."

"Be nice."

"My advice to teachers is that when you're telling someone what to do,
don't yell. Be more open-minded. Don't think, 'My way or no way.'"

"Teachers need to be more understanding or they won't last."

"Be humorous. Do not be mean to the kids. Don't be strict or very
demanding."

"I think anyone who wants to be a teacher better check to make sure they
have a sense of humor. It is important to be funny sometimes when
dealing with kids."

Interviews by Doda and Knowles (2008) with young adolescents have yielded the
following advice for teachers from an eighth grader:

I can imagine that teaching eighth graders must be pretty tough. Half of us don't even know who we
are, so how could teachers understand us? It's hard, but I can think of some ways. First of all, it must be
understood that we are all trying to fit in. Eighth grade is a hard year and everyone has insecurities. I'm
not saying to walk on eggshells around us, but be aware that our emotions can change like the wind. Be
firm but understanding and strict but gentle. Also, we need to get breaks from class work and homework.
We have a life outside of school. Parts of us wish we were older, but other parts wish we were still in
kindergarten, playing in the sandbox. If it's nice weather, don't give a lot of homework. We need time to
breathe and enjoy life while we're still kids. (32)

Sharing these students' comments is in keeping with a critical component of effective middle level teachers—listening to your students. David Virtue (2013), former
Middle School Journal editor, describes what effective middle level teachers should
aspire to do each day for their students:

For more than two decades, researchers have noted the importance of teacher quality in determining
student success; but good teachers do more than help their students learn academic content; they
build their students' self concepts, inspire their students to persevere, and help their students imagine
bright futures for themselves. In short, they transform lives. Transformative teaching is, to a great extent,
relational; teachers build positive, trusting relationships with their students intentionally and gradually over
time. (5)

You either already are or want to be a middle level teacher. You want to make a difference in the lives of young adolescents. Right now you are on top of the mountain. If you believe that you have what it takes to work with young adolescents, to validate them, encourage them, and help them learn, push your poles into the ground and go. It will be an exhilarating ride. You will surely fall. But you will also fly.

◆❙ References

Aalsma, M., D. K. Lapsley, and D. J. Flannery. 2006. "Personal Fables, Narcissism, and Adolescent Adjustment." *Psychology in the Schools* 43: 481–491.

Alexander, W. M. 1998a. "The Junior High School: A Changing View." In *Moving Forward from the Past: Early Writings and Current Reflections of Middle School Founders*, edited by R. David, 3–13. Columbus, OH, and Pittsburgh, PA: National Middle School Association and Pennsylvania Middle School Association.

American Heritage Dictionary. 2000. *American Heritage Dictionary*. 4th ed. Boston: Houghton Mifflin.

Anderson, S. E., G. E. Dallal, and A. Must. 2003. "Relative Weight and Race Influence Average Age at Menarche: Results from Two Nationally Representative Surveys of U.S. Girls Studied 25 Years Apart." *Pediatrics* 111: 844–850.

Anfara, Jr., V. A. 2001. "Introduction: Setting the Stage," An Introduction to Middle Level Education." In *The Handbook of Research in Middle Level Education*, edited by V. A. Anfara, Jr., vii–xx. Greenwich, CT: Information Age Publishing.

———. 2006. "The Evidence for the Core Curriculum—Past and Present." *Middle School Journal* 37 (3): 48–54.

Anfara, Jr., V. A., N. Flowers, M. M. Caskey, and S. B. Mertens. 2013. "Common Planning Time: A Review of the Literature." In *Common Planning Time in Middle Level Schools: Research Studies from the MLER SIG's National Project*, edited by S. B. Mertens, V. A. Anfara, Jr., M. M. Caskey, and N. Flowers, 13–26. Charlotte, NC: Information Age Publishing.

Anorexia Nervosa and Related Eating Disorders (ANRED). 2008. "Statistics: How Many People Have Eating Disorders?" *Anorexia Nervosa and Related Eating Disorders, Inc.* Available from www.anred.com/stats.html.

Archibald, A. B., J. A. Graber, and J. Brooks-Gunn. 2006. "Pubertal Processes and Physiological Growth in Adolescence." In *Blackwell Handbook of Adolescence*, edited by G. R. Adams and M. D. Berzonsky, 24–48. Malden, MA: Blackwell.

Arhar, J. M. 2013. "Disciplinary Teaming: A Context for Learning." *Research to Guide Practice in Middle Level Education*, edited by P. G. Andrews, 615–632. Westerville, OH: Association for Middle Level Education.

Association for Middle Level Education (AMLE). 2010. *This We Believe: Keys to Educating Young Adolescents*. Westerville, OH: Association for Middle Level Education.

Atwell, N. 2002. *Lessons That Change Writers*. Portsmouth, NH: Heinemann.

Aud, S., M. Fox, and A. Kewal Ramani. 2010. "Status and Trends in the Education of Racial and Ethnic Groups." *NCES 2010–015; U.S. Department of Education, National Center of Education Statistics*. Washington, DC: Government Printing Office.

Azmitia, M. 2002. "Self, Self-Esteem, Conflicts, and Best Friendships in Early Adolescence." In *Understanding Early Adolescent Self and Identity: Applications and Interventions*, edited by T. M. Brinthaupt and R. P. Lipka, 167–192. Albany, NY: State University of New York Press.

Barr, M. A. 2000. "Looking at the Learning Record." *Educational Leadership* 57 (5): 20–24.

Barth, R. S. 1991. *Improving Schools from Within*. San Francisco: Jossey-Bass.

Beane, A. L. 2011. *The New Bully Free Classroom: Proven Prevention and Intervention Strategies for Teachers K–8*. Minneapolis, MN: Free Spirit Publishing.

Beane, J. A. 1993. *A Middle School Curriculum: From Rhetoric to Reality*. 2nd ed. Columbus, OH: National Middle School Association.

———. 1997. *Curriculum Integration: Designing the Core of Democratic Education*. New York: Teachers College Press.

———. 1998. "A Process for Collaborative Teacher–Student Planning." *The Core Teacher* 48 (3): 3–4.

———. 2004. "Creating Quality in the Middle School Curriculum." In *Reforming Middle Level Education: Considerations for Policymakers: A Volume in the Handbook of Research in Middle Level Education*, edited by S. C. Thompson, 49–63. Greenwich, CT: Information Age Publishing.

———. 2005. *A Reason to Teach: Creating Classrooms of Dignity and Hope*. Portsmouth, NH: Heinemann.

———. 2007. "Curriculum for Early Adolescents, What Is It and Why?" *Middle Schooling Review: New Zealand Association for Intermediate and Middle Schooling* 1 (3): 7–9.

———. 2013. "A Common Core of a Different Sort: Putting Democracy at the Center of the Curriculum." *Middle School Journal* 44 (3): 6–14.

Beers, K. 2003. *When Kids Can't Read: What Teachers Can Do*. Portsmouth, NH: Heinemann.

Bell, J. H., and R. D. Bromnick. 2003. "The Social Reality of the Imaginary Audience: A Grounded Theory Approach." *Adolescence* 38: 205–219.

Bentley, M. K. 2002. "The Body of Evidence: Dangerous Intersections Between Development and Culture in the Lives of Adolescent Girls." In *Growing Up Girls: Popular Culture and the Construction of Identity*, edited by S. R. Mazzarella and N. Odom Pecora, 209–221. New York: Peter Lang Publishing.

Bergmann, J., and A. Sams. 2014. "Flipping for Mastery." *Educational Leadership* 71 (4): 24–29.

Berk, L. E. 2008. *Child Development*, 8th Edition. Boston, MA: Allyn & Bacon.

———. 2012. *Infants, Children, and Adolescents*, 7th Edition. Boston, MA: Allyn & Bacon.

Bizar, M., and H. Daniels. 2005. *Teaching the Best Practice Way: Methods That Matter, K–12*. Portland, ME: Stenhouse.

Blackburn, J. 1999. Conversation with the authors, West Chester, PA, 12 March.

Bogaert, A. F. 2005. "Age at Puberty and Father Absence in a National Probability Sample." *Journal of Adolescence* 28: 541–546.

Bordeaux, R. 1992–1994. Unpublished poetry for class project. Sinte Gleska University, Mission, SD.

Bosworth, K. 1995. "Caring for Others and Being Cared For: Students Talk About Caring in School." *Phi Delta Kappan* 76 (9): 686–93.

Brazee, E. 1995. "An Integrated Curriculum Supports Young Adolescent Development." In *Beyond Separate Subjects: Integrative Learning at the Middle Level*, edited by Y. Siu-Runyan and C. V. Faircloth, 16–28. Norwood, MA: Christopher-Gordon.

Brazee, E., and J. Capelluti. 1994. *Second Generation Curriculum: What and How We Teach at the Middle Level*. Topsfield, MA: New England League of Middle Schools.

Brendtro, L. M., M. Brokenleg, and S. Van Bockern. 1990. *Reclaiming Youth at Risk: Our Hope for the Future*. Bloomington, IN: National Education Service.

Brinthaupt, T. M. 2013. "Should Schools Be in the Business of Enhancing Student Self-Perceptions?" In *Middle Grades Curriculum: Voices and Visions of the Self-Enhancing School*, edited by K. Roney and R. P. Lipka, 1–16. Charlotte, NC: Information Age Publishing.

Brinthaupt, T. M., R. P. Lipka, and M. A. Wallace. 2007. "Aligning Student Self and Identity Concerns with Middle School Practices." In *The Young Adolescent and The Middle School*, edited by S. B. Mertens, V. A. Anfara, Jr., and M. M. Caskey, 201–218. Charlotte, NC: Information Age Publishing.

Brodhagen, B. 1998. "Varied Teaching and Learning Approaches." *Middle School Journal* 29 (3): 49–52.

Brookhart, S. M. 2008. *How to Give Effective Feedback to Your Students*. Alexandria, VA: Association for Supervision and Curriculum Development.

Brooks, J. G., and M. G. Brooks. 1993. *In Search of Understanding: The Case for Constructivist Classrooms*. Alexandria, VA: Association for Supervision and Curriculum Development.

Brooks-Gunn, J., and M. P. Warren. 1989. "The Psychological Significance of Secondary Sexual Characteristics in 9- to 11-year-old girls." *Child Development* 59: 161–169.

Brough, J. A. 1994. "Donald H. Eichhorn: Pioneer in Inventing Schools for Transescents." *Middle School Journal* 25 (4): 19–22.

Brown, B. B., and E. L. Dietz. 2009. "Informal Peer Groups in Middle Childhood and Adolescence." In *Handbook of Peer Interactions, Relationships, and Groups*, edited by K. H. Rubin, W. M. Bukowski, and B. Laursen, 21: 153–165. New York: Guilford.

Brown, D. F. 2001a. "Middle Level Teachers' Perceptions of the Impact of Block Scheduling on Instruction and Learning." *Research in Middle Level Education Annual* 24: 121–41.

———. 2001b. "Flexible Scheduling and Young Adolescent Development: A Perfect Match." In *The Handbook of Research in Middle Level Education*, edited by V. A. Anfara, Jr., 125–139. Greenwich, CT: Information Age Publishing.

———. 2002a. "Self-Directed Learning in an 8th Grade Classroom." *Educational Leadership* 60 (1): 54–58.

———. 2002b. *Becoming a Successful Urban Teacher*. Portsmouth, NH, and Westerville, OH: Heinemann and National Middle School Association.

———. 2002c. "Culturally Responsive Instructional Processes." In *Middle School Curriculum, Instruction, and Assessment*, edited by V. A. Anfara, Jr. and S. L. Stacki, 57–73. Greenwich, CT, and Westerville, OH: Information Age Publishing and National Middle School Association.

———. 2003. Informal Assessment of Middle Level Teachers' Perceptions of How Learning Occurs. Unpublished raw data. West Chester University, Pennsylvania, 25–30 June.

———. 2005. "The Significance of Congruent Communication in Effective Classroom Management." *The Clearing House: A Journal of Educational Strategies, Issues, and Ideas* 79 (1): 12–15.

———. 2006. "It's the Curriculum, Stupid: There's Something Wrong With It." *Phi Delta Kappan* 87 (10): 777–83.

———. 2011. "Curriculum Integration: Meaningful Learning Based on Students' Questions." *Middle Grades Research Journal* 6 (4): 193–206.

———. 2012. *Why America's Public Schools Are the Best Place for Kids: Reality vs. Negative Perceptions*. Lanham, MD: Rowman & Littlefield Education.

———. 2013a. "Developing Caring Humanistic Classrooms: Effects on Young Adolescents' Complete Growth." In *Middle Grades Curriculum: Voices and Visions of the Self-Enhancing School*, edited by K. Roney and R. P. Lipka, 17–31. Charlotte, NC: Information Age Publishing.

———. 2013b. "Educators' Perceptions of Legislative Actions on Instructional and Curricular Decisions." Ongoing research interviews by author. Ardmore, PA, 14 July 2013.

Brown, D. F., and M. Canniff. 2007. "Designing Curricular Experiences that Promote Young Adolescents' Cognitive Growth." *Middle School Journal* 39 (1): 16–23, 37.

Brown, D. F., and H. L. Leaman. 2006. "I'm White: They're Not: Helping Ethnically Diverse Students Develop Healthy Identities." Presentation at the Pennsylvania Middle School Association annual conference. 20 March, in State College, PA.

———. 2007. "Recognizing and Responding to Young Adolescents' Ethnic Identity Development." In *The Young Adolescent and The Middle School*, edited by S. B. Mertens, V. A. Anfara, Jr., and M. M. Caskey, 219–236. Charlotte, NC: Information Age Publishing.

Brown, D. F., and J. L. Morgan. 2003. "Students' Perceptions of a Curriculum Integration Experience on Their Learning." Paper presented at the American Educational Research Association annual conference. 23 April, in Chicago, IL.

Brown, J. D., and P. S. Bobkowski. 2011. "Older and Newer Media: Patterns of Use and Effects on Adolescents' Health and Well-Being." *Journal of Research on Adolescence* 21: 95–113.

Brown, K. 2001. "Get the Big Picture of Teaming: Eliminate Isolation and Competition Through Focus, Leadership, and Professional Development." In *The Handbook of Research in Middle Level Education*, edited by V. A. Anfara, Jr., 35–72. Greenwich, CT: Information Age Publishing.

Brown, K. M., K. Roney, and V. A. Anfara, Jr. 2003. "Organizational Health Directly Influences Student Performance at the Middle Level." *Middle School Journal* 34 (5): 5–15.

Brown, L., and C. Gilligan. 1992. *Meeting at the Crossroads: Women's Psychology and Girls' Development*. Cambridge, MA: Harvard University Press.

Brown, P. M. 2013. "Advocacy Through Advisory." *Research to Guide Practice in Middle Level Education*, edited by P. G. Andrews, 571–590. Westerville, OH: Association for Middle Level Education.

Brownlee, S. 2005. "Inside the Teen Brain." *Mysteries of the Teen Years: An Essential Guide for Parents. U.S. News and World Report*, 10 May.

Buis, J. M., and D. N. Thompson. 1989. "Imaginary Audience and Personal Fable: A Brief Review." *Adolescence* 24: 773–81.

Butler, D. L., and P. H. Winne. 1995. "Feedback and Self-Regulated Learning. A Theoretical Synthesis." *Review of Educational Research* 65: 245–281.

Burns, J. B., J. Behre Jenkins, and J. T. Kane. 2012. *Advisory: Finding the Best Fit for Your School*. Westerville, OH: Association for Middle Level Education.

Caine, R. N., and G. Caine. 1994. *Making Connections: Teaching and the Human Brain*. Menlo Park, CA: Addison-Wesley.

Cameron, J. 2012. *Canaries Reflect on the Mine: Dropouts' Stories of Schooling.* Charlotte, NC: Information Age Publishing.

Cameron, C. A., L. Theron, S. Tapanya, C. Li, C. L. Lau, L. Liebenberg, and M. Unger. 2012. "Visual Perspectives on Majority World Adolescent Thriving." *Journal of Research on Adolescence.* In press.

Carnegie Council for Adolescent Development. 1989. *Turning Points: Preparing American Youth for the 21st Century*. New York: Carnegie Corporation.

———. 1996. *Great Transitions: Preparing Adolescents for a New Century*. Abridged version. New York: Carnegie Corporation of New York.

Carskadon, M. A., C. Acebo, and O. G. Jenni. 2004. "Regulation of Adolescent Sleep: Implications for Behavior." In *Adolescent Brain Development: Vulnerabilities and Opportunities*, edited by R. E. Dahl and L. P. Spear, 276–291. New York: Academy of Sciences.

Carskadon, M. 1999. "When Worlds Collide: Adolescent Need for Sleep Versus Social Demands." In *Adolescent Sleep Needs and School Starting Times*, edited by K. Walstrom, 11–27. Bloomington, IN: Phi Delta Kappa Educational Foundation.

Caskey, M. M., V. A. Anfara, Jr., S. B. Mertens, and N. Flowers. 2013. "Common Planning Time Project: Findings, Implications, and Recommendations." In *Common Planning Time in Middle Level Schools: Research Studies from the MLER SIG's National Project*, edited by S. B. Mertens, V. A. Anfara, Jr., M. M. Caskey, and N. Flowers, 329–343. Charlotte, NC: Information Age Publishing.

Center for Applied Special Technology. 2014. *Universal Design for Learning*. Retrieved from www.cast.org, January 14, 2014.

Charles, C. M. 2000. *The Synergistic Classroom: Joyful Teaching and Gentle Discipline*. Reading, MA: Addison Wesley Longman.

Charney, R. S. 1991. *Teaching Children to Care*. Pittsfield, MA: Northeast Foundation for Children.

Chaskin, R. J., and D. Mendley Rauner. 1995. "Youth and Caring." *Phi Delta Kappan* 76 (9): 667–74.

Chen, M. Y., E. K. Wang, and Y. J. Jeng. 2006. "Adequate Sleep Among Adolescents is Positively Associated with Health Status and Health-related Behaviors." *BMC Public Health* 6: 59.

Chu, J. 2005. "You Wanna Take This Online?" *Time Special Report on Being Thirteen:* 52–55. 8 August.

Cisneros, S. 1984. *House on Mango Street*. Houston, TX: Arte Publico Press.

Clark, J. S. 1996. "Real Learning in My Classroom? Yes!" Unpublished manuscript. Westfield State College, Westfield, MA.

———. 1997. Unpublished presentation materials. Westfield State College, Westfield, MA.

Coiro, J., and J. Fogleman. 2011. "Using Websites Wisely." *Educational Leadership* 68 (5): 34–38.

Cole, C. 1992. *Nurturing a Teacher Advisory Program*. Columbus, OH: National Middle School Association.

Comer, J. P. 2005. "Child and Adolescent Development: The Missing Focus in School Reform." *Phi Delta Kappan* 86 (10): 757–63.

Cowan, K. C., and E. Rossen. 2014. "Responding to the Unthinkable: School Crisis, Response, and Recovery." *Phi Delta Kappan* 95 (4): 8–12.

Crowley, S. J., and M. A. Carskadon. 2010. "Modifications to Weekend Recovery Sleep Delay Circadian Phase in Older Adolescents." *Chronobiology International* 27: 1469–1492.

Daniel, L. 2007. *Research Summary: Multiage Grouping*. Retrieved from www.nmsa.org /Researchsummary/multigage grouping/tabid 1282/Default.aspx.

Daniels, H. 2002. *Literature Circles: Voice and Choice in Book Clubs and Reading Groups*. York, ME: Stenhouse Publishers.

Daniels, H., A. Hyde, and S. Zemelman. 2005. *Best Practice: Today's Standards for Teaching and Learning in America's Schools*. 3rd ed. Portsmouth, NH: Heinemann.

D'Augelli, A. R., A. H. Grossman, and M. T. Starks. 2008. "Families of Gay, Lesbian, and Bisexual Youth: What Do Parents and Siblings Know and How Do They React?" *Journal of GLBT Family Studies* 4: 95–115.

David, R., ed. 1998. *Moving Forward from the Past: Early Writings and Current Reflections of Middle School Founders*. Columbus, OH, and Pittsburgh, PA: National Middle School Association and Pennsylvania Middle School Association.

Davies, A. 2001. "Involving Students in Communicating About Their Learning." *National Association of Secondary School Principals Bulletin* 85 (621): 47–52.

Davis, J., and S. Hill. 2003. *The No-Nonsense Guide to Teaching Writing: Strategies, Structures, Solutions*. Portsmouth, NH: Heinemann.

Delpit, L., and J. Kilgour Dowdy, eds. 2002. *The Skin We Speak: Thoughts on Language and Culture in the Classroom*. New York: The New Press.

Demaria, T. P., and D. J. Schonfeld. 2014. "Do It Now: Short-term Responses to Traumatic Events." *Phi Delta Kappan* 95 (4): 13–17.

deVries, A. L. C., P. T. Cohen-Kettenis, H. D. Delemarre-Vander Waal. 2006. "Caring for Transgender Adolescents in BC: Suggested Guidelines" (cited 27 March, 2007). Available from www.vch.ca/transhealth/ resources/library/tcpdocs/guidelines -adolescent.pdf.

Dewey, J. 1938. *Experience and Education*. New York: Macmillan.

Diamond, J. 2012. "How to Raise a Child the Hunter-Gatherer Way." *Newsweek*, December 24, 32–38.

Dickinson, T., ed. 1993. *Readings in Middle School Curriculum: A Continuing Conversation*. Columbus, OH: National Middle School Association.

Doda, N. M., and T. Knowles. 2008. "Listening to the Voices of Young Adolescents." *Middle School Journal* 39 (3): 26–33.

Dong, Y. R. 2014. "The Bridge of Knowledge." *Educational Leadership* 71 (4): 30–36.

Dressel, P. 1957. "Facts and Fancy in Assigning Grades." *Basic College Quarterly* 2: 6–12.

Duffield, S. 2013. "Common Planning Time: Benefits and Barriers." In *Common Planning Time in Middle Level Schools: Research Studies from the MLER SIG's National Project*, edited by S. B. Mertens, V. A. Anfara, Jr., M. M. Caskey, and N. Flowers, 27–48. Charlotte, NC: Information Age Publishing.

Eccles, J. S., and C. Midgley. 1989. "Stage-environment Fit: Developmentally Appropriate Classrooms for Young Adolescents." In *Research on Motivation in Education: Goals and Cognitions*, Vol. 3, edited by C. Ames and R. Ames, 13–44. New York: Academic Press.

Eder, D. 2002. "Segregating the Popular from the Unpopular." In *Readings on Adolescence and Emerging Adulthood*, edited by J. J. Arnett, 151–60. Upper Saddle River, NJ: Prentice Hall.

Educators in Connecticut's Pomperaug Regional School District 15. 1996. *A Teacher's Guide to Performance-Based Learning and Assessment*. Alexandria, VA: Association for Supervision and Curriculum Development.

Eight Year Study. 1942. *Adventure in American Education*, vol. I. Retrieved from www.8year study.org.

Elias, M. J., J. E. Zins, R. P. Weissberg, K. S. Frey, M. T. Greenberg, N. M. Haynes, R. Kessler, M. E. Schwab-Stone, and T. P. Shriver. 1997. *Promoting Social and Emotional Learning: Guidelines for Educators.* Alexandria, VA: Association for Supervision and Curriculum Development.

Elkind, D. 1967. "Egocentrism in Adolescence." *Child Development* 38: 1025–34.

———. 1970. *Children and Adolescents: Interpretive Essays on Jean Piaget.* New York: Oxford University Press.

EL online. 2011. "What Screenagers Say About . . . " *Educational Leadership* 68 (5): 44–46.

Emdin, C. 2012. "Yes, Black Males Are Different, But Different Is Not Deficient." *Phi Delta Kappan* 93 (5): 13–16.

Englander, M. E. 1986. *Strategies for Classroom Discipline.* New York: Praeger.

Erb, T. 2005a. *This We Believe in Action.* Westerville, OH: National Middle School Association.

———. 2005b. "The Making of a New Urban Myth." *Middle School Journal* 37 (1): 2–3.

Erikson, E. H. 1950. *Childhood and Society.* New York: W. W. Norton.

———. 1968. *Identity: Youth and Crisis.* New York: W. W. Norton.

Ewing Flynn, J. 2012. "Critical Pedagogy With the Oppressed and the Oppressors: Middle School Students Discuss Racism and White Privilege." *Middle Grades Research Journal* 7 (2): 95–110.

Felner, R. D., A. W. Jackson, D. Kasak, P. Mulhall, S. Brand, and N. Flowers. 1997. "The Impact of School Reform for the Middle Years: Longitudinal Study of a Network Engaged in *Turning Points*–Based Comprehensive School Transformation." *Phi Delta Kappan* 78 (7): 528–32, 541–50.

Flegal, K. M., M. D. Carroll, C. L. Ogden, and L. R. Curtin. 2010. "Prevalence and Trends in Obesity Among U.S. Adults, 1999–2008." *Journal of the American Medical Association* 303: 235–241.

Finn, P. J. 2009. *Literacy with an Attitude: Educating Working-Class Children in Their Own Self-Interest.* 2nd ed. Albany, NY: State University of New York Press.

Forbes, E. 1944. *Johnny Tremain.* Boston: Houghton Mifflin.

Forte, I., and S. Schurr. 1993. *The Definitive Middle School Guide.* Nashville, TN: Incentive Publications.

———. 2002. *The Definitive Middle School Guide.* Rev. ed. Nashville, TN: Incentive Publications.

Frank, A. 1967. *The Diary of a Young Girl.* New York: Doubleday.

Gamson, D. A., X. Lu, and S. A. Eckert. 2013. "Challenging the Research Base of the Common Core State Standards: A Historical Reanalysis of Text Complexity." *Educational Researcher* 42 (7): 381–391.

Garcia, E. 1999. *Student Cultural Diversity: Understanding and Meeting the Challenge.* 2nd ed. Boston: Houghton Mifflin.

Gay, G. 1994. "Coming of Age Ethnically: Teaching Young Adolescents of Color." *Theory Into Practice* 33 (3): 149–55.

———. 2010. *Culturally Responsive Teaching: Theory, Research, and Practice*. 2nd ed. New York: Teachers College Press.

Ge, X., I. J. Kim, G. H. Brody, R. D. Conger, and R. Simons. 2003. "It's About Timing and Change: Pubertal Transition Effects on Symptoms of Major Depression Among African American Youths." *Developmental Psychology* 39: 430–439.

George, P. S. 2005. "K–8 or Not? Reconfiguring the Middle Grades." *Middle School Journal* 37 (1): 6–13.

———. 2011. "The American Middle School Movement: Taking the Long View." *Middle School Journal* 43 (2): 44–52.

George, P. S., and W. Alexander. 1993. *The Exemplary Middle School*. 2nd ed. New York: Holt, Reinhart, and Winston.

George, P. S., C. Stevenson, J. Thomason, and J. Beane. 1992. *The Middle School—and Beyond*. Alexandria, VA: Association for Supervision and Curriculum Development.

Giannetti, C., and M. Sagarese. 2001. *Cliques: 8 Steps to Help Your Child Survive the Jungle*. New York: Broadway Books.

Giedd, J. N., L. S. Clasen, R. Lenroot, D. Greenstein, G. L. Wallace, S. Ordaz, et al. 2006. "Puberty Related Influence of Brain Development." *Molecular and Cellular Endocrinology* 154–162: 254–255.

Gilliam, M., M. Stockman, M. Malek, W. Sharp, D. Greenstein, F. Lalonde, L. Clasen, J. Giedd, J. Rapoport, and P. Shaw. 2011. "Developmental Trajectories of the Corpus Callosum in Attention Deficit/Hyperactivity Disorder." *Biological Psychiatry* 69 (9): 839–846.

Glatthorn, A. A., and J. Baron. 1991. "The Good Thinker." In *Developing Minds: A Resource Book for Teaching Thinking*, edited by A. L. Costa, 63–67. Rev. ed. Alexandria, VA: Association for Supervision and Curriculum Development.

Goodman, J. F., V. Sutton, and I. Harkevy. 1995. "The Effectiveness of Family Workshops in a Middle School Setting: Respect and Caring Make a Difference." *Phi Delta Kappan* 75 (9): 694–700.

Gorski, P. C. 2013. "Building a Pedagogy of Engagement for Students in Poverty." *Phi Delta Kappan* 95 (1): 48–52.

Graber, J. A. 2003. "Puberty in Context." In *Gender Differences at Puberty*, edited by C. Hayward, 307–325. New York: Cambridge University Press.

Graber, J. A., P. M. Lewinsohn, J. R. Seeley, and J. Brooks-Gunn. 2002. "Effects of the Timing of Puberty." In *Readings on Adolescence and Emerging Adulthood*, edited by J. J. Arnett, 40–49. Upper Saddle River, NJ: Prentice Hall.

Grantes, J., C. Noyce, F. Patterson, and J. Robertson. 1961. *The Junior High We Need*. Washington, DC: Association for Supervision and Curriculum Development.

Hannaford, B., M. Fouraker, and V. Dickerson. 2000. "One School Tackles the Change to Block Scheduling." *Phi Delta Kappan* 82 (2): 212–13.

Hardiman, M. M. 2010. "The Creative Artistic Brain." In *Mind, Brain, & Education: Neuroscience Implications for the Classroom*, edited by D. A. Sousa, 227–246. Bloomington, IN: Solution Tree Press.

Harter, S. 2006. "The Self." In *Handbook of Child Psychology: Volume 3. Social, Emotional, and Personality Development*, Sixth Edition, edited by N. Eisenberg, 505–570. Hoboken, NJ: Wiley.

Hinshaw, S. 2009. *The Triple Bind: Saving Our Teenage Girls from Today's Pressures*. New York: Ballantine.

Howard, T. C. 2001. "Powerful Pedagogy for African American Students: A Case Study of Four Teachers." *Urban Education* 36 (2): 179–200.

———. 2013. "How Does It Feel to Be a Problem? Black Male Students, Schools, and Learning in Enhancing the Knowledge Base to Disrupt Deficit Frameworks." In *Review of Research in Education: Volume 37: Extraordinary Pedagogies for Working Within School Settings Serving Nondominant Students*, edited by C. Faltis and J. Abedi, 54–86. Washington, DC: American Educational Research Association.

Huddleson, J. and X. Ge. 2003. "Boys at Puberty: Psychosocial Implications." In *Gender Differences at Puberty*, edited by C. Hayward, 113–134. New York: Cambridge University Press.

Hurd, E. 2012. "A Framework for Understanding Multicultural Identities: An Investigation of a Middle Level Student's French-Canadian Honduran-American (Mestizo) Identity." *Middle Grades Research Journal* 7 (2): 111–127.

Imordino-Yang, M. H., and M. Faeth, 2010. "The Role of Emotion and Skilled Intuition in Learning." In *Mind, Brain, & Education: Neuroscience Implications for the Classroom*, edited by D. A. Sousa, 68–83. Bloomington, IN: Solution Tree Press.

Jackson, A. W., and G. A. Davis. 2000. *Turning Points 2000: Educating Adolescents in the 21st Century*. New York, and Westerville, OH: Teachers College Press and National Middle School Association.

James, M. 1986. *Adviser-Advisee Programs: Why, What and How*. Columbus, OH: National Middle School Association.

Jensen, E. 1998. "How Julie's Brain Learns." *Educational Leadership* 56 (3): 41–45.

———. 2009. *Teaching with Poverty in Mind: What Being Poor Does to Kids' Brains and What Schools Can Do About It*. Alexandria, VA: Association for Supervision and Curriculum Development.

Johnston, J., and R. Williamson. 1998. "Listening to Four Communities: Public and Parent Concerns About Middle Level Schools." *NASSP Bulletin*, 82 (597): 44–52.

Kasak, D., and E. Uskali. 2012. "Organizational Structures: Organizational Structures Foster Purposeful Learning and Meaningful Relationships." *This We Believe in Action: Implementing Successful Middle Level Schools*, edited by the Association for Middle Level Education, 119–131. Westerville, OH: Association for Middle Level Education.

Kellough, R. D., and N. G. Kellough. 2008. *Teaching Young Adolescents: Methods and Resources for Middle Grades Teaching*, 5th ed. Upper Saddle River, NJ: Pearson Merrill Prentice Hall.

Kerr, M. M. 2006. "Bullying: What the Research Tells Us." Presentation at the Pennsylvania Middle School Association Conference. 19 March, in State College, PA.

Kindlon, D. 2006. *Alpha Girls: Understanding the New American Girl and How She Is Changing the World*. New York: Rodale.

Kinney, P., M. B. Monroe, and P. Sessions. 2000. *A Student-Wide Approach to Student-Led Conferences*. Westerville, OH: National Middle School Association.

Kliebard, H. M. 1986. *The Struggle for the American Curriculum: 1893–1958*. Boston: Routledge and Kegan Paul.

Kline, L. W. 1995. "A Baker's Dozen: Effective Instructional Strategies." In *Educating Everybody's Children: Diverse Teaching Strategies for Diverse Learners*, edited by R. W. Cole, 21–45. Alexandria, VA: Association for Supervision and Curriculum Development.

Knowles, T. 2006. *The Kids Behind the Label: An Inside Look at ADHD for Classroom Teachers*. Portsmouth, NH: Heinemann.

———. 2007. "Understanding English Language Learners: Lessons from Honduras." www.teachhub.com/understanding-english-language-learners-lessons-honduras.

Kohlberg, L., and C. Gilligan. Fall 1971. "The Adolescent as a Philosopher: The Discovery of the Self in a Postconventional World." *Daedalus* 1051–86.

Kohn, A. 1986. *No Contest: The Case Against Competition, Why We Lose in Our Race to Win*. Boston: Houghton Mifflin.

———. 1998. *What to Look for in a Classroom . . . and Other Essays*. San Francisco, CA: Jossey-Bass.

———. 2000. *The Case Against Standardized Testing: Raising the Scores, Ruining the Schools*. Portsmouth, NH: Heinemann.

———. 2006. *The Homework Myth: Why Our Kids Get Too Much of a Bad Thing*. Cambridge, MA: DaCapo Press.

Kolb, L. 2011. "Adventures with Cell Phones." *Educational Leadership* 68 (5): 39–43.

Ladson-Billings, G. 1994. *The Dreamkeepers: Successful Teachers of African American Children*. San Francisco: Jossey-Bass.

Ladson-Billings, G. 2002. "I Ain't Writin' Nuttin': Permissions to Fail and Demands to Succeed in Urban Classrooms." In *The Skin We Speak: Thoughts on Language and Culture in the Classroom*, edited by L. Delpit and J. Kilgour Dowdy, 107–120. New York: The New Press.

Lane, B. 2005. "Dealing with Rumors, Secrets, and Lies: Tools of Aggression for Middle School Girls." *Middle School Journal* 36 (3): 41–47.

Lee, H. 1960. *To Kill a Mockingbird*. Philadelphia, PA: Lippincott & Company.

Lemhart, A. 2010. "Cyberbullying 2010: What the Research Tells Us." *Pew Internet and American Life Project*. Washington, DC: www.pewinternet.org/Presentations/2010/May/Cyberbullying-2010.aspx

Lenroot, R. K., and J. N. Giedd. 2011. "Annual Research Review: Developmental Considerations of Gene by Environment Interactions." *Journal of Child Psychology and Psychiatry* 52: 429–441.

Lipsitz, J. 1995. "Prologue: Why We Should Care About Caring." *Phi Delta Kappan* 76 (9): 665–66.

Lipsitz, J., A. W. Jackson, and L. M. Austin. 1997. "What Works in Middle Grades School Reform." *Phi Delta Kappan* 78 (7): 517–19.

Lounsbury, J. H., and E. N. Brazee. 2004. *Understanding and Implementing This We Believe First Steps*. Westerville, OH: National Middle School Association.

Lounsbury, J. H., and D. Clark. 1990. *Inside Grade Eight: From Apathy to Excitement*. Reston, VA: National Association of Secondary School Principals.

Lounsbury, J. H., S. Tarbet Carson, and P. G. Andrews. 2013. "Looping and Multiage Grouping: Providing Long-Term Student-Teacher Relationships—and Time." In *Research to Guide Practice in Middle Level Education*, edited by P. G. Andrews, 633–675. Westerville, OH: Association for Middle Level Education.

Lounsbury, J. H., and G. F. Vars. 1978. *A Curriculum for the Middle School Years*. New York: Harper & Row.

———. 2003. "The Future of Middle Level Education: Optimistic and Pessimistic Views." *Middle School Journal* 35 (2): 6–14.

MacLaury, S. 2002. *Student Advisories in Grades 5–12: A Facilitator's Guide*. Norwood, MA: Christopher-Gordon.

Madden, M., A. Lenhart, S. Cortesi, U. Gasser, M. Duggan, A. Smith, and M. Beaton. May 2013. "Teens, Social Media, and Privacy." Washington, DC: Pew Research Center.

Manning, M. 1993. *Developmentally Appropriate Middle Level Schools*. Wheaton, MD: Association for Childhood Education International.

Markham, C. M., D. Lormand, K. M. Gloppen, M. F. Peskin, B. Flores, B. Lowe, and L. D. House. 2010. "Connectedness as a Predictor of Sexual and Reproductive Health Outcomes for Youth." *Journal of Adolescent Health* 46 (3): Supplement 1, S23–S41.

Marzano, R. J. 2000. *Transforming Classroom Grading*. Alexandria, VA: Association for Supervision and Curriculum Development.

Mattox, K., D. R. Hancock, and J. A. Queen. 2005. "Block Scheduling Effects on Middle School Students' Mathematics Achievement." Paper presented at the American Educational Research Association annual meeting, 12 April, in Montreal, Canada.

May, F. B. 1998. *Reading as Communication: To Help Children Write and Read*. 5th ed. Upper Saddle River, NJ: Merrill Prentice Hall.

McCarthy, A. R. 1999. *Healthy Teens: Facing the Challenge of Young Lives*. 3rd ed. Birmingham, MI: Bridge Communications, Inc.

McEwin, C. K., and T. S. Dickinson. 2001. "Educators Committed to Young Adolescents." In *This We Believe . . . And Now We Must Act*, edited by T. O. Erb, 11–19. Westerville, OH: National Middle School Association.

McEwin, C. K., T. S. Dickinson, and M. G. Jacobson. 2005. "How Effective Are K–8 Schools for Young Adolescents?" *Middle School Journal* 37 (1): 24–28.

McEwin, C. K., T. S. Dickinson, and D. M. Jenkins. 1996. *America's Middle Schools: Practice and Progress—A 25-Year Perspective*. Columbus, OH: National Middle School Association.

McEwin, C. K., and M. W. Greene. 2011. *The Status of Programs and Practices in America's Middle Schools: Results From Two National Surveys*. Westerville, OH: Association for Middle Level Education.

———. 2013. "Programs and Practices in America's Middle Schools: A Status Report." In *Research to Guide Practice in Middle Grades Education*, edited by P. G. Andrews, 75–104. Westerville, OH: Association for Middle Level Education.

Mee, M., H. Rogers Haverback, and J. Passe. 2012. "For the Love of the Middle: A Glimpse Into Why One Group of Preservice Teachers Chose Middle Grades Education." *Middle Grades Research Journal* 7 (4): 1–14.

Merenbloom, E. Y., and B. A. Kalina. 2007. *Making Creative Schedules Work!* Thousand Oaks, CA: Corwin Press.

Mertens, S. B., V. A. Anfara, Jr., M. M. Caskey, and N. Flowers, eds. 2013. *Common Planning Time in Middle Level Schools: Research Studies from the MLER SIG's National Project*. Charlotte, NC: Information Age Publishing.

Mertens, S. B., and N. Flowers. 2003. "Middle School Practices Improve Student Achievement in High Poverty Schools." *Middle School Journal* 35 (1): 33–43.

Milgram, J. 1992. "A Portrait of Diversity: The Middle Level Student." In *Transforming Middle Level Education: Perspectives and Possibilities*, edited by J. L. Irvin, 16–27. Needham Heights, MA: Allyn & Bacon.

Milsom, A., and L. L. Gallo. 2006. "Bullying in Middle Schools: Prevention and Intervention." *Middle School Journal* 37 (3): 12–19.

Musser, P. M., M. M. Caskey, L. L. Samek, Y. M. Kim, W. L. Greene, J. M. Carpenter, and J. Casbon. 2013. "Imagine a Place Where Teaching and Learning Are Inspirational: A Decade of Collected Wisdom from the Field." *Middle School Journal* 44 (4): 6–13.

Muuss, R. E. 1988. *Theories of Adolescence*. 5th ed. New York: McGraw-Hill.

Nasir, N. S. 2012. *Racialized Identities: Race and Achievement Among African American Youth*. Stanford, CA: Stanford University Press.

National Association of Secondary School Principals. 2006. *Breaking Ranks in the Middle: Strategies for Leading Middle Level Reform*. Reston, VA: The National Association of Secondary School Principals.

National Forum to Accelerate Middle-Grades Reform. 1999. *Criteria*. Retrieved from www.middlegradesforum.org/index.php/schools-to-watch/our-criteria.

National Forum to Accelerate Middle-Grades Reform. 2004. *Policy Statement: Small School and Small Learning Communities* (Issue 4). Retrieved from www.mgforum.org/Portals/0/MGFdocs/SmallCommunities.pdf.

National Governors Association Center for Best Practices and Council of Chief State School Officers. 2010. *English Language Arts Standards*. Common Core State Standards Initiative. www.corestandards.org/ELA-literacy.

National Middle School Association. 1982. *This We Believe*: *A Position Paper of the National Middle School Association*. Columbus, OH: National Middle School Association.

———. 1995. *This We Believe: Developmentally Responsive Middle Level Schools*. Columbus, OH: National Middle School Association.

———. 2003. *This We Believe: Successful Schools for Young Adolescents*. Westerville, OH: National Middle School Association.

———. 2010. *This We Believe: Keys to Educating Young Adolescents*. Westerville, OH: National Middle School Association.

Nechochea, J., L. P. Stowell, J. E. McDaniel, M. Lorimer, and C. Kritzer. 2001. "Rethinking Middle Level Teacher Education for the 21st Century: A Systems Approach." In *The Handbook of Research in Middle Level Education*, edited by V. A. Anfara, Jr., 161–81. Greenwich, CT: Information Age Publishing.

Nesin, G., and E. N. Brazee. 2005. "Creating Developmentally Responsive Middle Schools." In *The Encyclopedia of Middle Grades Education*, edited by V. A. Anfara, Jr., G. Andrews, and S. B. Mertens, 3–44. Greenwich, CT: Information Age Publishing.

Nesin, G. and J. Lounsbury. 1999. *Curriculum Integration: Twenty Questions—With Answers*. Atlanta, GA: Georgia Middle School Association.

Newman, D. L., D. T. Spalding, and L. Yezzi. 2000. "Cognitive and Social Emotional Growth of Early Adolescents: A Longitudinal Study of Middle School." Paper presented at the American Educational Research Association Annual Conference. 5 April, in New Orleans.

No Child Left Behind Act. 2001. Retrieved from www.ed.gov/policy/elsec/eg/esea02/index. html. Public Law No. 107–110.

Noddings, N. 2005. "What Does It Mean to Educate the Whole Child?" *Educational Leadership* 63 (1): 8–13.

North Central Association. 1919. Bulletin. North Central Association of Colleges and Secondary Schools.

Nottelmann, E. D., E. J. Susman, J. H. Blue, G. Inoff-Germain, L. D. Dorn, D. L. Loriaux, G. B. Cutler, and G. P. Chrousos. 1987. "Gonadal and Adrenal Hormone Correlates of Adjustment in Early Adolescence." In *Biological-Psychological Interactions in Early Adolescence*, edited by R. M. Lerner and T. T. Foch, 303–323. Hillsdale, NJ: Erlbaum.

Nutter, M. L. 2013. "Beyond Bullying: Civil and Criminal Law Implications." Presentation at the Pennsylvania Association for Middle Level Education. 25 February, in State College, PA.

Ogbu, J. U. 1991. "Cultural Diversity and School Experience." In *Literacy as Praxis: Culture, Language, and Pedagogy*, edited by C. E. Walsh, 25–50. Norwood, NJ: Ablex Publishing.

Ogden, C. L., M. D. Carroll, L. R. Curtin, M. M. Lamb, and K. M. Flegal. 2010. "Prevalence of High Body Mass Index in U.S. Children and Adolescents, 2007–2008." *Journal of the American Medical Association* 303: 242–249.

Olweus, D., and S. Limber. 2007. *Olweus Bullying Prevention Program: Teacher Guide*. Center City, MN: Hazelden.

Ornstein, P. 1994. *School Girls: Young Women, Self-Esteem, and the Confidence Gap*. New York: Anchor Books, Doubleday.

Paddack, C. 1987. "Preparing a Boy for Nocturnal Emissions." *Medical Aspects of Human Sexuality* 21: 15–16.

Palmer, E. 2014. *Teaching the Core Skills of Listening and Speaking*. Alexandria, VA: Association for Supervision and Curriculum Development.

Pardini, P. 1999. "Battling Bullies: Teasing and Taunting Can Threaten School Safety." *Middle Ground* 3 (7): 25–29.

Parkey, F. W., and G. Hass. 2000. *Curriculum Planning: A Contemporary Approach*. 2nd ed. Needham Heights, MA: Allyn & Bacon.

Perry, B. D. 1996. *Maltreated Children: Experience, Brain Development, and the Next Generation*. New York: W. W. Norton.

Petersen, A. C. 1987. "Those Gangly Years." *Psychology Today*. September: 28–34.

Piaget, J. 1977a. *The Development of Thought: Elaboration of Cognitive Structures*. New York: Viking.

———. 1977b. *The Essential Piaget*. New York: Basic Books.

Pollock, S. L. 2006. "Counselor Roles in Dealing with Bullies and Their LGBT Victims." *Middle School Journal* 38 (2): 29–36.

Popham, W. J. 1999. "Why Standardized Tests Don't Measure Educational Quality." *Educational Leadership* 56 (6): 8–15.

Queen, J. A. 2000. "Block Scheduling Revisited." *Phi Delta Kappan*, 82 (2): 214–22.

Raevuori, A., H. W. Hoek, E. Susser, J. Kaprio, A. Rissanen, and A. Keski Rahkonen. 2009. "Epidemiology of Anorexia Nervosa in Men: A Nationwide Study of Finnish Twins." *PLoS ONE* 4: e4402.

Raskin, E. 1978. *The Westing Game*. New York: Puffin Books.

Ray, K. W. 2001. *The Writing Workshop: Working Through The Hard Parts (And They're All Hard Parts)*. Urbana, IL: National Council of Teachers of English.

Reither, G. 1999. "When There Aren't Enough Hours in the Day . . ." *Momentum* 30 (2): 63–67.

Rice, R. P., and K. G. Dolgin. 2005. *The Adolescent: Development, Relationships, and Culture*. 11th ed. Boston, MA: Pearson.

Rigby, K. 2001. *STOP the Bullying: A Handbook for Teachers*. Markham, Ontario, Canada: Pembroke Publishers Limited.

Rimm, S. 2005. *Growing Up Too Fast: The Rimm Report on the Secret World of America's Middle Schoolers*. New York: Rodale.

Ritchie, L. D., P. Spector, M. J. Stevens, M. M. Schmidt, G. B. Schreiber, R. H. Striegel-Moore et al. 2007. "Dietary Patterns in Adolescence Are Related to Adiposity in Young Adulthood in Black and White Females." *Journal of Nutrition* 137: 399–406.

Roake, J., and L. Varlas. 2013. "More than Words: Developing Core Speaking and Listening Skills." *Education Update* 55 (12): 1, 4–5.

Roeser, R. W., and S. Lau. 2002. "On Academic Identity Formation in Middle School Settings During Early Adolescence." In *Understanding Early Adolescent Self and Identity: Application and Interventions*, edited by T. M. Brinthaupt, and R. P. Lipka, 91–131. Albany, NY: State University of New York Press.

Roschewski, P., C. Gallagher, and J. Isernhagen. 2001. "Nebraskans Reach for the STARS." *Phi Delta Kappan* 82 (8): 611–15.

Rubenstein, J., D. Meyer, and J. E. Evans. 2001. "Executive Control of Cognitive Processes in Task Switching." *Journal of Experimental Psychology* 27 (4): 763–97.

Ruddell, R. B. 2006. *Teaching Children to Read and Write: Becoming an Effective Literacy Teacher*. 4th ed. Boston, MA: Pearson.

Saltman, K. 2005. *The Edison Schools: Corporate Schooling and the Assault on Public Education*. New York: Routledge.

Santrock, J. W. 2013. *Children*, 12th Edition. New York: McGraw-Hill.

Savin-Williams, R. C., and L. M. Diamond. 2004. "Sex." In *Handbook of Adolescent Development*, Second Edition, edited by R. M. Lerner, and I. Steinberg, 189–231. Hoboken, NJ: Wiley.

Schofield, H. L., K. L. Bierman, B. Heinrichs, R. L. Nix, and Conduct Problems Research Group. 2008. "Predicting Early Sexual Activity With Behavior Problems Exhibited at School Entry and in Early Adolescence." *Journal of Abnormal Child Psychology* 36 (8): 1175–1188.

Schurr, S. 1999. *Authentic Assessment: Using Product, Performance, and Portfolio Measures from A to Z*. Columbus, OH: National Middle School Association.

Schurr, S. and I. Forte. 2009. *The Definitive Middle School Guide: A Handbook for Success*, Revised Edition. Nashville, TN: Incentive Publications, Inc.

Shakespeare, W. 1992. *Romeo and Juliet*, edited by B. A. Mowat, and P. Werstine. New York: Washington Square Press.

Sheets, R. H. 2005. *Diversity Pedagogy: Examining the Role of Culture in the Teaching-Learning Process*. Boston, MA: Pearson/Allyn & Bacon.

Sheehy, A., T. Gasser, L. Molinari, and R. H. Largo. 1999. "An analysis of variance of the pubertal and midgrowth spurts for length and width." *Annals of Human Biology* 26: 309–331.

Slavin, R. E. 1991. "Synthesis of Research on Cooperative Learning." *Educational Leadership* 48 (5): 71–77, 79–82.

Sousa, D. A., ed. 2010. *Mind, Brain, & Education: Neuroscience Implications for the Classroom*. Bloomington, IN: Solution Tree Press.

———. 2011. *How the Brain Learns*. 4th ed. Thousand Oaks, CA: Corwin.

Sparrow, T., and A. Sparrow. 2012. "The Voices of Young Black Males." *Phi Delta Kappan* 93 (5): 42–47.

Sprenger, M. 2005. "Inside Amy's Brain." *Educational Leadership* 62 (7): 28–32.

Springer, M. 2006. *Soundings: A Democratic Student-Centered Education*. Westerville, OH: National Middle School Association.

———. 2013. "Charting the Course of Curriculum Integration." In *Research to Guide Practice in Middle Grades Education*, edited by P. G. Andrews, 187–215. Westerville, OH: Association for Middle Level Education.

Steinbeck, J. 1939. *The Grapes of Wrath*. New York: Viking Press.

Stiggins, R. 2004. "New Assessment Beliefs for a New School Mission." *Phi Delta Kappan* 86 (1): 22–27.

———. 2006. "Assessment for Learning: Creating a Culture of Confidence." Presentation at the National Middle School Association Annual Conference. 3 November, in Philadelphia, PA.

Strickland, M. J. 2012. "Storylines: Listening to Immigrant Students, Teachers, and Cultural Bridge Persons Making Sense of Classroom Interactions. *Middle Grades Research Journal* 7 (2): 77–93.

Sumaryono, K., and F. W. Ortiz. 2004. "Preserving the Cultural Identity of the English Language Learner." *Voices from the Middle* 11 (4): 16–19.

Swaim, S. 1993. "Curriculum Change—The Time Is Now." In *Readings in Middle School Curriculum: A Continuing Conversation*, edited by T. Dickinson, xi–xiii. Columbus, OH: National Middle School Association.

Tarbet, S. 2010. Anecdotal Notes and Student Reflections in a Looped Classroom. Unpublished data.

Thompson, S. C., L. Gregg, and L. Caruthers. 2005. "Using Action Research for Aspiring Middle Level Administrators: Going Beyond the Traditional Practicum Experience." In *Making a Difference: Action Research in Middle Level Education*, edited by M. M. Caski, 125–45. Greenwich, CT: Information Age Publishing.

Tice, D. M., J. Buder, and R. F. Baumeister. 1985. "Development of Self Consciousness: At What Age Does Audience Pressure Disrupt Performance?" *Adolescence* 20: 301–305.

Toepfer, C. 1998. "Curricular Imperatives for the Middle School." In *Moving Forward from the Past: Early Writings and Current Reflections of Middle School Founders*, edited by R. David, 134–39. Columbus, OH: National Middle School Association.

Tombari, M., and G. Borich. 1999. *Authentic Assessment in the Classroom: Applications and Practice*. Upper Saddle River, NJ: Merrill.

Tomlinson, C. A. 1999a. "Mapping a Route Toward Differentiated Instruction." *Educational Leadership* 57 (1): 12–16.

———. 1999b. *The Differentiated Classroom: Responding to the Needs of All Learners*. Alexandria, VA: Association for Supervision and Curriculum Development.

Tremblay, L., and J. Y. Frigon. 2005. "Precocious Puberty in Adolescent Girls: A Biomarker of Later Psychosocial Adjustment Problems." *Child Psychiatry and Human Development* 36: 73–94.

Tye, K. 1985. *The Junior High: School in Search of a Mission*. New York: University Press of America.

Umana-Taylor, A. J., and K. A. Updegraff. 2007. "Latino Adolescents' Mental Health: Exploring the Interrelations Among Discrimination, Ethnic Identity, Cultural Orientation, Self-Esteem, and Depressive Symptoms." *Journal of Adolescence* 30: 549–567.

Umana-Taylor, A. J., K. A. Updegraff, and M. A. Gonzales-Bracken. 2011. "Mexican-Origin Adolescent Mothers' Stressors and Psychological Functioning: Examining Ethnic Identity Affirmation and Familism as Moderators." *Journal of Youth and Adolescence* 40: 140–157.

Van Hoose, J. 1991. "The Ultimate Goal: AA Across the Day." *Midpoints* 2 (1): 1–7.

Van Hoose, J., and D. Strahan. 1988. *Young Adolescent Development and School Practices: Promoting Harmony*. Columbus, OH: National Middle School Association.

Varlas, L. 2013. "How We Got Grading Wrong, and What to Do About It." *Education Update* 55 (10): 1, 6–7. Alexandria, VA: Association for Supervision and Curriculum Development.

Vars, G. F. 1997. "Effects of Integrative Curriculum and Instruction." In *What Current Research Says to the Middle Level Practitioner*, edited by J. L. Irvin, 179–186. Columbus, OH: National Middle School Association.

———. 2001. "Can Curriculum Integration Survive in an Era of High-Stakes Testing?" *Middle School Journal* 33 (2): 7–17.

Virtue, D. C. 2013. "A Profession that Matters." *Middle School Journal* 44 (4): 5.

Vogler, K. E. 2003. "An Integrated Curriculum Using State Standards in a High-Stakes Testing Environment." *Middle School Journal* 34 (4): 5–10.

Wallis, C. 2005. "Is Middle School Bad For Kids?" *Time Magazine Special Report: Being 13*, 8 August.

Walsh, D. 2004. *Why Do They Act That Way? A Survival Guide to the Adolescent Brain for You and Your Teen*. New York: Free Press.

Ward, J. V., and B. C. Benjamin. 2004. "Women, Girls, and the Unfinished Work of Connection: A Critical Review of American Girls' Studies." In *All About the Girl: Culture, Power, and Identity*, edited by A. Harris, 15–27. New York: Routledge.

Weiner, L. 1999. *Urban Teaching: The Essentials*. New York: Teachers College Press.

Wheeler, R., and R. Swords. 2010. *Code-Switching Lessons: Grammar Strategies for Linguistically Diverse Writers*. Portsmouth, NH: Firsthand Heinemann.

Wiggins, G. 1993. "Assessment, Authenticity, Context, and Validity." *Phi Delta Kappan* 78 (3): 200–14.

Wilhelm, J. D. 1997. *"You Gotta BE the Book": Teaching Engaged and Reflective Reading with Adolescents*. New York: Teachers College Press.

———. 2006. *Engaging Readers and Writers with Inquiry*. New York: Scholastic.

Willis, S., ed. 1997. "Student-Involved Conferences." *Education Update* 39 (8): 1, 6. Alexandria, VA: Association for Supervision and Curriculum Development.

Willis, J. 2010. "The Current Impact of Neuroscience on Teaching and Learning." In *Mind, Brain, & Education: Neuroscience Implications for the Classroom*, edited by D. A. Sousa, 44–66. Bloomington, IN: Solution Tree Press.

Wlodkowski, R. J., and M. B. Ginsberg. 1995. *Diversity and Motivation: Culturally Responsive Teaching*. San Francisco: Jossey-Bass.

Wolfe, P. 2005. "Advice for the Sleep-Deprived." *Educational Leadership* 62 (7): 39–40.

Wolfe, P., and R. Brandt. 1998. "What Do We Know from Brain Research?" *Educational Leadership* 56 (3): 8–13.

Wolfson, A. R., and M. A. Carskadon. 1998. "Sleep Schedules and Daytime Functioning in Adolescents." *Child Development* 69: 875–87.

Worrell, F. C., and D. L. Gardner-Kitt. 2006. "The Relationship Between Racial and Ethnic Identity in Black Adolescents: The Cross-Racial Identity Scale and the Multigroup Ethnic Identity Measure." *Identity* 6: 293–315.

Zeehandelaar, D., and A. M. Winkler, eds. 2013. *What Parents Want: Education Preferences and Trade-Offs*. Washington, DC: Thomas B. Fordham Institute. Cited in *Phi Delta Kappan*, 95 (3): 7.

Ziegler, S., and L. Mulhall. 1994. "Establishing and Evaluating a Successful Advisory Program in a Middle School." *Middle School Journal* 25 (4): 42–46.

Zittleman, K. R. 2004. *Making Public Schools Great for Every Girl and Boy. Gender Equity in Mathematics and Science Classrooms*. Washington, DC: NEA.

———. 2007. "Gender Perceptions of Middle Schoolers: The Good and the Bad." *Middle Grades Research Journal* 2 (2): 65–97.

◆❚ Index